PRAISE FOR *THE NEW URBAN CRISIS*

"[Richard] Florida is right that there are really twin crises: inequality and segregation....The government should concentrate on helping poor people, not poor places. After all, the American economy will not benefit from stemming the flow of people from less productive places to more productive ones. The answer instead is, as Mr. Florida nicely puts it in his conclusion, a 'new and better urbanism.'"
—*Wall Street Journal*

"[Richard Florida] vividly expose[s] how gentrification, followed by rising housing costs, concentrated affluence, and glaring inequality, has pushed the displaced into deteriorating suburbs far from mass transit, employment, services, and decent schools....[*The New Urban Crisis* is] nuanced and proposes solutions."

—*Washington Post*

"*The New Urban Crisis* is well worth reading for the original research, clearheaded critique, and the skilled analysis of solid data....Florida writes in personally positioned transparent language without taking refuge in academic jargon, making the book accessible to a broad audience."

—*New York Journal of Books*

"Startling and illuminating."
—*Architectural Record*

"*The New Urban Crisis* is an important book."
—*Atlanta Studies*

"Florida lands on an intriguing mix of policy prescriptions for dealing with the new urban crisis."
—*Insider Higher Ed*

"*The New Urban Crisis* is underpinned by reams of data breezily and readably presented."
—*Miami Herald*

"Impeccable."
—800-CEO-READ

"Florida's book offers a groundbreaking vision for inclusive and prosperous cities and is a call to city dwellers and urban politicians alike to become better-informed and propose and follow through on hard but rewarding choices."

—*Winnipeg Free Press*

"[Richard Florida] is a serious scholar whose ideas must be wrestled with. I've found myself in agreement with him more often than not."   —*Seattle Times*

"Some of Florida's ideas—give more powers to mayors, resist NIMBYism, cut red tape for builders, construct more transit, push for more urban density—are sensible responses to these evolving urban challenges."   —*Globe and Mail*

"Urban planners should consider the case being made for the need to address a new urban crisis. A thought-provoking work for those interested in all stages of urban planning and place-making."   —*Library Journal*

"Florida draws subtle, thoughtful inferences from his research, and he writes in slick, approachable prose....Throughout, the author remains an idealistic, perceptive observer of cities' transformations. A sobering account of inequality and spatial conflict rising against a cultural backdrop of urban change."

—*Kirkus Reviews*

"Cities are engines for prosperity and progress, but it's essential that the benefits extend far and wide. Florida proposes promising ideas for building stronger cities that offer greater opportunities for all."

—Mayor Michael Bloomberg, New York City

"*The New Urban Crisis* deserves to stand alongside Thomas Piketty's *Capital in the Twenty-First Century* as an essential diagnosis of our contemporary ills, and a clear-eyed prescription of how to cure them. It's also a rare and compelling example of a great intellect displaying the courage to rethink his older ideas in the face of changing circumstances. Anyone interested in the crisis of inequality and in the vitality of our cities will want to read this book."

—Steven Johnson, author of *Emergence* and *How We Got to Now*

"Perceptions of urban crisis are steeped in the past, dominated by images of deindustrialization, economic decline, high crime, the hollowing out of cities, and rampant suburbanization. Urban divergence is the reality today—superstar cities like New York are thriving like never before while other cities continue to languish. Suburban communities are also tackling problems once thought unique to cities, and as the recent presidential election revealed, the divide between urban and rural has deepened. The urbanist Richard Florida, famous for his work on the creative class, turns his attention in *The New Urban Crisis* to the paradox of our times—the 'clustering force' of concentrated talent and economic activity is simultaneously an engine for urban growth and a driver of inequality. Not everyone will agree, but the general public, leaders, and students of cities will profit by engaging his provocative data and ideas. Don't be fooled by the title—*crisis* is double-edged and at the end, Florida lays out an ambitious but concrete plan for a renewed and more equitable urbanism. Rather than provoking angst, *The New Urban Crisis* is an inspired and pointed call to action."

—Robert J. Sampson, Harvard University, and author of *Great American City*

"*The New Urban Crisis*. Staying ahead of the curve. This is about how cities are failing the middle class throughout much of the world. At the same time, suburbs are seeing a new poverty and urbanization is not always translating into rising living standards around the world. This book is where the problems of urban economics 'are at' right now."

—Tyler Cowen, professor, George Mason University, College of Humanities and Social Sciences

"Richard Florida demonstrates again that he is one of the most discerning (and provocative) observers of the great metropolitan migrations of the past sixty years. Using masses of carefully curated demographic data, he identifies the winners and losers of the widespread 'urban resurgence' of the past couple of decades. His observations are disquieting on many levels, and Florida doesn't shy away from proposing bold and sometimes costly solutions. *The New Urban Crisis* is certain to be one of the most widely debated books of the year."

—Governor John Hickenlooper, Colorado

"This is the book we have been waiting for. Richard Florida is the greatest American urbanist of our time. In this book, he thoughtfully and forcefully confronts how Americans' return to our cities has brought incredible cultural and economic renewal but without careful and thoughtful land use, infrastructure, and economic justice initiatives, this renewal is leaving a disappearing middle class in its wake. This is an indispensable read for policy makers, students, educators, and all urban dwellers alike. Florida sketches an urgent roadmap to ensure that America's urban revival brings prosperity to everyone, not just a few."

—Mayor Eric Garcetti, Los Angeles

"A sweeping narrative of the most significant human movement of our times—global urbanization. Richard Florida lays out with unassailable facts and clear vision the convergence of an urgent human development—the drive for more livable cities and the quest for a more sustainable planet. Clear, compelling, and full of vision."

—Governor Martin O'Malley, Maryland

"Richard Florida is the great pioneer thinker who first explained how the influx of creative people was reviving cities. Now he takes the next step: looking for ways to make this urbanism more inclusive. Florida takes a hard look at the problems and, as usual, comes up with some smart new policies. Making cities work for all residents is one of the great economic, political, and moral issues of our time."   —Walter Isaacson

THE NEW URBAN CRISIS

THE NEW

URBAN

CRISIS

HOW OUR CITIES ARE INCREASING INEQUALITY,
DEEPENING SEGREGATION, AND FAILING THE
MIDDLE CLASS—AND WHAT WE CAN DO ABOUT IT

RICHARD FLORIDA

BASIC BOOKS
NEW YORK

Basic Books
Hachette Book Group
1290 Avenue of the Americas, New York, NY 10104
www.basicbooks.com

Printed in the United States of America

First Trade Paperback Edition: May 2018

Published by Basic Books, an imprint of Perseus Books, LLC, a subsidiary of Hachette Book Group, Inc. The Basic Books name and logo is a trademark of the Hachette Book Group.

The Hachette Speakers Bureau provides a wide range of authors for speaking events. To find out more, go to www.hachettespeakersbureau.com or call (866) 376-6591.

The publisher is not responsible for websites (or their content) that are not owned by the publisher.

Designed by Jack Lenzo

The Library of Congress has cataloged the hardcover edition as follows:

Names: Florida, Richard L., author.
Title: The new urban crisis : how our cities are increasing inequality, deepening segregation, and failing the middle class—and what we can do about it / Richard Florida.
Description: New York : Basic Books, [2017] | Includes bibliographical references and index.
Identifiers: LCCN 2016042401 (print) | LCCN 2016057434 (ebook) | ISBN 9780465079742 (hardcover) | ISBN 9780465097784 (ebook)
Subjects: LCSH: Urbanization—United States. | Urban policy—United States. | Equality—United States. | Sociology, Urban—United States.
Classification: LCC HT123 .F6195 2017 (print) | LCC HT123 (ebook) | DDC 307.760973—dc23
LC record available at https://lccn.loc.gov/2016042401

ISBNs: 978-0-465-07974-2 (hardcover), 978-0-465-09778-4 (ebook), 978-1-5416-4412-0 (paperback)

LSC-C

10 9 8 7 6 5 4 3 2

For Mila and Valentina

CONTENTS

Any city, however small, is in fact divided into two, one the city of the poor, the other of the rich.

—Plato, *The Republic*

Cities have the capability of providing something for everybody, only because, and only when, they are created by everybody.

—Jane Jacobs, *The Death and Life of Great American Cities*

PREFACE

I was born in Newark, New Jersey, in 1957, back when it was a thriving city, bustling with iconic department stores, morning and evening newspapers, libraries and museums, a busy downtown, and a large middle class. My parents both came of age in the city's Italian district, and they still lived there when I was born, in an apartment near the city's verdant Branch Brook Park. My father had left school in the seventh grade to work in a factory alongside Italian, Polish, Irish, German, Hispanic, and black laborers. Except for his stint in the military, when he stormed the beaches at Normandy and fought in some of the great battles of World War II, he walked through its doors every working day of his life, starting as a laborer, climbing the ladder to foreman, and ultimately becoming one of the plant's managers.

My parents, like millions of other Americans, moved to the suburbs when I was a toddler. They chose the small town of North Arlington, about a fifteen-minute drive from Newark. They did so, as they often reminded me, because of the good schools the town offered, particularly the Catholic school, Queen of Peace, which they believed would prepare my brother and me for college, putting us on a path to a better life. One of my mother's sisters, my aunt Lonnie, already lived there; her husband, my uncle Walter, put himself through night school at Newark College of Engineering for both his bachelor's and master's degrees in chemical engineering, and then rose through the ranks to become a senior executive at Colgate Palmolive. Blue-collar families like mine and more affluent ones like my aunt and uncle's still lived side by side in the same neighborhoods. Despite our different economic circumstances, we were all part of the same American Dream. Even though we had moved out of Newark, we still visited the old neighborhood on most Sundays, joining my grandmother and the rest of the family who still lived there for large Italian suppers.

Then, one hot July day in 1967, when I was nine years old, I saw the city overtaken by turmoil. As my father drove us into the city, the air grew thick with smoke: Newark was engulfed in its infamous riots, and police, National Guardsmen, and military vehicles lined its streets. Eventually, a policeman flagged us down to warn us about "snipers." As my father anxiously turned the car around, he instructed me to lie down on the floor for safety. More than two dozen people, mostly African Americans, died in Newark over the next several days; 750 more were injured, and another 1,000 jailed. Property damage was estimated in millions of dollars. The devastating riots boiled over into many other cities, including nearby New Brunswick and Plainfield, New Jersey; Detroit and Cincinnati in the Rustbelt; and Atlanta in the South. It would become known as the "long, hot summer of 1967." In most cases, the precipitating event was police violence toward blacks, but the root causes ran deeper. Jobs and economic activity, as well as the largely white working and middle classes, had been moving out of those cities for some time, and many blacks, who had been moving into them as part of their Great Migration from the South, were packed into urban ghettos.[1]

I didn't realize it at the time, but I was witnessing the unfolding of what would come to be called "the urban crisis." For all of my life up to that point—and, as I would later learn, for all of modern history—cities had been centers of industry, economic growth, and cultural achievement. By the late 1960s and 1970s, that was no longer the case. Middle-class people and jobs were fleeing cities like Newark for the suburbs, leaving their economies hollowed out. By the time I entered high school in the early 1970s, huge stretches of Newark had fallen victim to economic decay, rising crime and violence, and racially concentrated poverty. The year I graduated, 1975, New York City teetered on the brink of bankruptcy. Not long after, my father's factory closed its doors forever, putting him and hundreds of others out of work. Hope, prosperity, and the American Dream had moved to the suburbs.

These stark realities haunted me. What was causing people, companies, and stores to abandon Newark? Why had the city exploded into racial turmoil and entered into such a steep decline? Why had the factory where my father worked closed down? My early experience of that original urban crisis left a deep imprint on me.

When I went off to Rutgers College that fall, I found myself drawn to courses about cities and the urban issues of race, poverty, urban decay, and industrial decline. When I was a sophomore, my urban geography professor, Robert Lake, gave us an assignment to tour Lower Manhattan and chronicle what we saw. I was transfixed by the incredible urban change that was under way in SoHo, the East Village, and surrounding areas, captivated by the energy of the streets and of the artists, musicians, designers, and writers who lived and worked there. Old industrial warehouses and factories were being transformed into studios and living spaces. Punk, new wave, and rap were electrifying the area's music venues and clubs—the first tender shoots of what would later become a full-blown urban revival.

But it was in Pittsburgh, where I taught for almost twenty years at Carnegie Mellon University (CMU), that I began to sort out the main factors acting on America's cities. Pittsburgh had been devastated by deindustrialization, losing hundreds of thousands of people and considerable numbers of high-paying factory jobs. Thanks to its world-class universities, medical centers, and corporate research and development units, as well as its major philanthropies, the city was able to stave off the worst. Its leaders were working hard to change its trajectory, and as a professor of economic development I was involved in the thick of it. Yet, for all its leading-edge research and innovation potential, the talent at Pittsburgh's universities was not staying in the region; my computer science and engineering colleagues and my own students were leaving in droves for high-tech hubs like Silicon Valley, Seattle, and Austin. When the Internet pioneer Lycos, which had its roots at

CMU, abruptly announced that it was moving from Pittsburgh to Boston, all at once a lightbulb seemed to go off in my head.

The traditional thinking that people followed companies and jobs, it seemed to me, was not working. Following the established economic development wisdom, Pittsburgh's leaders had attempted to lure companies by offering them tax breaks and similar incentives; they'd poured money into subsidized industrial and office parks; they'd built a state-of-the-art convention center and two gleaming stadiums. But companies weren't looking for those things, and neither were my students or the other talented people who were leaving. Boston had not offered Lycos any tax breaks or other bribes; in fact, the costs of doing business in Boston, from rents to salaries, were much higher than in Pittsburgh. Lycos was moving because the talent it needed was already in Boston.

The key to urban success, I argued in my 2002 book, *The Rise of the Creative Class*, was to attract and retain talent, not just to draw in companies. The knowledge workers, techies, and artists and other cultural creatives who made up the creative class were locating in places that had lots of high-paying jobs—or a thick labor market; lots of other people to meet and date—what I called a thick mating market; and a vibrant quality of place, with great restaurants and cafés, a music scene, and lots of other things to do.[2]

By the turn of the twenty-first century, the ranks of the creative class had grown to some 40 million members, a third of the US workforce. It was the advantaged and dominant class of our time, I argued, and its members' tastes, preferences, and proclivities were reshaping not just our cities but our culture, workplace practices, and society at large. I also identified two less advantaged classes that together made up the rest of the workforce: the larger and much-lower-paid service class, roughly 60 million workers, about half of the workforce, who toiled in low-paid food prep, retail, and personal service jobs, and the shrinking ranks of the blue-collar working class, who worked in factories, construction, the trades, and transportation and logistics and constituted about one-fifth of the workforce.

The cities and the larger metropolitan areas that were most successful economically, I argued further, were those that excelled at what I called the "3Ts of economic development": technology, talent, and tolerance. They had clusters of technology industry; they had great school systems and research universities that produced talent; and they were open-minded and tolerant, which allowed them to attract and retain talent regardless of gender, race, ethnicity, and sexual orientation.

Cities were the places that brought together these 3Ts; and in doing so, they had become the fundamental organizing units of the economy. This was what the mega-corporations like General Motors, US Steel, and IBM had done for the old industrial economy: providing good jobs for a broad middle class of blue-collar workers, like my dad, and white-collar managers and engineers, like my uncle. Place itself had become the central organizing unit of the new knowledge-based economy—the basic platform for attracting talent, for matching people to jobs, and for spurring innovation and economic growth.

I traveled across the country and the world, taking this message to mayors, economic developers, and city leaders who still believed that the surest way to grow their cities was to lure big companies with tax subsidies and other incentives, or to dazzle people with downtown mega-projects like stadiums and outdoor malls. Instead, I told them, enduring success in the new people-driven, place-based economy turned on doing the smaller things that made cities great places to live and work—things like making sure there were walkable, pedestrian-friendly streets, bike lanes, parks, exciting art and music scenes, and vibrant areas where people could gather in cafés and restaurants. Cities needed more than a competitive business climate; they also needed a great people climate that appealed to individuals and families of all types—single, married, with children or without, straight or gay.

In time, my work generated a considerable following among mayors, arts and cultural leaders, urbanists, and even some enlightened real estate developers who were looking for a better way to spur urban development in their communities. But my message also generated a backlash on both sides of the ideological spectrum. Some conservatives questioned the connection I drew between diversity and urban economic growth, countering that it was companies and jobs, not the creative class, that moved the economy forward. Others, mainly on the left, blamed the creative class and me personally for everything from rising rents and gentrification to the growing gap between the rich and the poor. Although some of the more personal attacks stung, this criticism provoked my thinking in ways I could never have anticipated, causing me to reframe my ideas about cities and the forces that act on them.

Slowly but surely, my understanding of cities started to evolve. I realized I had been overly optimistic to believe that cities and the creative class could, by themselves, bring forth a better and more inclusive kind of urbanism. Even before the economic crisis of 2008, the gap between rich and poor was surging in the cities that were experiencing the greatest revivals. As techies, professionals, and the rich flowed back into urban cores, the less advantaged members of the working and service classes, as well as some artists and musicians, were being priced out. In New York's SoHo, the artistic and creative ferment I had observed as a student was giving way to a new kind of homogeneity of wealthy people, high-end restaurants, and luxury shops.

Truth be told, the downsides of the urban revival had captured my attention fairly early on. Back in 2003, well before Occupy Wall Street drew attention to the rise of the "one percent," or Thomas Piketty's *Capital in the Twenty-First Century* opened our eyes to global inequality, I warned that America's leading creative cities were also the epicenters of economic inequality. My research found that the metros with the highest levels of wage inequality were also those with the most dynamic and successful creative economies—San Francisco, Austin, Boston, Seattle, Washington, DC, and New York.[3] But even as I was documenting these new divides, I had no idea how fast they would metastasize, or how deeply polarized these cities would become. In little more than a decade, the revitalization of our cities and our urban areas that I had predicted was giving rise to rampant gentrification and unaffordability, driving deep wedges between affluent newcomers and struggling longtime residents.

What troubled me most of all was the decline of the great middle-class neighborhoods that had formed the backbones of our cities and broader society for most of my life. This was the kind of neighborhood I'd been born into, in Newark, and grown up in, in North Arlington. This was the kind of neighborhood I had hoped the new creative class was bringing back to our cities. But now, these once sturdy middle-class neighborhoods were disappearing right before my eyes.

I entered into a period of rethinking and introspection, of personal and intellectual transformation, of which this book is the result. I began to see the back-to-the-city movement as something that conferred a disproportionate share of its benefits on a small group of places and people. I found myself confronting the dark side of the urban revival I had once championed and celebrated.

Our divides were causing greater inequality both within cities and metro areas, and between them. As I pored over the data, I could see that only a limited number of cities and metro areas, maybe a couple of dozen, were really making it in the knowledge economy; many more were failing to keep pace or falling further behind. Many Rustbelt cities are still grappling with the devastating combination of suburban flight, urban decay, and deindustrialization. Sunbelt cities continue to attract people to their more affordable, sprawling suburban developments, but few are building robust, sustainable economies that are powered by knowledge and innovation. Tens of millions of Americans remain locked in persistent poverty. And virtually all our cities suffer from growing economic divides. As the middle class and its neighborhoods fade, our geography is splintering into small areas of affluence and concentrated advantage, and much larger areas of poverty and concentrated disadvantage.

It became increasingly clear to me that the same clustering of talent and economic assets generates a lopsided, unequal urbanism in which a relative handful of superstar cities, and a few elite neighborhoods within them, benefit while many other places stagnate or fall behind. Ultimately, the very same force that drives the growth of our cities and economy broadly also generates the divides that separate us and the contradictions that hold us back.

My research ultimately brought me face to face with the troubling reality of our new geography. Both the conventional wisdom and economic research tell us that people do better economically in large, dense, knowledge-based cities where they earn higher wages and salaries. But when a colleague and I looked into how the members of each of the three different classes fared after paying for housing, we uncovered a startling and disturbing pattern: The advantaged knowledge workers, professionals, and media and cultural workers who made up the creative class were doing fine; their wages were not only higher in big, dense, high-tech metros, but they made more than enough to cover the costs of more expensive housing in these places. But the members of the two less advantaged classes—blue-collar workers and service workers—were sinking further behind; they actually ended up worse off in large, expensive cities and metro areas after paying for their housing.[4]

The implications were deeply disturbing to me. The greatest driver of innovation, economic growth, and urban prosperity—the clustering of talent and other economic assets in cities—conferred the lion's share of its benefits on the already privileged, leaving a staggering 66 percent of the population behind. When I wrote up these findings, it set off a minor firestorm. One critic went so far as to trumpet that I had "conceded the limits" of creative-class theory. I responded directly at the time.[5] But my longer and more considered answer is the book you are holding in your hands.

My perspective on cities and urbanism was also deeply affected by what I saw happening in my adopted hometown of Toronto. I had moved there in 2007 to head up a new institute on urban prosperity at the University of Toronto. For me, the city was a bastion of the very best of progressive urbanism. Toronto had as diverse a population as can be found anywhere in North America; a thriving economy that was barely dented by the economic crisis of 2008; safe streets, great public schools, and a cohesive social fabric. Yet, somehow, this progressive, diverse city—a place that Peter Ustinov had famously dubbed "New York run by the Swiss"—chose Rob Ford as its mayor.

While his personal foibles and dysfunctions may have endeared him to his Ford Nation of supporters, he was, to me, perhaps the most anti-urban mayor ever to preside over a major city. Once elected, Ford went about tearing down just about everything that urbanists believe make for great cities. He ripped out bike lanes on major thoroughfares in his quest to reverse what he called a "war on the car." He developed plans to turn a prime stretch of the city's downtown lakefront into a garish mall, complete with a giant Ferris wheel. Ford had become mayor, it seemed, because he wanted to make the city more like the suburbs.[6]

Ford's rise was the product of the city's burgeoning class divide. As Toronto's once sizable middle class declined and its old middle-class neighborhoods faded, the city was splitting into a small set of affluent, educated areas packed in and around the urban core and along the major subway and transit lines and a much larger expanse of disadvantaged neighborhoods located far from the city center and transit.[7] Ford's message resonated powerfully with his constituency of working people and new immigrants, who felt that the benefits of the city's revitalization were being captured by a downtown elite and passing them by.

I came to see this mounting class divide as a ticking time bomb. If a city as progressive, diverse, and prosperous as Toronto could fall prey to such a populist backlash, then it could happen anywhere.

At the time I said Ford was just the first signal of this brewing backlash: more and worse would follow. It did. In short order came England's stunning and wholly unexpected decision to leave the European Union with the Brexit. Vehemently opposed by affluent, cosmopolitan London, it was backed by the struggling residents of working-class cities, suburbs, and rural areas who were being left behind by the twin forces of globalization and re-urbanization.

But what came next was even more unanticipated—and even more frightening: the election of Donald Trump to the presidency of the most powerful country on the planet. Trump rose to power by mobilizing anxious, angry voters in the left-behind places of America. Hillary Clinton took the dense, affluent, knowledge-based cities and close-in suburbs that are the epicenters of the new economy, winning the popular vote by a substantial margin. But Trump took everywhere else—the farther-out exurbs and rural areas—which provided his decisive victory in the Electoral College. All three—Trump, Ford, and Brexit—reflect the deepening fault lines of class and location that define and divide us today.

These political cleavages ultimately stem from the far deeper economic and geographic structures of the New Urban Crisis. They are the product of our new age of winner-take-all urbanism, in which the talented and the advantaged cluster and colonize a small, select group of superstar cities, leaving everybody and everywhere else behind. Much more than a crisis of cities, the New Urban Crisis is the central crisis of our time.

This book is my attempt to grapple with the New Urban Crisis and the deep contradictions of our cities and our society writ large. In writing it, I have three primary objectives: to spell out the key dimensions of this crisis; to identify the fundamental forces that are shaping it; and to outline what we need to do to bring about a new and more inclusive urbanism that encourages innovation and wealth creation while generating good jobs, rising living standards, and a better way of life for all.

The stakes could not be higher. How we come to grips with the New Urban Crisis will determine whether we become more divided and slide backward into economic stagnation, or forge ahead to a new era of more sustainable and inclusive prosperity.

1

THE URBAN CONTRADICTION

Imagine that you could travel back in time to 1975, snatch a random New Yorker off the street, and set him loose in the city today. The New York he knew was a place in steep economic decline. People, jobs, and industry were fleeing to the suburbs. Grimy, dangerous, and violent, New York teetered on the brink of bankruptcy. What would that same New Yorker make of the city today?

He wouldn't have any trouble finding his way around. The Bronx would still be up, the Battery down, and Lady Liberty would continue to preside over the harbor. Most of the city's great landmarks—the Empire State and Chrysler buildings, Rockefeller and Lincoln Centers—would look much as they did in his heyday. The streets would still be clogged with traffic. He could take the same subways across Manhattan and out to the edges of Brooklyn, Queens, and the Bronx, the PATH train to New Jersey, and New Jersey Transit and Metro North into the outer suburbs.

But many other things would have dramatically changed. Sadly, the Twin Towers, brand new in his day, would be gone. The city's rebuilt financial district would be teeming not just with businesspeople but also with the sort of affluent families who would have made their homes in the suburbs back in his day. Nearby, on what was once a wasteland of rubble and sagging piers, a long, green park with a bike path would run along the Hudson River across the entire length of Manhattan. Times Square would still have its lights and flickering billboards, but where seedy theaters and sex shops once stood, he would find an urban version of

1

Disneyland teeming with tourists, some of them relaxing in the rocking chairs placed there for their enjoyment. Where the squatting artists of SoHo and the hippies and punks of the West and East Villages once roamed, he would find upscale restaurants, cafés, and bars filled with well-off investment bankers, techies, tourists, and more than the occasional celebrity.

The once functioning meat-processing plants, industrial warehouses, and off-the-beaten-path gay leather bars of the Meatpacking District would be gone; instead, a linear park built atop the neighborhood's derelict elevated rail line would be crowded with people. Spanning its length would be shiny new condos and office towers, a brand-new Whitney Museum, boutique hotels, and upscale stores. The nearby Nabisco factory would be turned into a high-end food court, and the gargantuan old Port Authority building would be filled with techies working for Google, one of the many high-tech companies in the neighborhood. Crossing the East River or the Hudson, he would see the factories, run-down tenements, and row houses of Brooklyn, Hoboken, and Jersey City transformed into neighborhoods where young professionals and families live, work, and play. He could walk the streets at night without worrying about crime.

But as polished and well-appointed as the city would appear on the surface, he would also feel the tensions simmering underneath. Living there would be far less affordable for a working person like him than it had been in 1975. Apartments that had sold for $50,000 in his day would now be fetching millions; others that he could have rented for $500 a month would now cost $5,000, $10,000, or more. He would see glistening towers rising along Fifty-Seventh Street's billionaires' row, many of them almost completely dark and lifeless at night. He would hear people complaining about increasing inequality, the rise of the "one percent," and how the city had become increasingly unaffordable for the middle class.

Amid all the new money and the tourists, he would see vast stretches of persistent disadvantage, often cheek by jowl with the new bastions of wealth. He would find that the poverty and social problems, such as crime and drug use, that had plagued the city in his day had moved out to what used to be solidly middle-class suburbs. He might be surprised to learn that a Democrat had been returned to the mayor's office in 2014, after two decades of rule by conservatives, one of them a multibillionaire who served for three full terms. He would be even more amazed to find that the new mayor—a former community activist from Brooklyn—won office in a campaign that railed against the transformation of New York City into two cities: one rich and one poor. How this happened, "the tale of two cities," as the new mayor put it, would largely be the story of what he had missed in those forty years.

I have lived in and around cities and observed them closely my entire life, and I have been an academic urbanist for more than three decades. I have seen cities decline and die, and I have seen them come back to life. But none of that prepared me for what we face today. Just when it seemed that our cities were really turning a corner, when people and jobs were moving back to them, a host of new urban challenges—from rising inequality to increasingly unaffordable housing and more—started to come to the fore. Seemingly overnight, the much-hoped-for urban revival has turned into a new kind of urban crisis.

Although many commentators have identified and grappled with elements of this crisis, few appreciate how deep it runs and how systemic it has become. A gaping intellectual divide splits leading urban experts into two distinct camps: urban optimists and urban pessimists. Each camp describes important realities of urbanism today—and yet the one-sidedness of their perspectives has prevented us from grasping the full dimensions of the current urban crisis so we can figure our way out of it.

The urban optimists focus on the stunning revival of cities and the power of urbanization to improve the human condition.[1] For these thinkers (myself among them, not too long ago), cities

3

are richer, safer, cleaner, and healthier than they have ever been, and urbanization is an unalloyed source of betterment. The world, they say, would be a better place if nation-states had less power, and cities and their mayors had more.

In stark contrast, the urban pessimists see modern cities as being carved into gilded and virtually gated areas for conspicuous consumption by the super-rich with vast stretches of poverty and disadvantage for the masses nearby. Urban revitalization, in the pessimists' view, is driven by rapacious capitalists who profit by rebuilding some neighborhoods and running others down. Global urbanization is being foisted on the world by an unrelenting neo-liberal capitalist order, and its defining feature is not progress and economic development, but slums, along with an economic, humanitarian, and ecological crisis of staggering proportions.[2] Gentrification and inequality are the direct outgrowths of the re-colonization of the city by the affluent and the advantaged.

So, which is it: Are cities the great engines of innovation, the models of economic and social progress, that the optimists cele-brate, or are they the zones of gaping inequality and class division that the pessimists decry? The reality is that they are both. Urban-ism is every bit as powerful an economic force as the optimists say, and it is simultaneously as wrenching and divisive as the pessi-mists claim. Like capitalism itself, it is paradoxical and contradic-tory. Understanding today's urban crisis requires taking both the urban pessimists and the urban optimists seriously. In my attempt to grapple with it, I have tried to draw from the best and most im-portant contributions of each.

What exactly is the New Urban Crisis?

For the past five years or so, I have focused my research and my intellectual energy on defining it. Working with my research team, I developed new data on the scope and sources of urban inequality, the extent of economic segregation, the key causes and dimensions of gentrification, the cities and neighborhoods where the global super-rich are settling, the challenges posed by the concentration of high-tech startups in the cities, and the al-leged dampening of artistic and musical creativity as cities have grown more expensive. Marrying my own long-held interest in urban economic development with the insights of urban sociologists on the corrosive effects of concentrated poverty, I mapped the deep new divides that isolate the classes in separate neighborhoods and traced the growth of poverty and economic disadvantage in the suburbs. I delved deep into the many challenges that face the rapidly growing cities of the world's emerging economies, where urbanization is failing to spur the same kind of economic growth and rising living standards that it did for the advanced nations.[3]

The New Urban Crisis is different from the older urban crisis of the 1960s and 1970s. That previous crisis was defined by the economic abandonment of cities and their loss of economic function. Shaped by deindustrialization and white flight, its hallmark was a hollowing out of the city center, a phenomenon that urban theorists and policymakers labeled the hole-in-the-donut. As cities lost their core industries, they became sites of growing and persistent poverty: their housing decayed; crime and violence increased; and social problems, including drug abuse, teen pregnancy, and infant mortality, escalated. As urban economies eroded and tax revenues declined, cities became increasingly dependent on the federal government for financial support.[4] Many of these problems remain with us to this day.

But the New Urban Crisis stretches even further and is more all-encompassing than its predecessor. Although two of its core features—mounting inequality and rising housing prices—are most often discussed in relation to rising and reviving urban centers such as New York, London, and San Francisco, the crisis also hits hard at the declining cities of the Rustbelt and in sprawling Sunbelt cities with unsustainable economies driven by energy, tourism, and real estate. Other core features—economic and racial segregation, spatial inequality, entrenched poverty—are becoming as common in the suburbs as they are in the cities. Seen in this light, the New Urban Crisis is also a crisis of the suburbs, of urbanization itself, and of contemporary capitalism writ large.

As I have come to understand it, this New Urban Crisis encompasses five key dimensions.

The first is the deep and growing economic gap between a small number of superstar cities, such as New York, London, Hong Kong, Los Angeles, and Paris, along with leading technology and knowledge hubs, such as the San Francisco Bay Area, Washington, DC, Boston, Seattle, and other cities across the world. These superstar places have wildly disproportionate shares of the world's leading high-value industries, high-tech innovation and startups, and top talent. To take but one example: just six metro areas—the San Francisco Bay Area, New York, Boston, Washington, DC, San Diego, and London—attract nearly half of all high-tech venture capital investment across the entire world.[5] The rise of this *winner-take-all urbanism* creates a new kind of inequality between cities, with the economic gulf growing wider and wider between the winners and the much broader ranks of other cities that have lost their economic footing as a result of globalization, deindustrialization, and other factors.

The second dimension is the crisis of success that vexes these same superstar cities. These winners face extraordinarily high and increasingly unaffordable housing prices and staggering levels of inequality. In these places, mere gentrification has escalated into what some have called "plutocratization."[6] Some of their most vibrant, innovative urban neighborhoods are turning into deadened trophy districts, where the global super-rich park their money in high-end housing investments as opposed to places in which to live. It's not just musicians, artists, and creatives who are being pushed out: growing numbers of economically advantaged knowledge workers are seeing their money eaten up by high housing prices in these cities, and they have started to fear that their own children will never be able to afford the price of entry in them. But it is the blue-collar and service workers, along with the poor and disadvantaged, who face the direst economic consequences. These groups are being driven out of the superstar cities, and they are being denied the economic opportunities, the services and amenities, and the upward mobility these places have to offer. It's hard to sustain a functional urban economy when teachers, nurses, hospital workers, police officers, firefighters, and restaurant and service workers can no longer afford to live within reasonable commuting distance to their workplaces.

The third, much broader, and in many ways more problematic dimension of the New Urban Crisis is the growing inequality, segregation, and sorting that is taking place within virtually every city and metro area, winners and losers alike. If the hole-in-the-donut epitomized the urban crisis of the 1960s and 1970s, the New Urban Crisis is marked by the *disappearing middle*—the fading of the once large middle class and of its once stable neighborhoods, which were the physical embodiment of the American Dream. From 1970 to 2012, the share of American families living in middle-class neighborhoods declined from 65 to 40 percent, while the share living in either poor or affluent neighborhoods grew substantially. Over the past decade and a half, nine in ten US metropolitan areas have seen their middle classes shrink.[7] As the middle has been hollowed out, neighborhoods across America are dividing into large areas of concentrated disadvantage and much smaller areas of concentrated affluence. In place of the old class divide of poor cities versus rich suburbs a new pattern has emerged—a *Patchwork Metropolis* in which small areas of privilege and large swaths of distress and poverty crisscross city and suburb alike.

The fourth dimension of the New Urban Crisis is the burgeoning crisis of the suburbs, where poverty, insecurity, and crime are mounting, and economic and racial segregation are growing deeper. Forget those *Brady Bunch* images of middle-class suburban life: today, there are more poor people in the suburbs than there are in cities—17 million versus 13.5 million. And the ranks of the suburban poor are growing much faster than they are in cities, by a staggering 66 percent between 2000 and 2013, compared to 29 percent in urban areas.[8] Some of this suburban poverty is being imported from the cities as displaced families seek more affordable places to live. But much of it is also homegrown: more and more people who were once members of the middle class have fallen out of it, as a result of either job loss or rising housing prices. Suburbia has long been home to the wealthiest communities in America, but now its inequalities increasingly rival those of cities.

The fifth and final dimension of the New Urban Crisis is the crisis of urbanization in the developing world. The urban optimists believe that urbanization will ultimately bring economic growth, rising living standards, and a growing middle class to these places, just like it did for the United States, Europe, Japan, and more recently, China. Cities, after all, have historically driven the development of national economies. But this connection between urbanization and a rising standard of living has broken down in many of the most rapidly urbanizing areas of the world. We are seeing the rise of a troubling phenomenon of urbanization without growth, in which people pour into rapidly urbanizing areas of the developing world, but see little or no improvement in their living standards. More than 800 million people—two and a half times the entire population of the United States—live in destitute poverty and substandard conditions in slums, barrios, and favelas, and their numbers will continue to grow as the world's urban population surges.[9]

Although the New Urban Crisis has multiple manifestations, it is shaped by the fundamental contradiction brought on by urban clustering. This clustering force is Janus-faced; along with its positive attributes, it has significant negative ones, too. On the one hand, the clustering of industry, economic activity, and talented and ambitious people in cities is now the basic engine of innovation and economic growth. It is no longer natural resources or even large corporations that drive economic progress, but the ability of cities to cluster and concentrate talented people, enabling them to combine and recombine their ideas and efforts, which massively increases our innovation and productivity. Out of that ferment come the new inventions and entrepreneurial enterprises that power prosperity. The extent to which economic activity has become concentrated in the world's cities and metropolitan areas is staggering. The fifty largest metros across the globe house just 7 percent of the world's total population but generate 40 percent of global economic activity. Just forty mega-regions—constellations of cities and metros like the Boston–New York–Washington corridor—account for roughly two-thirds of the world's economic output and more than 85 percent of its innovation, while housing just 18 percent of its population. The amount of economic activity packed into small urban spaces within the leading cities is even more astonishing. Just one small sliver of downtown San Francisco, for instance, attracts billions of dollars in venture capital annually, more than any nation on the planet save for the United States.[10] This is why I believe it is more useful to refer to contemporary capitalism as *urbanized* knowledge capitalism as opposed to knowledge-based capitalism.

On the other hand, even as urban clustering drives growth, it also carves deep divides into our cities and our society. Not everything can cluster in the same limited space; some things ultimately crowd others out. This is the essence of the *urban land nexus*—a product of the extreme clustering of economic activity in very limited parts of a very limited number of cities and the increasingly fierce competition over them.[11] As with most things in life, the winners in the competition for urban space are those with the most money to spend. As the affluent and advantaged return to cities, they colonize the best locations. Everyone else is then crammed into the remaining disadvantaged areas of the city or pushed farther out into the suburbs. This competition in turn shapes a related economic paradox: the *paradox of land*. There are seemingly endless amounts of land across the world, but not nearly enough of it where it is needed most.

In this new age of urbanized knowledge capitalism, place and class combine to reinforce and reproduce socioeconomic advantage. Those at the top locate in communities that afford them privileged access to the best schools, the best services, and the best economic opportunities, while the rest get the leftover neighborhoods, which have inferior versions of all of those things and hence offer less of a chance for moving up in life. The well-off, living in a relatively small number of advantaged cities, and an even smaller number of advantaged neighborhoods within them, capture a disproportionate share of the economic gains for themselves and their offspring.

Sadly, these divides will only deepen and harden in the age of Trump. For all of his populist rhetoric about fighting for forgotten

blue-collar workers and rebuilding the middle class, his administration and the Republican congressional majority are unlikely to
address the deep structural forces that created them, and even less
likely to help the people and places that are being left behind.

As vexing and worrisome as this New Urban Crisis is, I believe it is possible for us to find our way out of it in time. Even as
my urban optimism has been tempered, I have not lost my faith in
urbanism. The word crisis, after all, has two meanings. It can describe a time of extreme stress and danger when a whole array of
threats are lined up against us; but it also refers to a critical inflec-
tion point, a time when, depending on the choices we make, things
can still tip one way or the other.

This brings me to the most important point of this book: if
the crisis we face is urban, so is its solution. For all of the challenges and tensions they generate, cities are still the most powerful economic engines the world has ever seen. The way out of the
New Urban Crisis is more, not less, urbanism.

Getting there will require a new framework and strategy for
a fuller and fairer urbanism. In the 1950s and 1960s, America's
economy grew largely as a result of strategic investments in the
system of highways and housing that undergirded the rise of suburbia. The rapid expansion of the suburbs, in turn, helped to generate demand for the cars, televisions, washers and dryers, and
other durable goods that were produced in the factories that employed millions of American workers. But our sprawling suburbs
are increasingly at odds with the clustering that now powers innovation and economic growth. Today, we need a new, improved,
and more inclusive model of urbanism that I call *urbanism for all*.

For much of the time I was writing this book, I was optimistic
that a new Democratic administration, backed and supported by
big-city mayors, would undertake the sustained national investment that a more inclusive urbanism requires. Sadly, that will not
happen now. As I was putting the finishing touches on the book,
I was brought up against our sobering new reality. The stunning
victory of Trump and the Republicans means that over at least
the next four years we will have scant federal investment in our

cities and little if any investment in affordable housing. While the Trump administration has pledged to spend more on infrastructure, its priorities will likely be roads and bridges as opposed to transit. Some combination of local government, nonprofit organizations, and philanthropic foundations will have to try to fill in the gaps that result from Republican inaction and the deep cuts that are likely to be made in America's already fraying social safety net, which will hit hard at disadvantaged people and neighborhoods. Now more than ever, mayors and local officials will have to take the lead on transit, affordable housing, poverty, and other pressing urban issues.

Ultimately, the urbanism for all that is required to move us forward must take shape around seven key pillars:

- Reform zoning and building codes, as well as tax policies, to ensure that the clustering force works to the benefit of all.
- Invest in the infrastructure needed to spur density and clustering and limit costly and inefficient sprawl.
- Build more affordable rental housing in central locations.
- Expand the middle class by turning low-wage service jobs into family-supporting work.
- Tackle concentrated poverty head-on by investing in people and places.
- Engage in a global effort to build stronger, more prosperous cities in rapidly urbanizing parts of the emerging world.
- Empower communities and enable local leaders to strengthen their own economies and cope with the challenges of the New Urban Crisis.

In the final chapter of this book, I will have much more to say about all of this. But first, I want to lay out the full parameters of the New Urban Crisis, systematically and empirically. Chapter 2 describes the rise of winner-take-all urbanism and details the winners and losers between and within cities in the competition for urban space. Chapter 3 outlines the rise of a new "city of elites," which pits relatively advantaged groups of people—knowledge

workers, techies, and creatives—against one another in the battle for urban space. Chapter 4 takes a hard empirical look at the
myths and realities of the hot-button issue of gentrification, examining where and how it is happening, the thorny issue of displacement, and the even more vexing problem of the chronically poor
neighborhoods that are being bypassed altogether, and whose residents are left further behind.

The next few chapters focus on the class division and sorting
that are reshaping our cities and metropolitan areas. Chapter 5
looks at the close connection between cities and inequality, laying
out how inequality is worse in large cities and urban areas than in
other places and how, in many ways, it is a product of the clustering and density that power economic growth. Chapter 6 provides
a detailed empirical examination of the decline of the middle class
and of middle-class neighborhoods and the ongoing sorting and
segregation of Americans by income, education, and occupation.
Chapter 7 maps the changing class geography of America's cities
and metro areas, showing how the old fault line of disadvantaged
city and advantaged suburb has given way to a new Patchwork
Metropolis crisscrossed by class divisions.

The last three chapters look both outward and forward.
Chapter 8 tackles the deepening crisis of the suburbs, while Chapter 9 examines the troubling rise of urbanization without growth
in the developing world. Finally, Chapter 10 charts the path forward, highlighting what our cities, our nation, and the world must
do to overcome the deepening divides of winner-take-all urbanism
and inaugurate a new era of urbanism for all.

2

WINNER-TAKE-ALL URBANISM

In the fall of 2013, in a hotel suite overlooking New York City's Times Square, the computer gaming giant Electronic Arts unveiled *Cities of Tomorrow*, the latest addition to its hugely successful SimCity franchise. Rather than racking up points the usual way, by killing bad guys, players of SimCity games take charge of cities. In the role of mayor, they have the power to change things like tax rates, zoning ordinances, and land use regulations, and to do things that boost economic development and create jobs. Then, by clicking on individual citizens, players can see the effects their changes are having on people's lives. In the grim future world in which *Cities of Tomorrow* is set, the city's technologically advanced infrastructure is owned by an über-elite cadre known as ControlNet. The mayor can do things to limit their power, but only at the risk of stifling the city's economic growth. Too little growth and the city devolves into dystopian squalor; too much and it becomes so unequal that its citizens cannot afford to live in it. To succeed, players must find and navigate the precarious path between those two equally unpalatable urban alternatives.[1]

Sound familiar? The futuristic city might be science fiction, but the basic dilemma that the game describes is playing out in real cities today.

Thanks to the clustering force, the most important and innovative industries and the most talented, ambitious, and wealthiest people are converging as never before in a relative handful of leading superstar cities and knowledge and tech hubs.[2] This small group of elite places forges ever forward, while many—if not most—others struggle, stagnate, or fall behind. I call this process winner-take-all urbanism.

While that phrase is my own coinage, the broader phenomenon of winner-take-all economics has been recognized for quite a while. Robert H. Frank and Philip J. Cook popularized the concept of the winner-take-all society nearly two decades ago. They drew on the research of economist Sherwin Rosen, who had laid out the economics behind the rise of superstar talent some two decades before that. The rudiments of the theory are easy to grasp. As high as the salary of the average professional athlete may be, the pay gap between middling players and superstars is enormous. A basketball superstar like LeBron James, Kevin Durant, or Steph Curry, or a star quarterback like Tom Brady or Aaron Rogers, makes many times what an average player makes. Similarly, a superstar entertainer like Taylor Swift or Beyoncé hauls in exponentially more money than the average working musician. The same is true for big-name movie stars like Jennifer Lawrence, Scarlett Johansson, Tom Cruise, Bradley Cooper, or Dwayne "The Rock" Johnson. The economics are straightforward. Superstar musicians generate big bucks by attracting large numbers of fans who are willing to pay a premium to see them or purchase their albums. Marquee movie stars sell tickets for sequel after sequel. Sports superstars draw fans to stadiums and help their teams make the playoffs and win championships.[3]

But Frank and Cook saw the winner-take-all phenomenon spreading throughout the broader economy, too, as large pay disparities appeared in industries ranging from consulting, banking, and management to design, fashion, medicine, and law. The gap between CEOs and the average worker soared. In the nearly four decades spanning 1978 to 2015, CEOs enjoyed pay increases of more than 940 percent, while the typical worker's wages grew by just 10 percent. The average CEO earned 20 times what the average worker did in 1965; by the 2000s, the ratio had grown to more than 300 to 1, where it has remained since. The rise in CEO pay was fueled largely by the increased use of stock options and other forms of equity compensation—the basic idea being that this would provide a powerful incentive for better performance. It didn't turn out that way. There ends up being little actual correlation between CEO pay and company performance. The companies run by the highest-paid CEOs had the worst overall performance between 2004 and 2014, according to a study of 800 CEOs at 429 corporations.[4]

Cities have also been caught up in this winner-take-all phenomenon. Just as superstar talent in our economy garners disproportionate rewards, superstar cities tower above the rest. Superstar cities generate the greatest levels of innovation; control and attract the largest shares of global capital and investment; have far greater concentrations of leading-edge companies in the finance, media, entertainment, and high-tech industries; and are home to a disproportionate share of the world's talent. They are not just the places where the most ambitious and talented people want to be— they are where such people need to be. The dynamic is cumulative and self-reinforcing. Their expanding economies spur demand for more and better restaurants, theaters, nightclubs, galleries, and other amenities. Successful businesspeople and entrepreneurs endow their museums, concert halls, private schools, and universities. Their growing tax revenues are plowed into new and better schools, more transit, better libraries, more and better parks, and so on, which further reinforces and perpetuates their advantages. All of this attracts still more industry and talent. It's a powerful, ongoing feedback loop that compounds the advantages of these cities over time.[5] The gap between these superstar cities and other cities around the world—from the older, stagnating industrial cities of the United States and Europe to the impoverished and economically disconnected cities of the Global South—is enormous, and it is growing.

But just which cities make up the ranks of the world's superstars? There are many rankings of global cities, each capturing particular dimensions, such as economic strength, competiveness, or livability. A comprehensive assessment can be created by combining these analyses. To do so, my team and I developed an overall

Superstar City Index, putting together five key rankings.[6] We calculated a city's final score by awarding ten points to a first-place ranking, nine points to a second-place ranking, and so on. These scores should not be read as being cast in stone, but rather as providing an approximation of how each city compares to others and how global superstar cities fall into broad tiers (see Table 2.1).

Table 2.1: The World's Superstar Cities

Rank	City	Score
1	New York	48
2	London	40
3	Tokyo	29
4	Hong Kong	21
5	Paris	19
6	Singapore	17
7	Los Angeles	13
8	Seoul	11
9	Vienna	10
10	Stockholm	9
10	Toronto	9
12	Chicago	8
13	Zurich	6
14	Sydney	5
14	Helsinki	5
16	Dublin	4
16	Osaka-Kobe	4
18	Boston	3
18	Oslo	3
18	Beijing	3
18	Shanghai	3
22	Geneva	2
23	Washington	1
23	San Francisco	1
23	Moscow	1

Source: Martin Prosperity Institute, based on five key rankings of global cities.

New York and London represent the apex of superstar power (with scores of 48 and 40, respectively). Tokyo, Hong Kong, Paris, Singapore, and Los Angeles occupy the second tier of global urban power (with scores ranging from 13 to 29). The rest—Seoul, Vienna, Stockholm, Toronto, Chicago, Zurich, Sydney, Helsinki, Dublin, and so on—occupy a third tier, functioning as important regional financial and economic centers with key global functions. Boston, Washington, DC, and San Francisco play additional roles as specialized knowledge and tech hubs. Superstar cities, in effect, form a league of their own, often sharing more in common with each other than they do with other cities across their own nations.[7]

Superstar cities have unique kinds of economies that are based on the most innovative and highest value-added industries, particularly finance, media, entertainment, and technology.[8] Everything in these cities happens fast—information travels at lightning speed, innovation occurs at a rapid pace, businesses form and scale up more quickly—and this speed, along with their sheer size, underpins their advantage in productivity. That rapid pace is not just an impression one gets, as in the old cliché "in a New York minute"; it is an objective, scientific phenomenon. Scientists at the Santa Fe Institute, a think tank specializing in complex adaptive systems, have discovered that cities have unique kinds of metabolisms. In contrast to all biological organisms, whose metabolic rates slow down as they get larger in size, the metabolisms of cities get faster as they grow larger. With each doubling of population, the Santa Fe scientists concluded, a city's residents become, on average, 15 percent more innovative, 15 percent more productive, and 15 percent wealthier.[9]

The advantages that accrue to superstar cities are substantially more enduring than those that accrue to superstar talent. No matter how big the name, talent rises and falls. Professional athletes have relatively short careers and can always be sidelined by injuries, and even the biggest draws at the movie box office grow old and fade with time. Big cities can and do decline, of course—Detroit was a very big city at one time—but the biggest and most dominant ones tend to redouble their strengths. Over a period of less than two decades, New York City was hit by several disasters: a massive terrorist attack in 2001, the collapse of its tech economy in the dot-com bust, a globe-shaking financial crisis in 2008, and Superstorm Sandy in 2012, and yet it remains the most economically powerful city in the world.[10]

Winner-take-all urbanism has reordered the world's cities in a way that is analogous to, and in some ways the outgrowth of, the dramatic globalization of industry.[11] Historically, each of the advanced nations had its own manufacturers of automobiles, steel, electronics, chemicals, and so on. As barriers to trade came down and those national industries faced global competition, some of those companies were acquired by others and many more went out of business. Instead of numerous small companies each playing on its own turf, there are now a relative handful of giant multinational conglomerates in each industry; meanwhile, the smaller companies that survive scramble for smaller and smaller shares of the pie.

Globalization has similarly reshuffled the ranks of the world's cities. As capitalism's spatial division of labor—the distribution of economic activities across locations—becomes more finely honed, fewer and fewer cities are able to hold on to the most economically valuable spaces and niches. The most highly prized talent and the most profitable industries, which used to be spread across many smaller and medium-sized cities, increasingly concentrate in a few superstar behemoths. These cities constitute the tallest peaks of the world economy: these peaks thrive, while the smaller hills stagnate; and the plains and valleys, which are large, suffer.

A skeptic might point out here that superstar cities like New York, London, and LA, and knowledge hubs like San Francisco, Washington, DC, and Boston, haven't experienced the levels of population growth that Sunbelt metros like Phoenix, Dallas, and Atlanta have. But population growth does not capture the dynamic that lies at the heart of superstar power. The superstar advantage is one of quality rather than quantity. Superstar cities are bastions of the most affluent and the most advantaged. Their high and rising costs of living mean that large numbers of people are priced out and ultimately move to less expensive regions like the Sunbelt, spurring the growth of these areas. Others say that the high prices in superstar cities and tech hubs will gradually cause some firms in their key industries to relocate to other, less expensive places, shaping what they refer to as the "rise of the rest." That would indeed take some of the pressure off the real estate prices. But, as the next chapter will show, there is little evidence that high-tech industries are decentralizing away from superstar cities and tech hubs; if anything, they are becoming even more concentrated in the superstars.

Real estate prices provide a clear indicator of the dominant position of superstar cities and the large gap between them and the rest. To get at this, my team and I tracked housing prices in more than 11,000 ZIP codes across America using data from the on-line real estate firm Zillow. There were just 160 ZIP codes where the median home price was $1 million or more, and 80 percent of them were located in the New York, Los Angeles, and San Francisco metro areas. All but 4 of the 28 ZIP codes where median home values were more than $2 million were located in these three metros: 11 in the San Francisco Bay Area, 7 in LA, and 6 in New York. In 2016, roughly 6 in 10 homes in the San Francisco metro area (57.4 percent) were valued at more than $1 million, up from less than 20 percent in 2012.[12] Consider this in light of the fact that more than half (56.2 percent) of the ZIP codes for which data are available have median home values of less than $200,000, and roughly 15 percent have median home values of less than $100,000.

Figure 2.1 provides a visualization of the enormous gap between superstar cities by simply adding up the number of houses you can buy in cities across the United States for the price of just one in New York's SoHo neighborhood. For the price of one SoHo apartment (with a median value of about $3 million) you could buy 18 homes in Las Vegas, 20 in Nashville, 23 in Atlanta, 29 in Detroit, 30 in Cleveland, 34 in St. Louis, and 38 in Memphis. The disparities are even more staggering when you zero in on specific ZIP codes. That one SoHo apartment is worth as many as 50 houses in parts of Toledo and 70 in parts of Detroit. In one

Figure 2.1: How Many Houses You Can Buy for the Price of One in SoHo

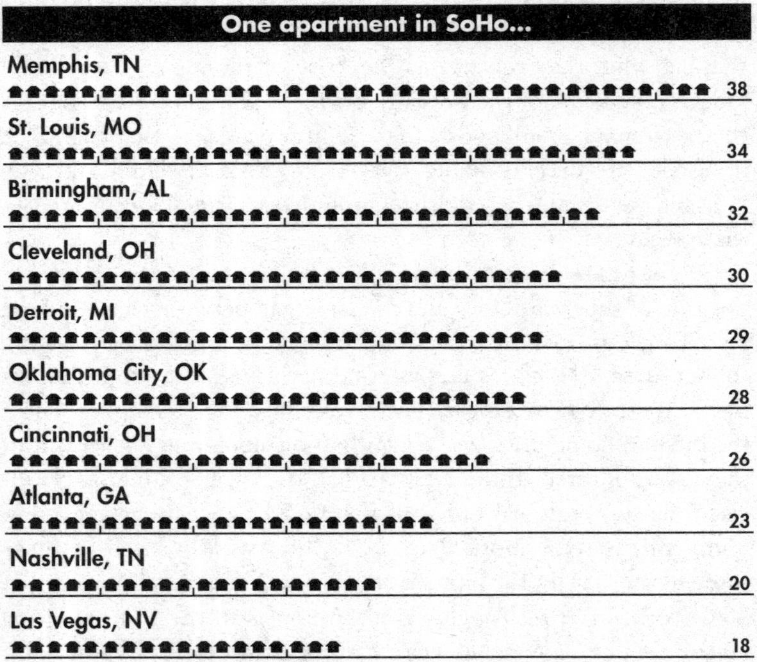

One apartment in SoHo...

Memphis, TN
🏠🏠🏠🏠🏠,🏠🏠🏠🏠🏠,🏠🏠🏠🏠🏠,🏠🏠🏠🏠🏠,🏠🏠🏠🏠🏠,🏠🏠🏠🏠🏠,🏠🏠🏠🏠🏠,🏠🏠🏠   38

St. Louis, MO
🏠🏠🏠🏠🏠,🏠🏠🏠🏠🏠,🏠🏠🏠🏠🏠,🏠🏠🏠🏠🏠,🏠🏠🏠🏠🏠,🏠🏠🏠🏠🏠,🏠🏠🏠🏠   34

Birmingham, AL
🏠🏠🏠🏠🏠,🏠🏠🏠🏠🏠,🏠🏠🏠🏠🏠,🏠🏠🏠🏠🏠,🏠🏠🏠🏠🏠,🏠🏠🏠🏠🏠,🏠🏠   32

Cleveland, OH
🏠🏠🏠🏠🏠,🏠🏠🏠🏠🏠,🏠🏠🏠🏠🏠,🏠🏠🏠🏠🏠,🏠🏠🏠🏠🏠,🏠🏠🏠🏠🏠   30

Detroit, MI
🏠🏠🏠🏠🏠,🏠🏠🏠🏠🏠,🏠🏠🏠🏠🏠,🏠🏠🏠🏠🏠,🏠🏠🏠🏠🏠,🏠🏠🏠🏠   29

Oklahoma City, OK
🏠🏠🏠🏠🏠,🏠🏠🏠🏠🏠,🏠🏠🏠🏠🏠,🏠🏠🏠🏠🏠,🏠🏠🏠🏠🏠,🏠🏠🏠   28

Cincinnati, OH
🏠🏠🏠🏠🏠,🏠🏠🏠🏠🏠,🏠🏠🏠🏠🏠,🏠🏠🏠🏠🏠,🏠🏠🏠🏠🏠,🏠   26

Atlanta, GA
🏠🏠🏠🏠🏠,🏠🏠🏠🏠🏠,🏠🏠🏠🏠🏠,🏠🏠🏠🏠🏠,🏠🏠🏠   23

Nashville, TN
🏠🏠🏠🏠🏠,🏠🏠🏠🏠🏠,🏠🏠🏠🏠🏠,🏠🏠🏠🏠🏠   20

Las Vegas, NV
🏠🏠🏠🏠🏠,🏠🏠🏠🏠🏠,🏠🏠🏠🏠🏠,🏠🏠🏠   18

Source: Martin Prosperity Institute, based on Zillow data for 2015.

neighborhood in Mahoning County, home of Youngstown, Ohio, a SoHo apartment owner could afford more than 100 homes.

The reality, however, is that the superstar-ness of cities turns on a relatively small number of superstar areas within them. As of late 2015, when the average Manhattan apartment cost more than $2 million, the median home value in the city as a whole was just $600,000—and it was substantially lower than that in many parts of it. The owner of the average SoHo apartment could have bought 30 residences in Parkchester, for instance, where the average home would have cost just $107,067. Superstar cities fall victim to a winner-take-all urbanism of their own, as they, too, are divided into a small number of extremely advantaged superstar districts and much larger numbers of less advantaged neighborhoods.

The astronomical real estate prices of superstar neighborhoods and cities—and the staggering gap between their prices and those of almost everywhere else—are the product of the underlying motor of capitalist development: the clustering force. Two key kinds of clustering take place in cities. First, and most obviously, is the clustering of certain firms and industries. The nineteenth-century economist Alfred Marshall identified the gains that occur when competing firms agglomerate. Paul Krugman won his Nobel Prize in part for his insights into the ways that clusters of firms shape our economic geography and power economic growth. Big, populous cities develop thriving industry clusters, such as finance in New York and London, motion pictures in LA, fashion in Milan and Paris, and technology in San Jose. But second, and perhaps even more importantly, skilled and ambitious people cluster in cities. Jane Jacobs originally showed how the clustering of diverse groups of people and skills power urban economies. The Nobel Prize–winning economist Robert Lucas formalized her insights about talent clustering into a theory of economic growth based on what he called human capital externalities. Superstar cities push together talented people from all corners of the world across lines of ethnicity, race, national origin, and sexual orientation. Anywhere from a third to half of the high-tech startups that have been launched in the San Francisco Bay Area in the past decade or so include at least one immigrant among their founders.[13]

But this self-reinforcing process generates its own fundamental contradiction. Although clustering drives growth, it also increases the competition for limited urban space; the more things cluster in space, the more expensive land gets; the more expensive land gets, the higher housing prices become, and the more certain things get pushed out. In a classic 1960 essay, "A Theory of the Urban Land Market," urban economist William Alonso developed a simple but elegant economic model of the competition for urban space. In his view, the price of land followed a series of urban bid rent curves in which land decreased in value with distance from the center.[14] Back then, the headquarters of big companies occupied the most valuable land in and around urban cores.

Factories and warehouses that needed to be located centrally came next, and then housing for the less affluent working classes, who lived in the congested, noisy, and dirty districts around those industrial areas. More affluent households located farther out in the suburbs to avoid all of this. Today, affluent people are taking over the areas once occupied exclusively by industry and commerce, and they are bidding up their prices. The supply of land that is densely developed and highly productive is limited, giving rise to the fierce competition for space that lies at the heart of the urban land nexus.

Consider the premium paid for prime urban land and property. In broad terms, the total value of all land across the United States was $23 trillion in 2009, equivalent to some 160 percent of the nation's economic output, according to a detailed enumeration by the US Bureau of Economic Analysis (BEA).[15] But just the 6 percent of that land that is developed accounts for more than half of that value, $11.7 trillion. The average price for an acre of developed land across the continental United States is sixteen times higher than the price of an acre of undeveloped land—$106,000 versus $6,500. In large metro areas (with populations of 1 million or more), land values average out to $64,800 per acre, compared to $16,600 per acre in metros with fewer than 1 million people, and just $6,700 per acre in metros with populations between 10,000 and 49,000.

Property in superstar neighborhoods in New York, London, LA, and San Francisco is far more expensive than it is anywhere else, routinely selling for $1,500, $2,000, $3,000, or more per square foot—many times the $150 or $200 per square foot for the average US home. In fact, the overall value of real estate in superstar cities rivals the gross domestic product of nations. As of 2015, the value of real estate in the New York metro area was roughly $2.9 trillion, equal to the GDP of the United Kingdom, the world's fifth-largest national economy. The value of real estate across greater Los Angeles was roughly $2.8 trillion, about the size of the economy of France, the world's sixth largest. Greater San Francisco's real estate added up to about $1.4 trillion, comparable to Australia's or South Korea's economy. The total value of residential property across America was nearly $35 trillion ($28.4 trillion for owner-occupied homes and another $5.8 trillion for rental properties), more than the total economic output of America and China combined.[16]

The reality is that housing prices in superstar cities have long outdistanced housing prices in other places. They were twice the national average already in 1950, but by 2000 that gap had quadrupled.[17] And they have risen at a considerably faster pace than prices elsewhere. Between 1950 and 2000, housing prices grew by 3.5 percent per year in San Francisco, more than double the average of 1.7 percent across all large metro areas in the United States (those with more than 1 million people in 2000).

But the real surge in real estate prices in superstar cities has occurred in just the past decade or two, as extreme clustering has heightened the competition for scarce land. As Figure 2.2 shows, land in New York City appreciated at a rate of less than half of 1 percent per year in the four decades spanning 1950 and 1993. Land values zoomed up after that, crashed briefly in the aftermath of the economic crisis of 2008, and then climbed back to record highs. If an investor had bought a plot of land in 1950 and sold it in 1993, it would have returned less than half of 1 percent of value per year in inflation-adjusted dollars. If that same investor purchased a plot of land in 1993 and sold it in 2014, its value would have risen by a factor of 28, returning 16.3 percent per year.

Land values in Manhattan have risen much more dramatically than the value of other forms of real estate. In the two decades spanning 1994 to 2014, investments in land realized an annual return of 15 percent (14.9 percent, to be exact), three times as much as the return for investments in condominiums (4.4 percent).[18] This is the nub of the urban land nexus: barring incredible feats of civil engineering, land in superstar neighborhoods is limited to what is already there.

The urban land nexus is not just a consequence of natural economic forces—that is, of limited supply in the face of surging

Figure 2.2: The Recent Spike in New York City Land Values

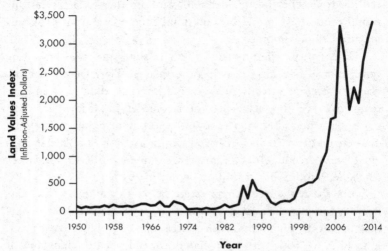

Note: The Land Value Index reflects inflation-adjusted values of $100 invested in a standard plot of land in January 1950.

Source: Data from Jason Barr, Fred Smith, and Sayali Kulkarni, "What's Manhattan Worth? A Land Values Index from 1950 to 2014," Working Paper #2015-002, Rutgers University, March 2015, http://econpapers.repec.org/paper/runwpaper/2015-002.htm. Graph from Anna Scherbina and Jason Barr, "Manhattan Real Estate: What's Next?," *Real Clear Markets*, February 8, 2016, www.realclearmarkets.com/articles/2016/02/08/manhattan_real _estate_whats_next_101995.html.

demand. It also stems from the efforts of urban landlords and home-owners—some of re-urbanization's biggest winners—to restrict what is built, and in doing so to keep the prices of their own real estate holdings high. Over the past several years, a growing chorus of urban economists has decried the way that NIMBY sentiment (an acronym for "not in my backyard") keeps urban housing prices un-necessarily high. Traditionally, NIMBYs were concerned residents who were motivated to keep "bad" things, like prisons or waste treatment plants, out of their neighborhoods. But NIMBYism has grown substantially over time. Across the United States, the number of court cases that mentioned the term land use—a proxy for NIM-BYism—has increased substantially since 1970.[19]

I became the target of NIMBY wrath when I wrote an op-ed suggesting that Toronto should take a closer, harder look at allowing a new generation of small, quiet jets to fly into Billy Bishop Airport, which is on an island very close to Toronto's downtown. It was based on my research, which had found that airports were one of the most important economic generators for cities. The airport was limited to operating turbo-prop planes to relatively close-by places like Montreal, New York, Boston, Washington, DC, and Chicago. The question was whether it should be permitted to extend its runway to accommodate small jets that could fly to cities farther away, such as Vancouver, Los Angeles, and Miami, and potentially even London and Paris. My basic point was that Toronto should try to assess the costs in terms of noise or traffic in and around the waterfront against the economic benefits of a vibrant downtown airport with direct connections to a greater number of cities. Since Toronto's waterfront was busy and noisy already, I wrote, wouldn't it make sense to take into account the economic value that the airport could add to the city if we allowed these small, quiet jets to use its runways?[20] We'll never know. I was accused of being a sellout, more interested in my own convenience than the welfare of the city, when that was hardly my point. Thanks to unrelenting pressure from residents and activists, the newly elected administration of Prime Minister Justin Trudeau kept its campaign promise and nixed the plan.

While there is certainly a place for neighborhood preservation and environmental conservation, NIMBYs do more than keep "bad" things out of cities and neighborhoods. Well-intended or not, when they reflexively block any and all development, they not only preserve their own housing values but also put a brake on the very clustering that drives innovation and economic growth.

In many cases, NIMBYism reflects what economists refer to as rentier or rent-seeking behavior. An economic rent is essentially an extraordinary return that comes about through little or no real effort. And what could be easier than sitting on property and watching its value go up, especially since the gain comes largely from what is going on in the city and neighborhood? Concern over unproductive rentier behavior hearkens all the way back to eighteenth-century economists, who were writing at a time when land, not capital, was the dominant factor of production. In the 1730s, the classical economist Richard Cantillon laid out his "land theory of value," which was in some ways the precursor to Karl Marx's own labor theory of value. Cantillon divided the economy into two groups or classes.[21] On the one hand there were laborers, who traded their work for wages that they used to purchase life's necessities. On the other hand, there were the members of an advantaged class, but instead of Marx's capitalists, Cantillon's advantaged class was made up of landlords, who made their money off the rent they charged for the use of their land. Later, David Ricardo developed his own "law of rent" to describe the economic windfall that accrues to landlords simply by virtue of their owning land, or, as he put it, "that portion of the produce of the earth which is paid to the landlord for the use of the original and indestructible powers of the soil." In *The Wealth of Nations*, Adam Smith decried the selfish "indolence" of landlords.

Today's urban rentiers have more to gain from increasing the scarcity of usable land than from maximizing its productive and economically beneficial uses. The end result is the rise of what *The Economist*'s Ryan Avent has dubbed the "parasitic city," in which wealthy homeowners and landlords capture a disproportionate share of economic output and wealth. As one economist scathingly put it, "It's *landlords*, not corporate overlords, who are sucking up the wealth in the economy."[22]

This behavior isn't just selfish; it's destructive. By limiting density and clustering, NIMBYs hold back the urban innovation that powers growth. That's why I prefer to call them the New Urban Luddites instead of NIMBYs, which sounds more benign. The original Luddites, named after their semi-mythical leader, Ned Ludd, took hammers to the weaving machines that were taking away their livelihoods during England's Industrial Revolution.[23] Over the course of the next century, ironically, those factories would lift living standards to higher levels than the Luddites could have ever imagined. The original Luddites, at least, were poor. The New Urban Luddites aren't exploited workers, but some of the biggest winners of winner-take-all urbanism.

This New Urban Luddism is codified in the enormous and complex thicket of zoning laws and other land use regulations that restrict the supply of housing in many cities. While that may not have been their original intention (much urban zoning began as an effort to keep noxious industrial operations a safe distance away from people's housing), when added up and taken together, these regulations have a substantial negative effect on the economy.

A 2015 study by two leading urban economists found that, taken together, policies that restrict housing development cost the US economy a great deal in lost productivity and economic growth over nearly half a century from 1964 to 2009. New York, they pointed out, was responsible for 12 percent of the nation's overall growth in economic output during that period, but more than half of it was sucked up by artificially inflated housing costs. If the housing and land use restrictions that constrain development were eliminated, so that everyone who wanted to work in San Francisco could afford to live there, the city would see a 500 percent increase in jobs, they calculated. New York's increase would be 800 percent. On a national basis, this would add up to an annual wage increase of $8,775 for the average worker. All told, they estimated that policies which restrict housing development cost the US economy roughly 9 percent of GDP per year, an estimated $1.3 trillion annually in 2009 dollars. These estimates provide a stark reminder of the very real hit the US economy takes every year because of its inefficient and suboptimal use of land. The problem has become so acute that the President's Council of Economic Advisers highlighted the deleterious consequences of land use restrictions on the US economy in its 2016 report.[24]

The New Urban Luddism does not just limit the construction of new homes and apartments; more troublingly, it also puts an artificial cap on the further development and expansion of entire cities. Schools, sewer lines, electric power grids, and, even more importantly, the transit and subway lines required to move people around get much costlier to develop as a place grows bigger. This is why there are so few New Yorks and Londons to begin with. In many aspiring cities, New Urban Luddites effectively limit and block the investments that are required for such further scaling. Less scaling means less clustering; less clustering means lower levels of innovation and productivity. This, in turn, means lower economic output and smaller tax bases, which further constrains the ability of these cities to invest in urban development and to expand their redistributive policies and programs.

There's no doubt that the New Urban Luddism of today's cities is a big contributor to the New Urban Crisis. Yet this does not mean that the solution is to simply rid our cities of all land use regulation. Certainly, there is much that can and should be done to limit NIMBYism and to streamline outdated land use restrictions. But the basic notion, advocated by the growing chorus of so-called market urbanists, that we can make our cities more affordable, more equal, and more productive simply by getting rid of existing land use restrictions is one of those ideas that is simply too good to be true. On the one hand, the high cost of land in superstar neighborhoods makes it very hard, if not impossible, for the private market to create affordable housing in their vicinity. Combine the high costs of land with the high costs of high-rise construction, and the result is more high-end luxury housing, and very little, if any, of the truly affordable housing these superstar cities need. On the other hand, there is a tipping point where too much density can actually deaden neighborhoods. The world's most innovative and creative places are not the high-rise canyons of Asian cities but the walkable, mixed-use neighborhoods in San Francisco, New York, and London. As I will show in Chapter 10, what our cities need is not just deregulation, but a reformed land use system that, together with broad changes in the tax system, increased investment in transit, and a shift from single-family homes to rental housing, can help create the kinds of density, clustering, and talent mixing that the urbanized knowledge economy requires.

The fact of the matter is that the urban land nexus is shaped by an even more powerful and immutable constraint than just land use restrictions—that of basic geography. Cities and metro areas like Los Angeles, San Francisco, Seattle, and Chicago face hard physical boundaries like mountains and water, which, in addition to regulations that limit height or density, hinder their capacity for development. Figure 2.3 tells the basic story, illustrating the inverse relationship between outward expansion and housing price growth. (The chart arrays metro areas across two dimensions: their increase in housing prices between 1980 and 2010 and their expansion of residential development.) The more a metro is able to expand outward and create new housing supply, the less its housing prices tend to rise. Metros in the upper left-hand quadrant, such as San Francisco, New York, LA, Seattle, and Washington, DC, have high housing prices and have seen relatively little residential expansion. Metros in the lower right-hand quadrant, including Las Vegas and Atlanta—as well as the tech hub of Austin, and Raleigh in the North Carolina Research Triangle—have seen more

Figure 2.3: Geography and Housing Values

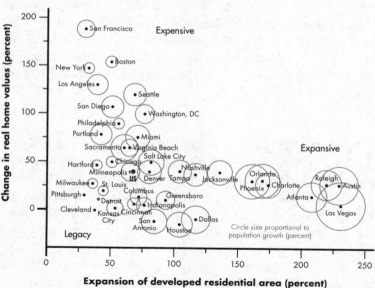

Source: Issi Romem, "Has the Expansion of American Cities Slowed Down?" BuildZoom, April 18, 2016, www.buildzoom.com/blog/cities-expansion-slowing.

modest housing price increases alongside much more residential development.[25]

Geography can push up housing prices in other ways. Older cities like New York, Boston, and San Francisco are ringed by suburbs that make it impossible for them to expand outward, unlike younger Sunbelt cities, which have been able to annex and accumulate the land at their peripheries. In fact, the cities that have seen significant population growth in their already-built-up areas in and around their urban centers are those that have hit such geographic limits to outward expansion—cities like New York, Chicago, the San Francisco Bay Area, LA, and Miami. The expansionary city of Houston lost roughly 120,000 people in its already-built-up urban neighborhoods between 1960 and 2014, while San Francisco—the veritable poster child for restrictive land use policy—gained more than 70,000 people in its already-developed urban areas over the same time period.

Geography ultimately plays an even bigger role than land use restrictions in housing prices, according to a 2010 study by Massachusetts Institute of Technology economist Albert Saiz. Even when such geographically constrained places as New York, San Francisco, LA, and Boston have restrictive land use policies, geography is the key factor in the extraordinary run-up of their housing prices.[26]

D espite high land and housing prices, the conventional wisdom is that workers tend to be better off in superstar cities and tech hubs, which offer higher wages and salaries. Then there are the additional gains that come from the multiplier effect of the knowledge and high-tech jobs that cluster in superstar cities, where high-tech jobs spur additional jobs in related industries and support services.[27]

The overall data support this view. Table 2.2 shows the top five large metros (those with over 1 million people) where the average worker has the most left over after paying for housing and the five where the average worker has the least.[28] The top five are a who's

Table 2.2: Money Left Over After Paying for Housing

	Average Worker	Creative Class	Service Class	Working Class
Metros with the Most Left Over				
San Jose	$48,566	$80,503	$14,372	$23,109
San Francisco	$45,200	$71,741	$16,806	$26,920
Washington, DC	$43,308	$70,030	$13,925	$21,539
Boston	$42,858	$66,871	$16,206	$25,233
New York	$42,120	$71,245	$17,861	$27,343
Metros with the Least Left Over				
Orlando	$25,774	$50,002	$12,903	$21,173
Las Vegas	$26,194	$53,137	$14,394	$27,103
Riverside, CA	$27,296	$54,191	$13,501	$20,777
Miami	$27,482	$53,809	$14,099	$20,452
Virginia Beach-Norfolk	$28,448	$51,601	$13,284	$22,939

Source: Martin Prosperity Institute, based on data from the US Department of Labor, Bureau of Labor Statistics, and US Census.

who of tech hubs and superstar cities. The average worker in San Jose (the heart of Silicon Valley) has $48,566 left over; in San Francisco, it's $45,200. In Washington, DC, it's $43,308, and in Boston and New York it's $42,858 and $42,120, respectively, considerably more than Orlando, $25,774, or Las Vegas, $26,194. In fact, the wages for the "average worker," as well as for each of the three main classes of workers—highly paid creative-class workers, lower-paid working-class workers, and service workers—are all higher in larger metros, being positively correlated with population size.[29]

But these relatively large average amounts left over are mainly the product of the higher wages that accrue to the members of the advantaged creative class. The picture looks very different when the three classes are broken out individually. While advantaged creative-class workers make more than enough to cover their increased housing costs, working-class and service-class workers are worse off. In fact, while the average creative-class worker in San Jose has a whopping $80,503 left over after paying for housing, the average blue-collar worker has just $23,109 left over, and the average service-class worker ends up with just $14,372. The average creative-class worker in San Francisco has $71,741 left over compared to $26,920 and $16,806, respectively, for his working-class and service-class peers. The average creative-class worker in New York pockets $71,245, compared to just $27,343 for the average blue-collar worker and $17,861 for the average service-class worker.

This pattern may be most pronounced in these expensive places, but it holds across all 350-plus metro areas as well. The amount of wages that the members of the creative class have left over after paying for housing is positively correlated with housing costs, while the correlations between housing costs and the amount of wages left over after paying for housing are negative for both the working class and the service class.[30] The takeaway is daunting: as innovative and productive as the economies of superstar cities may be, their most advantaged residents haul in the lion's share of the gains. Their less advantaged working and service classes are falling further behind, unable to keep pace with rising housing costs.

On a more macro scale, the exorbitant real estate prices in superstar cities and tech hubs are a key factor, if not the key factor, in the staggering rise in economic inequality across the world. Thomas Piketty's now-famous formula "r > g" denotes a rate of return on capital that is greater than the rate of overall economic growth, a huge driver of generational inequality. But the reality is that the outsized gains to capital have accrued more from increased real estate values than from returns to assets like stocks and bonds. The share of capital income derived from housing tripled between 1950 and today, according to research by Matthew Rognlie, which is substantially more than for any other form of capital. "Since housing has relatively broad ownership," Rognlie wrote, "it does not conform to the traditional story of labor versus capital, nor can its growth be easily explained with many of the stories commonly proposed for the income split elsewhere in the economy—the bargaining power of labor, the growing role of technology, and so on." In other words, these gains are pure rents to location. Simply put, land and real estate owners in expensive superstar cities and tech hubs have been capitalism's biggest winners. Their trophy penthouses, luxury townhomes, and other real estate holdings amount to the visible, geographic manifestation of Piketty's $r > g$.[31]

This brings us face to face with both the central element of the New Urban Crisis and the central contradiction of contemporary capitalism. The clustering force is at once the main engine of economic growth and the biggest driver of inequality. The concentration of talent and economic activity in fewer and fewer places not only divides the world's cities into winners and losers, but ensures that the winner cities become unaffordable for all but the most advantaged. This unrelenting cycle is great news for wealthy landlords and homeowners, but bad news for almost everyone else.

In the next chapter we'll delve still deeper into the conflicts and tensions brought on by the land nexus, showing how it has pitted three elite groups of urbanites—the super-rich; techies and businesspeople; and artists and cultural creatives—against one another in the escalating competition for space, and how, in doing so, it has created some of the most visible fault lines of the New Urban Crisis.

3
CITY OF ELITES

"If the 1% stifles New York's creative talent, I'm out of here," musician David Byrne warned in 2013.[1] New York City's incredible economic success, he wrote, was threatening to become its cultural undoing. "Most of Manhattan and many parts of Brooklyn are virtual walled communities, pleasure domes for the rich," he continued. "Middle-class people can barely afford to live here anymore, so forget about emerging artists, musicians, actors, dancers, writers, journalists and small business people. Bit by bit, the resources that keep the city vibrant are being eliminated."

Byrne, the front-man of the famed new wave band Talking Heads, is not alone in sounding this alarm. "New York has closed itself off to the young and the struggling," is how the seminal punk rocker, poet, and National Book Award–winning memoirist Patti Smith put it, when asked if young artists could still forge a career in the city. "There are other cities. Detroit. Poughkeepsie. New York City has been taken away from you. So my advice is: Find a new city."[2]

Then there's electronic music artist Moby: "When I lived on 14th Street in the late '80s, I paid $140 a month to share an apartment with a bunch of other odd and dysfunctional musicians and artists," he wrote in 2014. "AIDS, crack and a high murder rate kept most people away from New York back then. But even though it was a war zone, or perhaps to some extent because it was a war zone, Manhattan was still the cultural capital of the world. Of course everything's changed since. New York has, to state the obvious, become the city of money. People say your rent should be 30 percent of your salary; in Manhattan today, at least for many people, it feels like it hovers around 300 percent."[3]

For a growing number of musicians and artists, the transformation of our cities is personal and palpable.[4] And they're not the only ones concerned about the possible creative demise of superstar cities. Pundits and policymakers have piled on, and not just in New York. As Rohan Silva, a key player in London's high-tech boom who served as a senior adviser to former British prime minister David Cameron put it: "In New York, people are decamping to LA and I think we've really got to be careful in London that people don't pick another city and choose to go there. Because the moment a city starts to lose its artists, things can fall apart and the city might lose its edge."[5]

There's little doubt that creative urban ecosystems exist in a precarious balance. Take away the ferment that comes from urban mixing, and the result is a sterile sameness. In SoHo today, luxury stores seem to outnumber performance spaces and studios. But even if rising housing prices are making it harder for a new generation of artists and creatives to get a toehold in SoHo and neighborhoods like it, that doesn't mean that entire cities have become creative dead zones. Despite the influx of wealthy people into the urban core and the transformation of some leading creative neighborhoods, there is little evidence of any substantial diminution of these cities' overall creative capacities. In fact, as we will see, cities like New York, London, Los Angeles, and San Francisco have thus far been able to consolidate their overall creative advantages by adding innovation and high-tech industry to their economic mixes. Cities are big places, after all; creativity can and does move from neighborhood to neighborhood. In time, the ongoing transformation of these cities may truly jeopardize their creative impetus, but that hasn't happened yet.

What Byrne's, Moby's, and Smith's complaints really reflect is the increasingly intense competition for urban space. Artists, musicians, and other creatives were just about the only people who cared enough to transform old, neglected urban spaces into their studios and work spaces in the 1970s and 1980s; today they are being elbowed out of those same places by investment bankers, business professionals, techies, and even the global super-rich. Take New York City's West Chelsea, for example. Just a couple of decades ago, it was a grimy, industrial neighborhood where few people wanted to live. But then artists and other creative people, many of them gays and lesbians, moved in to take advantage of its cheap lofts and apartments. Nightclubs, galleries, and restaurants followed. As the neighborhood became less dangerous and more desirable, more affluent people came in, along with higher-end shops, restaurants, and even hotels. Some of the same old industrial spaces that had once housed artists' lofts and studios were taken over by startups and tech companies. Then the High Line opened up and the neighborhood hit a tipping point, becoming an area of concentrated luxury development for an even wealthier group of people.

Creatives accurately see their adversaries in today's urban land wars as people who are far richer than they are. But even though the vast majority of creatives are not truly wealthy (Byrne, Smith, and Moby excepted), they are relatively advantaged by the standards of most urbanites and most Americans. This becomes abundantly clear when we take into account the amount of money that artists and cultural creatives have left over after paying for housing. In New York, artists and other cultural creatives have, on average, $52,750 left over after paying for housing, less than tech workers ($65,900) and business and financial professionals ($88,770), but nearly three times more than service workers ($17,860). In LA, artists and other cultural creatives have a similar amount left over ($53,760), less than techies ($64,350) and business professionals ($75,870), but three and a half times more than members of the service class ($15,350). In San Francisco, artists and other cultural creatives end up with $47,200 left over, again less than techies ($70,000) and business professionals ($84,900), but nearly three times more than service workers ($16,800).[6]

This is not to say that all artists and creatives in these places are doing fine. Many are undoubtedly struggling and being priced out of their neighborhoods. But, empirically speaking, their aggregate economic situation puts them closer to the company of a more advantaged urban elite, and a world away from that of the less advantaged service class.

In this chapter, I will look into the sources and nature of this new competition for urban space, starting with the influx of the super-rich into leading superstar cities like New York and London. Then I'll turn to the shift in startups, venture capital, and techies from their traditional suburban outposts to more central urban locations. After that, I will array data to address the central concerns that Byrne, Smith, and Moby raised—that rising housing prices and the influx of wealthier people threaten to dampen the creative impetus of cities. On this issue the numbers are clear: up to this point, the alleged death of urban creativity is largely a myth. The real nub of the New Urban Crisis is not the conflicts among different factions of the new urban elite, but the increased economic isolation and insecurity of far less advantaged urbanites.

Over the past several years, every time I've visited London I've invariably heard the same story from my taxi driver. As we've driven past Hyde Park on the way to or from the airport, he'll nod toward a modern glass tower next to the Mandarin Oriental hotel and say something like, "You see that building? Some of the apartments cost £50 million or more. And no one lives there—it's always dark." He has a point: in 2014, there were at least 740 uninhabited properties worth £5 million or more being warehoused in London's elite neighborhoods.

A similar trend is occurring in New York City. The number of Manhattan apartments occupied by absentee owners and renters grew from 19,000 in 2000 to nearly 34,000 by 2011—a jump of nearly 70 percent. In just a three-block stretch of the Upper East Side, 57 percent of the apartments were vacant ten months a year.[7]

According to a growing number of commentators, cities like London, New York, and Paris are being overtaken by an invasion of the global super-rich. In 2013 and 2014, for example, foreign buyers (including residents and nonresidents of the city) purchased almost half of the £1 million–plus residences sold in prime central London locations. The increasingly ferocious competition for space in London's poshest districts means that what we used to think of as gentrification is morphing into a new phase of plutocratization or "oligarchification." According to a 2016 London School of Economics study, it is no longer just the poor and the working class who are being pushed out of the city's upscale neighborhoods, but long-established elites and old-money families who are losing out and in some cases being driven out by much wealthier foreign buyers. No one is going to feel sorry for rich people who are selling their homes to wealthy foreigners for astronomical sums and humongous profits, especially in cities where inequality is reaching record levels, where working people can't afford to live, and the poor are packed into areas of concentrated disadvantage. Still, it highlights the extent to which certain highly prized areas of superstar cities are being turned into gilded enclaves for a global plutocracy of largely absentee owners.[8]

It's not just wealthy plutocrats who are buying into superstar cities. Giant corporations, real estate investment trusts, hedge funds, and sovereign wealth funds are investing huge amounts in real estate there as well. Global cities expert Saskia Sassen estimated that by 2015 corporations had accumulated more than $1 trillion in urban real estate. Many of the super-rich hide their identities behind shell companies, as a detailed *New York Times* investigation of just one hyper-luxury complex, the Time Warner Center, revealed. The identities of more than three-quarters of the owners of units at the more recently built One 57, which commands some of the highest prices per square foot in New York City, are protected by anonymous corporations.[9]

The global super-rich who are snapping up real estate in superstar cities aren't really buying homes, in the conventional sense of that term, to live in and use. They aren't looking for places to raise their families or to do productive work. Instead, they're looking for safe places to park their money. If luxury real estate was the most obvious way to measure and display wealth as "conspicuous consumption" around the turn of the twentieth century, when Thorstein Veblen coined the term, it has become something more mundane today—a new class of economic asset used to store and grow wealth.[10]

The broader evidence indicates that New York and London do have considerable shares of the world's wealthiest people, the former leading in the location of billionaires, the latter in the location of multimillionaires. New York has more billionaires than any other city in the world, with 116 of them, who collectively control $537 billion in total wealth (see Figure 3.1). The San Francisco Bay Area (including Silicon Valley) is second, with 71 billionaires (with $365 billion in total wealth), and Moscow is third with 68 ($290 billion). (It's worth noting that Moscow's billionaires are mostly oligarchs whose wealth has dwindled as resource prices have fallen and the ruble crumbled. Moscow also ranks well down the list of superstar cities, as we saw in Chapter 2.) Hong Kong is fourth, with 64 billionaires, Los Angeles fifth with 51,

Figure 3.1: Where the World's Billionaires Live

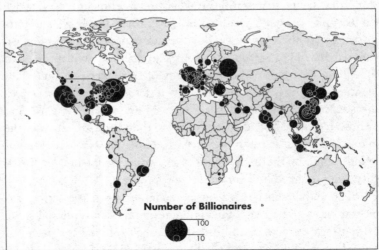

Number of Billionaires

100

10

Source: Martin Prosperity Institute, based on data from Forbes, 2015.

and London sixth with 50. London is more dependent on foreign money than New York is: more than half of London's billionaires (26 out of 50) hail from outside the United Kingdom, compared to less than 10 percent of the billionaires in New York (10 of 116). Beijing (with 46 billionaires), Mumbai (33), Miami (31), and Istanbul (30) fill out the top ten. An additional seven cities—Seoul, Paris, São Paolo, Shenzhen, Taipei, Dallas, and Singapore—each have more than 20 billionaires, and 30 others, including DC, Boston, Atlanta, Phoenix, Seattle, Toronto, and Mexico City, have between 10 and 20. Overall, the larger a city's population, the more globally competitive it is economically, and the larger its finance and tech industries, the greater the number of billionaires it has and the greater their net worth.[11]

Figure 3.2 charts the global locations of a wider pool of wealthy people, so-called ultra-high net worth individuals with $30 million or more in assets. Across the world, there are 173,000

Figure 3.2: Locations of Ultra-High Net Worth Households

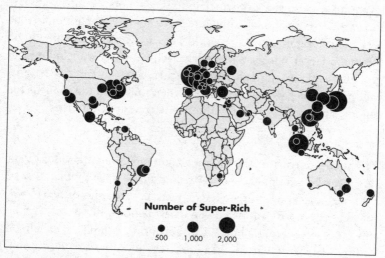

Number of Super-Rich

500   1,000   2,000

Note: Households $30 million or more in assets.
Source: Martin Prosperity Institute, based on data from Knight Frank, *The Wealth Report—2015*, www.knightfrank.com/research/the-wealth-report-2015-2716.aspx.

of these multimillionaires—a 0.002 percent slice of the global population that controls a total of roughly $20 trillion in wealth.[12] On this metric, London comes out on top, with 4,364 of these ultra-rich. Tokyo is second, followed by Singapore, with New York in fourth place and Hong Kong in fifth.

But is this a problem? Do the super-rich really damage great cities? Although rarely occupied trophy apartments and lights-out buildings certainly make certain neighborhoods less vibrant, there are simply not enough super-rich people to deaden an entire city or even significant parts of it. New York City, after all, has more than 8 million inhabitants and some 3 million housing units, and its 116 billionaires and 3,000 or so ultra-high net worth multimillionaires wouldn't fill half the seats in Radio City Music Hall. The global real estate buying spree that occurred in the wake of the 2008 economic and financial crisis had abated somewhat by 2016, as the world's emerging economies—and especially the oil-rich nations—came on harder times themselves and their currencies lost ground, and the United States has cracked down on foreign real estate transactions, some of which amount to money laundering. Ultimately, it's not so much an incursion of super-rich plutocrats that is transforming many of the world's great cities as an incursion of the much larger numbers of merely well-off people, including the growing ranks of startup entrepreneurs, venture capitalists, and well-paid techies who are trading in their houses in the suburbs for condos, apartments, and townhouses in the superstar cities.

The urban shift of the high-tech startup companies and talent is a real sea change—one I would never have predicted even a decade ago. The leading-edge high-tech companies of the 1970s, 1980s, and 1990s, and even the early 2000s—like Intel, Apple, and Google—were all housed in corporate campuses in Silicon Valley. Microsoft had its headquarters in suburban Redmond, Washington, and other high-tech companies clustered along the Route 128 suburbs outside of Boston, in the suburbs of Austin, or the office parks of North Carolina's Research Triangle. Back in the late 1980s, when I conducted my early studies of the geography of venture capital and high-tech industry with Martin Kenney, the lion's share of venture capital–backed startups were in these suburban areas.[13]

That geography has changed dramatically, with venture capital investment and startup companies becoming much more urban. With nearly $6.5 billion in venture capital investment, San Francisco topped the $4.2 billion that the San Jose metro (which encompasses Silicon Valley) received in 2012, ranking as the world's number one location for venture capital investment that year. Greater New York took in more than $2 billion, the bulk of it in Lower Manhattan. Those figures grew even larger in 2013. In that year, the San Francisco metro took in a whopping $8.5 billion in venture capital investment, with $6.2 billion of that flowing into the city itself, compared to $4.8 billion in venture capital investment in the San Jose metro. Venture capital investment in Greater New York grew to more than $3 billion.[14]

Across the United States, more than half of venture capital investment (54 percent) and nearly six in ten startups (57 percent) were in urban ZIP codes in 2013. Roughly 60 percent of venture investment in the Bay Area went to dense, walkable neighborhoods in urban ZIP codes, and in New York, more than 80 percent did. In the ZIP codes that received venture capital investment nationwide, the share of workers who walked, biked, or used transit to get to work was nearly twice the national average (16.6 percent in venture capital neighborhoods versus 8.4 percent overall). More than a quarter of venture capital investment nationally was concentrated in neighborhoods where more than half of all workers walked, biked, or used transit, and more than a third was located in neighborhoods where more than 30 percent did so. Two neighborhoods in the United States, both in downtown San Francisco, each took in more than $1 billion in venture capital in 2013. In these neighborhoods, roughly 60 percent of workers walked, biked, or used transit to get to work.

Indeed, urban density has become one of the most important factors in the propagation of high-tech startups and the attraction of venture capital investment. The amount of venture capital invested in startups is more strongly correlated with population density than it is with either the concentration of highly educated people or the concentration of the creative class, and only slightly less strongly correlated with population density than it is with the concentration of high-tech industry—which is the very thing that attracts venture capital investment to begin with.[15]

Even when venture capital investment flows to startups in smaller cities and suburbs, it tends to go to the ones that have the most urban characteristics. With more than $1.5 billion in

Table 3.1: Leading Global Cities for Venture Capital Investment

Rank	Metro	Venture Capital Investment
1	San Francisco	$6,471
2	San Jose	$4,175
3	Boston	$3,144
4	New York	$2,106
5	Los Angeles	$1,450
6	San Diego	$1,410
7	London	$842
8	Washington, DC	$835
9	Beijing	$758
10	Seattle	$727
11	Chicago	$688
12	Toronto	$628
13	Austin	$626
14	Shanghai	$510
15	Mumbai	$497
16	Paris	$449
17	Bangalore	$419
18	Philadelphia	$413
19	Phoenix	$325
20	Moscow	$318

Note: Millions of US dollars.

Source: Martin Prosperity Institute, based on data from Thomson Reuters for 2012.

investment, the leading center for venture capital investment in Silicon Valley is the densest part of Palo Alto surrounding Stanford University. Cambridge, Massachusetts, home to the Massachusetts Institute of Technology and Harvard, attracted close to $1 billion, more than the suburbs out along Route 128. Dense, walkable Santa Monica attracted double the amount of venture capital that the much larger but more sprawling city of Los Angeles received.

The urban shift in high-tech startups extends beyond the United States. Once a high-finance center with little in the way of tech, London is now home to thousands of high-tech firms and tens of thousands of high-tech jobs. Its startups pull in more than $800 million a year in venture capital, more than Seattle or Austin.[16] Beijing and Shanghai, Mumbai and Bangalore, Toronto, Paris, and Moscow all number among the world's twenty leading locations for venture capital investment and startup companies. Urban startup hubs are also emerging in Berlin, Amsterdam, Liverpool, and Munich in Europe, and Tel Aviv and Amman in the Middle East (see Table 3.1).

There is considerable overlap between the world's leading startup cities and its most important superstar cities. The two preeminent superstar cities, New York and London, rank fourth and seventh, respectively, for venture capital investment, and Los Angeles is fifth. San Francisco, Boston, Washington, DC, and Chicago, as well as Beijing and Shanghai, all rank high as both startup and global cities. Overall, eleven of the world's leading global cities also rank among the top twenty-five cities for high-tech venture capital investment.[17] The startups that power innovation and growth draw their strength and inspiration from cities.

Startups and cities are a natural match. Urban areas provide the diversity, creative energy, cultural richness, vibrant street-life, and openness to new ideas that startup founders are looking for. While many large, well-established tech companies—like Microsoft, Apple, and Facebook, to name a few—require large headquarter sites and remain in the suburbs, startups can make use of the flexible and adaptable work spaces that urban industrial and warehouse buildings provide.

In the past, the most successful startups were those that focused on developing and manufacturing software or hardware, and the large facilities and campuses they required could be more cheaply accommodated in the suburbs. Today's hottest startups involve digital and social media, games, and creative applications, which draw on the deep pools of designers, composers, scenarists, musicians, marketers, and copywriters that can be found in cities. Tumblr and Buzzfeed launched in New York City to take advantage of the proximity of leading media and advertising agencies.[18] Other urban startups, such as Uber and Airbnb, hope to actually make some aspect of cities work more efficiently—transportation and short-term housing, respectively. Cities aren't just locations for these companies, but the sites of the very problems their technologies aim to solve and the platforms for innovation itself.

Indeed, the cultural creativity of great cities has proven to be a big draw for startup talent. New York venture capitalist Fred Wilson told me of a meeting he had with Etsy's founder, Rob Kalen. Wilson found him sitting in his office playing his guitar. When Wilson remarked that he hadn't realized what a talented musician he was, Kalen said, "Fred, you know I'm really an artist. If I had grown up in the 1960s, I would have been a folk musician. If I'd grown up in the 1920s, I would have been a painter. But I grew up in this generation, and my art is making websites." Wilson added, "There's more art than science in this kind of tech, and artists, for the most part, congregate in cities."[19]

Back in 2002, in *The Rise of the Creative Class*, I noted the connection between bohemian values, vibrant art and music scenes, and the places that incubate high-tech startups. San Francisco was a font of 1960s psychedelia and the home of bands like the Grateful Dead, Jefferson Airplane, Big Brother and the Holding Company, and the Mamas and the Papas. Seattle was the birthplace of Jimi Hendrix, who had such a powerful influence on Microsoft cofounder Paul Allen that Allen opened the Experience Music Project in that city's downtown; it was also the birthplace of the grunge scene that later produced Nirvana. Austin, too, has a vibrant alternative music scene that grew up alongside its tech scene. New York and London are among the world's artistic and cultural leaders. These are not mere coincidences: great cities are creative and innovative across the board. In fact, my research shows empirically that artistic and cultural creativity acts alongside the high-tech industry and business and finance to power economic growth.

The current urban trend in high tech is not so much a startling reversal as a correction of a historical aberration. The venture capital icon Paul Graham saw the writing on the wall in 2006. For all its advantages and power, he wrote, Silicon Valley had a great weakness. This high-tech "paradise," with its roots in the 1950s and 1960s, had become "one giant parking lot," he observed. "San Francisco and Berkeley are great, but they're 40 miles away. Silicon Valley proper is soul-crushing suburban sprawl. It has fabulous weather, which makes it significantly better than the soul-crushing sprawl of most other American cities. But a competitor that managed to avoid sprawl would have real leverage."[20] He was right—and that's exactly what's happening today.

Still, as technology companies and the techies who work for them head back to the cities, they are increasingly being blamed for the deepening problems of housing affordability and urban inequality. In spring 2014, protests broke out in Oakland against the private buses that shuttled tech workers from their homes in the city's gentrifying urban core to their jobs in the corporate campuses of Silicon Valley. "You are not innocent victims," a flyer that was handed out to the bus passengers read. "You live your comfortable lives surrounded by poverty, homelessness and death, seemingly oblivious to everything around you, lost in the big bucks and success." Several protesters climbed atop a Yahoo bus, and one, as was widely reported, vomited on its windshield. In San Francisco's Mission District, protesters dressed as clowns formed human pyramids, bounced giant exercise balls, and performed the can-can in front of a Google bus.

For the San Francisco–based activist and writer Rebecca Solnit, those buses were akin to "spaceships on which our alien overlords have landed to rule over us." "A Latino who has been an important cultural figure for forty years is being evicted while his wife undergoes chemotherapy," she wrote. "One of San Francisco's most distinguished poets, a recent candidate for the city's poet laureate, is being evicted after 35 years in his apartment and his whole adult life here: whether he will claw his way onto a much humbler perch or be exiled to another town remains to be seen, as does the fate of a city that poets can't afford." As she framed it, the Bay Area's conflict pitted "writers, artists, activists, environmentalists, eccentrics" against the newly moneyed tech elite. But artists are sometimes seen as the enemy as well. In 2016, protests erupted against artists and art galleries, who were seen as the new colonizers of parts of downtown Los Angeles.[21]

These sorts of conflicts are not new; they have been playing out in San Francisco for a long time. I also wrote in *The Rise of the Creative Class* about San Francisco's SoMa Wars, which were fought over Proposition L, a narrowly defeated proposal in 2000 to ban high-tech development and other forms of gentrification from SoMa, the Mission, and other downtown neighborhoods. People have been protesting gentrification in the city since the late 1970s and 1980s. "San Francisco has become perhaps the most gentrified large city in the nation. Districts that a decade ago were blue collar are now ghettos for young urban professionals, who have spawned a consumptive economy in which one highly successful new chain mass markets croissants," is how one critic put it back in 1985. "The change has created a new vocabulary: Yuppification, croissantification, Manhattanization."[22] Techies and tech startups are just the latest players in a much longer running battle over urban space.

That said, the incredible wealth generated by tech startups can and does contribute to the growing gaps between the advantaged and less advantaged. It's not just lefties and activists who are raising concerns. In a hotly debated essay, venture capitalist Paul Graham argued that startup cities and high-tech districts are "manufacturers of inequality," but nevertheless defended them as the price of progress: "You can't prevent great variations in wealth without preventing people from getting rich, and you can't do that without preventing them from starting startups," he wrote. He went on to point out that the real problem is persistent poverty and declining social mobility, and that our focus on inequality fixates us more on a symptom than on the underlying disease.[23]

Yet, to what extent are urban startups and the techies who are increasingly settling in cities responsible for rising urban housing prices, inequality, and gentrification? On this, the empirical evidence is actually mixed. There's no question that the urban tech incursion has put pressure on housing costs, especially in cities like San Francisco, New York, Boston, and Seattle. Housing prices are closely correlated with several key measures of innovation and high-tech industry.

The connections between economic inequality and urban tech are less clear-cut, however. On the one hand, the concentration of high-tech startups and venture capital is closely associated with higher levels of wage inequality. This makes sense, since wage inequality reflects the divided job markets of cities, where knowledge workers make much more money than service workers and the working class. On the other hand, the statistical correlations between urban tech and the broader measure of income inequality are statistically insignificant, meaning there is no observable association between the two. I'll have more to say in Chapter 5 about the differences between these two forms of inequality and the factors that drive them. But for now, it's fair to say that urban startups and venture capital are not the primary drivers of the increase in urban inequality, which stems from other features of large, knowledge-based cities, the very ones that have made these cities attractive to techies and tech companies in the first place.[24]

Other research comes to similar conclusions. A detailed 2015 study looked closely at the connection between innovation and inequality over the past several decades across all fifty US states. While it found a reasonably strong connection between innovation and the increase in the share of income going to the top 1 percent of the population, there was little, if any, connection between innovation and the broader income inequality between the rich and the poor.[25] In fact, metro areas with higher levels of innovation had higher rates of economic mobility as well. Innovation was positively and significantly associated with the likelihood that children would end up in a higher income bracket than their parents. Despite the high housing costs and extreme wage inequality of superstar cities and knowledge hubs, the poor and working classes have better prospects for upward mobility in them than in other places.

Many people, including many San Franciscans, have an intuitive feel for these contradictions. Two-thirds of San Francisco residents who participated in an April 2014 survey said that techies were "squeezing out others" and making the city less diverse and more exclusive. But nearly three-quarters (73 percent) of them said they believed that tech companies were good for the city, and more than half (56 percent) said the city should continue to nurture and attract them.[26]

Of course, the migration of high-tech startups and tech workers into urban neighborhoods does put pressure on real estate, and this is especially the case in San Francisco. But tech companies are also huge drivers of innovation, economic progress, jobs, and the much-needed tax revenues that cities can use to address and mitigate the problems that come with them. High tech doesn't deaden cities; it increases their innovative capability considerably. Techies and startup companies may be convenient scapegoats for the very real problems of some places, but it makes little economic sense to discourage them from continuing to move back to cities.

There can be no doubt that the recent influx of the very rich, of tech startups and their employees, and of financial and other professionals into cities is generating real challenges and prompting highly charged conflicts. But has it blunted cultural creativity in those cities, as some have charged? In a word, no: the creative strengths of superstar cities have actually increased.

New York's comeback after the 2008 financial crisis was driven not by its traditional strengths in finance, banking, or even real estate, for instance, but by the incredible expansion of its creative economy, which grew by 13 percent between 2003 and 2013.

Though New York's 8.4 million people make up just 2.6 percent of the US population, the city is home to 8.6 percent of the nation's creative jobs, up from 7.1 percent in 2003. It accounts for 28 percent of the country's fashion designers, 14 percent of its movie and television producers and directors, 12 percent of its print and media editors, and 12 percent of its art directors.[27] This makes it by far the nation's preeminent creative center.

Across the Atlantic, London's dominance in the creative industries is even more pronounced. Greater London accounts for 40 percent of all the creative-industry jobs in the United Kingdom, although it is home to just 12.5 percent of the country's population. These creative jobs include 58 percent of the jobs in TV, film, and radio in the United Kingdom, and 43 percent of the jobs in music and the performing arts. And London's dominance has been growing: between 2007 and 2014, it accounted for by far the largest share of employment growth in the United Kingdom's creative industries.[28]

The concentration of creative industries and jobs in superstar cities goes far beyond what their large size alone can account for. When my colleagues and I examined the geography of America's creative economy broadly, spanning music, the visual arts, acting, and dance, we found that New York and Los Angeles had much larger concentrations of those jobs than any other metros, substantially more than what their populations alone would have predicted.[29]

How much do New York and Los Angeles dominate other places in arts and creativity? The short answer is a lot. LA's concentration of jobs in the artistic and creative fields across the board is nearly three times the national average, while New York's is more than double the national average. LA's concentration of people in the fine arts, including painters and sculptors, is nearly four times as high as the national average; New York's is one and a half times as high. New York has nearly three times and LA more than twice the national average for musicians and singers. LA's concentration of actors is roughly ten times the national average; New York's is two and a half times the average. LA has nearly seven times and New York four and a half times the national average for producers and directors. Both metros have more than three times the national average for writers and authors. And New York's concentration of fashion designers is ten times higher than the national average, while LA's is nearly eight times higher.[30]

Certainly, there has been a certain amount of sorting and shuffling between these two leading superstar cities. Moby said in 2014 that he left New York for Los Angeles "because creativity requires the freedom to fail," and LA's cheaper rents made that prospect less daunting. His anecdotal perception is backed up by empirical data. Artistic and cultural creatives are moving from New York to LA in numbers that are not trivial, according to research from the US Census Bureau.[31] But together, the two stand far above other American cities.

Figure 3.3: Winner-Take-All Creativity

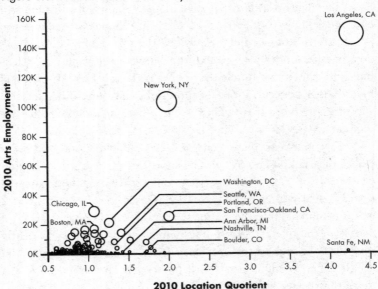

Source: Carl Grodach, Elizabeth Currid-Halkett, Nicole Foster, and James Murdoch, "The Location Patterns of Artistic Clusters: A Metro- and Neighborhood-Level Analysis," *Urban Studies* 51, no. 13 (2014): 2822–2843.

The dominance of New York and Los Angeles in the creative fields can be seen in Figure 3.3, which arrays metros on their concentrations of twenty-two leading arts and cultural industries spanning the visual arts, music, theater, and design and their overall employment in them. Both metros are significant outliers, especially Los Angeles (see the upper right-hand corner of the graph).[32] The concentration of the arts and cultural industries in these metros and associated employment opportunities in them are far greater than in any other metro area in the United States, even when their large populations are taken into account.

Digging deeper into the data on popular music provides another way of seeing the creative supremacy of these two superstar cities. New York and LA are among the world's leading centers for popular music and have been for decades. In fact, popular music follows an even more pronounced winner-take-all pattern than finance, media, or high tech. In an analysis of the geographic locations of ten popular music genres in 2007, my team and I found that LA led in six of them—pop, rock, electronic, Latin, folk, and experimental music—and took second place in three others—urban, country, and jazz. New York topped the list in jazz and was second in rock, pop, electronic, folk, and Latin. The only other places that registered at all were Nashville, which topped the list for country and Christian, and Atlanta, which leads in urban music.[33]

Just three cities—New York, Los Angeles, and London—have dominated popular music globally for the better part of a half century—an era that spans Frank Sinatra, Elvis, and the Beatles and extends all the way to Beyoncé, Jay-Z, and Taylor Swift.[34] Nearly two-thirds (63.2 percent) of hit-makers between 1950 and today were located in these three cities (21 percent in New York, 22 percent in LA, and 20 percent in London). Of course, there's a difference between where musicians go to make music and where they were actually born: only 14 percent of the pop stars in our dataset were born in or around New York City, 7 percent were born in London, and just 2 percent were born in LA. But that's not a new phenomenon either. The Beatles were incubated in Liverpool and Hamburg before making it in London. America's great indigenous art form, the blues, was born in the Mississippi Delta and came of age in Chicago before it was massively commercialized in New York, LA, and London. Madonna moved from Detroit to New York, and Miley Cyrus from a suburb of Nashville to LA. Taylor Swift, who grew up in Reading, Pennsylvania, moved to Nashville and then to New York. Max Martin, the Swedish producer who has had more hits than Michael Jackson, keeps a residence with a studio in LA. These cities may not be as hospitable as they once were to young musicians and artists at the beginnings of their careers, but they continue to be the places musicians go to become successful and stay on top.

Why are these three superstar cities so dominant? For one thing, because they have great economic scope over and above just their large size and scale. They benefit not just from being big cities with big markets, but from being home to vibrant clusters of the varied talent and skills these industries require—not just the performers and the artists, but also the companies, and the venues and producers, and the agents and writers, and the composers, choreographers, and designers, and the engineers. Hits are unpredictable: many more releases fail than succeed, and it takes many, many bets to create just one big winner. Large superstar cities have the best hit-makers, the most complete support structures required to launch them, and the fast metabolisms needed to process many bets quickly and efficiently. They are also the centers of the major media, which remain a central ingredient of the pop culture and its star-making machinery.

Cities with fully innovative and creative economies with capabilities spanning arts, culture, technology, and management are indeed rare. Just 5 percent of all US metros—19 out of 364—stand out as having high-performing, fully functional creative economies across these domains. These include the superstar cities of New York and LA along with the knowledge and tech hubs of San Francisco, San Jose, Boston, Washington, DC, Seattle, and Austin. Besides dominating in creative, high-tech, and management fields, they also have stronger, more diverse, and more robust economies across the board.[35]

While a growing number of commentators believe the high housing prices in these superstar places will dampen innovation and economic growth, so far that has not happened. Between 2014 and 2015, the San Jose metro area posted the second-fastest rate of growth in the United States, with an 8.9 percent increase in economic output, more than three times the national average of 2.5 percent, while nearby San Francisco grew at a 4.1 percent clip.[36] Rather than seeing their creativity deadened and driven out, leading superstar cities and tech hubs continue to outdistance the rest.

There's no denying that New York, London, Los Angeles, and San Francisco have become more expensive places to live; that younger, struggling artists and musicians have been priced out of some parts of these cities; and that some of the neighborhoods that were once the leading artistic centers have lost their creative verve. Superstar cities and knowledge hubs are in great demand. Land in them is finite, and the competition for space is fierce.

And yet, for all of the dire warnings coming from established musicians and artists, these cities are at least as artistically creative as they ever were, and they are even more technologically innovative. For me, there's a certain irony in the spectacle of highly successful rock stars pining after the good old days of low rent, cheap drinks, and creative nirvana, even though it burns me up, too, that the seminal punk-rock and new-wave venue, CBGB's, is now an upscale clothing store. On the whole, the creative economies of these cities are considerably stronger than they were back in the 1970s and 1980s. Would anyone *really* want to trade the economies of New York and Los Angeles today for their economic situation back in the 1970s or 1980s? The answer, it seems to me, is obvious. The addition of high-tech companies to the traditional strengths of these cities in artistic creativity has made their economies stronger.

Put bluntly, some of the noisiest controversies regarding our changing cities spring from the competing factions of a new urban elite. The much bigger problem is the widening gap between this relatively advantaged class and everyone else. It's the poor and the working classes who are truly being displaced and shunted aside in our thriving cities, and the way to help them is not to turn off the spigot of wealth creation, but to make their flourishing economies more encompassing and inclusive.

The challenges facing the poor and working classes are often framed as a problem of gentrification, which has become perhaps the biggest flashpoint in the current conversation about cities. While the debate over gentrification has more substance to it than the charge that expensive cities are becoming culturally dead, or that techies are to blame for the woes of leading knowledge hubs, it, too, suffers from its own myths and mystifications, which the next chapter will unpack and explore.

4

GENTRIFICATION AND
ITS DISCONTENTS

"When you see white mothers pushing their babies in strollers, three o'clock in the morning on 125th Street, that must tell you something," Brooklyn native Spike Lee declared in February 2014. The acclaimed director of *Do the Right Thing* and *Malcolm X* had opened the floor for questions after giving a talk at Brooklyn's Pratt Institute as part of a Black History Month series. A member of the audience asked him about gentrification, and, as it turned out, Lee had quite a lot to say on the subject. Gentrification isn't something that happens to neighborhoods, he asserted. It's something that is done to the people who live in them. It's little more than a neocolonialist land grab: "the motherfuckin' Christopher Columbus Syndrome," is how he put it.[1]

For Lee, gentrification amounts to rich white people pushing poor black ones out of their neighborhoods and their homes. He's not alone. Numerous critics have long decried it as an exploitative process that occurs as wealthy developers buy up land and buildings and drive the original residents out of their neighborhoods.[2]

Gentrification is as much an emotional issue as it is an economic one. (I should know, I've been blamed for it.[3]) Many newcomers understandably feel guilty that they are changing the character of the neighborhoods they move into and possibly forcing some of their neighbors out of their homes. ("There's Basically No Way Not to Be a Gentrifier," is how one 2014 article put it.[4])

Longtime residents have a strong sense of attachment to the places in which they live; even if they're not forced to leave, they are understandably upset when newcomers who are very different and much more well-to-do change their neighborhood in ways that make it feel unfamiliar. We all care deeply about where we live and want others to respect our right to be there. When they do not, anger and anxiety mount, and tensions flare.

Yet a number of experts who have researched the subject see the standard complaints about gentrification as overblown and inaccurate. Lance Freeman, an urban planning professor at Columbia University who has studied the gentrification of Harlem and other New York neighborhoods extensively, thinks that the concern over the direct displacement of poor residents by wealthy gentrifiers is based more on myth than reality. Douglas Massey, a sociologist at Princeton University and a leading expert on racial and economic segregation, argues that gentrification is a proverbial "drop in the bucket" compared to the broader movement of people into and out of cities. For him, the anti-gentrification stance taken by some urbanists is hypocritical. "On the one hand, liberal urban specialists rail against the suburbanization of America and the abandonment of the cities by the nation's whites," he wrote. "On the other hand, when a very few and highly selected whites buck the trend and stake a claim in the city, they are berated as opportunists and decried for gentrifying the inner city."[5]

My objective in this chapter is to focus on the facts in order to restore some sorely needed balance and perspective to the conversation. As we will see, the pace of gentrification has picked up as the back-to-the-city movement has accelerated since the year 2000. But as of yet, it has mainly affected the rather exclusive club of superstar cities and tech hubs. And though a large body of research finds that relatively few people are directly displaced by gentrification, the bigger problem lies in the way the back-to-the-city movement has driven up urban housing prices in these cities across the board, with the burden falling most heavily on the poor and disadvantaged. Ultimately, the media's obsession with gentrification deflects attention from the far more serious problem of chronic and concentrated urban poverty. It's important to understand gentrification as it actually exists, both for its own sake and as a prerequisite to understanding the deeper dynamics of the New Urban Crisis.

G enerally speaking, gentrification describes a process in which a neighborhood gains wealth and sees its population become more affluent, whiter, and younger. The term was coined back in the early 1960s by Ruth Glass, who used it to describe the transformation of working-class London neighborhoods by the middle- and upper-class gentry. "Once this process of 'gentrification' starts in a district," she wrote, "it goes on rapidly until all or most of the working class occupiers are displaced and the whole social character of the district is changed."[6]

Back in the 1960s and 1970s, gentrification occurred in two basic ways. The first way, which Glass wrote about, took place when affluent and educated people began moving back into formerly upscale residential neighborhoods, like New York's Greenwich Village, Boston's Beacon Hill, Society Hill in Philadelphia, or Georgetown in Washington, DC. Hollywood portrayed this type of gentrification in the 1970 film *The Landlord*, in which Beau Bridges plays a feckless child of privilege who invests some of his inherited money in a slum rooming house, intending to evict its African American tenants and restore it as a private townhouse for himself (of course, things take a rather different turn). Set in the then blighted neighborhood of Park Slope, Brooklyn, the film was a box-office dud, but its vision of Park Slope's economic and racial future proved more prophetic than it seemed at the time the movie was released.[7]

One of the earliest empirical studies of the phenomenon examined this form of gentrification in two Washington, DC, neighborhoods.[8] The first, Mount Pleasant, was transitional, with a lot of run-down residential buildings that required substantial renovation. Its longtime residents were fairly varied by race, ethnicity, age, marital status, and social class, but the gentrifiers were mostly young single men who were willing to shoulder the risks that came with the neighborhood's higher crime rate in order to afford a historical, architecturally interesting townhome. The second neighborhood, Capitol Hill, was further along in the process of gentrification, and it attracted a different kind of newcomer. The majority of its buildings had already been renovated, and the neighborhood was close to its residents' workplaces. In addition to single men, its newer residents included older people, more single and married women, and even some families with children. These people were much less transient than the single men in Mount Pleasant. They were heavily committed to the neighborhood and much more invested in its future. Some displacement was already occurring, especially in Capitol Hill, and blacks, other minorities, and the elderly were disproportionately affected by it. The study warned policymakers to watch this trend.

The second way gentrification occurred in the 1960s and 1970s was through the repurposing of older industrial and warehouse districts, largely by artists and creatives. As industry moved out to the suburbs, artists, musicians, and designers began transforming old factory lofts and warehouse spaces into studios and performance spaces. The nascent careers of artists like the noted minimalist Donald Judd were nurtured in Lower Manhattan lofts, while surrounding clubs and bars, including the Café Wha?, The Mudd Club, and CBGB, provided musicians from Bob Dylan and Jimi Hendrix to David Byrne and the Ramones with the venues where they honed their acts and were eventually discovered.

Gentrification has been happening for decades, and, for just as long, people have been worrying about the harm it can do to neighborhoods and cities. Back in 1981, one expert warned about its ill effects on San Francisco in language that is eerily similar to what we hear today: "At this rate we would become a place only the elite can afford," Kenneth Rosen of the University of California at Berkeley told the *New York Times*. "Ten years from now, unless we adopt some sort of policy to insure income integration, we will crowd out all the middle-income people. I think San Francisco is going to become a very rich living area, a lot of single and retired people who have money, executives who work down in the financial district. It's going to be very difficult for a nonwealthy person to live here."[9]

It is useful to see gentrification, as we experience it today, in its broader historical context. Over this longer time frame, it becomes clear how neighborhoods continuously shift and change, going from residential areas to centers of commerce and industry and back, and from rich to poor and back again to rich. This process of neighborhood transformation is a natural, if wrenching, feature of cities, which are perpetual works in progress. As they grow and change, their demography and class structures shift. While their buildings may look the same from the outside, what goes on inside them changes substantially over time.

A study by the economist William Easterly and a team of his students in 2014 illuminates how urban neighborhoods are constantly being built and rebuilt over time, tracking the development of a single 486-foot stretch of SoHo's Greene Street over three centuries.[10] Back in 1641, Dutch settlers granted the land to freed African slaves to farm, in the hope that they would provide a buffer between the colonists and the Indians. After the Dutch departed, the city's population increased and the land became more valuable. Eventually it was incorporated into a larger farm, which went bankrupt at the end of the eighteenth century. By the early 1800s the block had been developed into fashionable townhouses for the bankers and merchants who worked in the port and financial district on the southern tip of Manhattan. When a yellow fever epidemic broke out, Greene Street's toniest inhabitants moved farther north, and by the middle of the nineteenth century its houses and hotels had devolved into brothels.

As the city started to industrialize, the neighborhood transformed once more, and by the 1890s all but two of its original houses had been demolished and replaced with five- and six-story warehouses and factories. Greene Street became an epicenter of New York's garment trade, hat-making in particular. But then in 1911, a fire at the Triangle Shirt Waist Factory, six blocks north on the corner of Greene and Washington Place, became the catalyst for changing the neighborhood's fortunes yet again, as its buildings became uninsurable. The garment trade followed the red-light district uptown, and Greene Street fell into desuetude for some time—though an ill-fated midcentury plan by Robert Moses to turn Lower Manhattan into a set of Le Corbusier-esque superblocks, crisscrossed with elevated expressways, brought the neighborhood back into the public eye for a while. By the 1960s and 1970s, artists began moving into its empty industrial lofts, and today those artists are being supplanted by high-end shops and luxury housing. As Easterly's detailed data on real estate prices show, the past twenty or so years—the period that is commensurate with current gentrification—has seen by far the largest jump in the area's real estate values.

Indeed, gentrification has become a much more contentious issue today than it was in the 1970s and 1980s, as the back-to-the-city movement has accelerated and real estate prices have skyrocketed in superstar cities. Between 1990 and 2014, more than half of America's one hundred largest cities saw population growth in neighborhoods close to their urban centers. This is a dramatic reversal of previous patterns—by way of comparison, just six of those cities experienced population growth in these same areas between 1970 and 1980.[11] This recent re-urbanization trend has been overwhelmingly driven by the upscale, affluent, educated, and white. The group most likely to move back to dense urban neighborhoods between 2000 and 2014, according to data put together by real estate economist Jed Kolko, was the richest 10 percent of US households. This back-to-the-city movement of the affluent and advantaged has been most noticeable in New York, Los Angeles, the Bay Area, Boston, DC, Chicago, Seattle, Portland, and Denver, but it is occurring in other metros as well. At the same time, less advantaged residents of those cities have been pushed out. The poorest 10 percent of households were the most likely to leave America's cities between 2000 and 2014.[12]

Young people have also been an increasing force in gentrification, so much so that the urban planner Markus Moos has coined a term for it: youthification. Large swaths of Manhattan and adjacent parts of Brooklyn, along with downtown Chicago, Toronto, and San Francisco, have been taken over by the young, according to his maps and research. Over the past decade, the population of college-educated young people between the ages of twenty-five and thirty-four grew three times faster in downtown areas than in the suburbs of America's fifty largest metro areas. These close-in urban neighborhoods accounted for 25 percent of the total increase in young college-educated people across the nation, even though they accounted for just 5 percent of the population overall. For all this, the biggest demographic force in the back-to-the-city movement is not the Millennials, who were born in the early 1980s through about 2000, but the slightly older Generation Xers, who were born between the mid-1960s and the early 1980s, particularly the youngest among them, who are now in their late thirties. A big reason for this is that young people are getting married later in life and postponing having children, which enables them to stay in urban areas longer. Today's young urbanites are overwhelmingly singles, childless couples, or couples with very young children. But, any way you slice it, it's a privileged subset of young people that is headed back to cities.[13]

If affluent whites have been the driving force behind gentrification and the broader back-to-the-city movement, middle-class blacks have also played a role. A third of the income gains that occurred in more than 15,000 urban neighborhoods between 1990 and 2000, for instance, were attributable to the highly educated black households moving in, according to one study. Urban neighborhoods are especially attractive to middle-class blacks, who are less likely to suburbanize, largely as a result of discrimination. Long denied equal housing options in the suburbs, middle- and upper-class black families are far more concentrated in urban centers than their white peers. When they are priced out, they are more likely to move to and thus gentrify less advantaged black neighborhoods.[14]

The deepest dive into recent gentrification comes from my University of Toronto colleague Nathaniel Baum-Snow and Daniel Hartley of the Federal Reserve of Chicago, who tracked the transformation of downtown neighborhoods (within a three-mile radius of the central business district) in 120 US metros between 1970 and 2010.[15] Their study generates three big takeaways that help inform our understanding of the driving forces behind gentrification and its winners and losers.

First, gentrification is a recent phenomenon, having accelerated greatly since the year 2000. Between 1980 and 2000, most downtown neighborhoods were poor and black; gentrification was a relatively limited phenomenon, occurring mainly in cities like New York, Boston, Washington, DC, and San Francisco. During this time, both affluent and less affluent residents were leaving cities, including educated and working-class whites. But all of this changed sharply after 2000 as people began flowing back to urban centers.

Second, the back-to-the-city movement has been overwhelmingly driven by affluent and highly educated whites. In 1980, only two metros—New York and Santa Barbara—had large shares of affluent, highly educated whites living in and around their downtowns. Since 2000, affluent college-educated whites have poured back into the urban centers. By 2010, many more cities—from Washington, DC, and Chicago to Houston and Atlanta—had large shares of affluent educated whites living downtown. Between 2000 and 2010, the share of high-income, highly educated white households living downtown increased in roughly two-thirds of the metros the study examined.

Several factors have driven affluent, educated whites back to the urban core. One is access to the large concentration of the higher-paying knowledge, professional, tech, and creative jobs that are located there. Another is the growing tendency for the affluent to want to locate in closer proximity to work to avoid long commutes. But the most important factor driving the back-to-the-city movement of affluent, educated whites is access to the amenities cities offer—from libraries and museums to restaurants and cafés. By moving back to the urban core, affluent whites are able to simultaneously reduce their commutes, locate near high-paying economic opportunities, and gain privileged access to the better amenities that come from urban living.

Third, as these more advantaged types have come in, lower-income, less educated racial minorities have moved out—or been pushed out—of these areas, mainly as a result of rising housing prices. This outflow of the less affluent is especially troubling, because urban centers offer both better job opportunities and greater levels of the kinds of amenities that can help boost wages and increase prospects for economic mobility. The end result is growing inequality and spatial segregation as less advantaged blacks and whites are pushed out of the urban core and become increasingly concentrated in declining suburbs or in less advantaged and more economically isolated areas of the city, something I will look at more closely in Chapters 6, 7, and 8.

Ultimately, gentrification is the product of forces that go far beyond the individual desires and preferences of the young, educated, and affluent who are moving into cities today, or of the artists and musicians who occupied the lofts of the 1970s and 1980s. Gentrification is shaped by much bigger and broader forces, among them the large-scale public and private investments that structure the choices individuals make, and in doing so, alter the trajectories of neighborhoods and cities.[16]

The location of transit lines, for example, have long shaped real estate development patterns. A century ago, streetcar lines shaped the location of early suburbs.[17] Today, transit similarly spurs gentrification by encouraging the clustering of affluent people around it. It does so in two ways. On the one hand, it is a large-scale investment that signals a substantial commitment to neighborhood transformation and thus helps attract more affluent residents, helping to drive up property values. On the other, it allows more privileged groups to give up their arduous commutes. Highly educated professionals and knowledge workers are increasingly willing to pay a premium to be located near their jobs in the urban center or close to subway and transit stops that will get them there quickly.[18] This process feeds on itself. As more affluent households locate around transit lines and nodes, those

neighborhoods see their housing values improve, and quality amenities follow. They gain more and better shops, cafés, and restaurants and better schools, parks, and other amenities, making them
even more attractive and driving prices up further. The gentrification of neighborhoods around transit reflects scarcity: prices are
highest around transit lines because we don't have enough transit
and transit-served neighborhoods.

Transit, of course, is one of many forms of public investment
that can help to spur gentrification. Schools are another. Along
with crime, both the perception and the reality of lower-quality
schools has historically pushed middle-class families out of cities.
The creation of new charter and magnet schools in recent decades
and the overall improvement of existing schools has drawn more
affluent families back in and induced them to stay even when they
start having children. As advantaged groups reach a critical mass
in urban neighborhoods, increased political pressure generates
even more investment in local schools.

Universities and colleges and their affiliated medical centers—
so-called eds and meds—are another channel through which public investment attracts educated, affluent residents back to cities.
Both public universities and private research universities receive
substantial federal support, and many offer housing or housing
subsidies to university faculty and staff, who often live in and spur
gentrification in adjacent neighborhoods.

Public investment in parks and green spaces also boosts gentrification. New York's High Line park, for example, has generated
billions of dollars of residential development along its corridor.
Parks are attractive amenities in their own right, and they signal
that a neighborhood is rising. Of course, large-scale publicly subsidized redevelopment efforts, such as Hudson Yards in New York
City, Toronto's waterfront initiative, and Pittsburgh's North Side
urban stadium district, pour massive amounts of taxpayer dollars
into the transformation of formerly industrial districts, producing
mixed-use developments that are magnets for knowledge workers and new urbanites and that lead to gentrification in adjacent
neighborhoods.

The great irony is that the influx of the affluent and the educated is making cities less urban and more suburban in character. Today's new urban apartments and condo buildings offer a raft of suburban-like amenities, such as wine storage areas, theater rooms, gyms, outdoor decks and pools, and parking garages. In one exclusive building on Eleventh Avenue in New York's Chelsea area, residents have elevators that lift their cars right to their doorsteps. The suburbanization of gentrifying areas of cities is reflected in the space their residents take up as well. Today's urbanites consume almost as much square footage as suburbanites. The average urban family lives in 1,678 square feet, compared to 1,800 for suburbanites. And the average individual urbanite uses 767 square feet per person, just slightly less than the 800 square feet used by suburbanites. What we are seeing is the replacement of the gritty and crowded with the renovated and spacious.

Although gentrification is growing across the United States, it is a much bigger problem in expensive superstar cities and tech hubs. In three-quarters of America's fifty-five largest metros, less than 10 percent of the neighborhoods had gentrified, and in 40 percent of them, 5 percent or less of all neighborhoods had gentrified during the decade of the 2000s, according to a detailed study by the Federal Reserve Bank of Cleveland. (The study defined gentrification as the share of neighborhoods in a metro area that moved from the bottom half to the top half in the distribution of home prices between 2000 and 2007.[19]) By this metric, extensive gentrification was only occurring in a small number of metro areas, such as New York, Boston, and Washington, DC, on the East Coast and San Francisco, Portland, and Seattle on the West Coast (see Figure 4.1).

When my team and I correlated the Federal Reserve's data with a set of key economic, social, and demographic indicators for those same metro areas, it became clear that gentrification is occurring in a distinct set of expensive and advantaged cities and metros. Gentrification was positively correlated with the size and

Figure 4.1: Gentrification Varies Widely by Metro

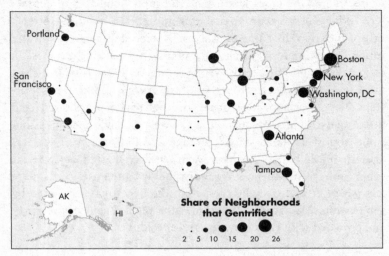

Source: Map by Martin Prosperity Institute, based on data from Daniel Hartley, *Gentrification and Financial Health*, Federal Reserve Bank of Cleveland, 2013.

density of a metro; its wealth and affluence; the concentration of high-tech industry; and the share of science and technology workers, artistic and cultural creatives, and college graduates. It was also positively associated with transit use and negatively correlated with sprawl, measured as the share of commuters who drive alone to work.[20] In other words, gentrification is the product of the very attributes that define knowledge hubs and superstar cities. When all is said and done, acute gentrification is more a symptom of urban success than it is a general characteristic of cities and metro areas across the board.

The fact that gentrification takes place mainly in superstar cities is a big part of the reason it attracts so much attention to begin with. These are the places where the most influential writers, journalists, and academics live and work. Today, one in five reporting jobs are located in New York, DC, and LA, up from one in eight in 2004.[21] (Journalism reflects the same superstar-city clustering we've seen in other fields.) It's not surprising that journalists write about gentrification in the cities where they live and where the publications they work for are located, but it can bias the coverage in less obvious ways. A 2015 study tracked the neighborhoods the *New York Times* identified as gentrified or gentrifying over three decades (1980–2009) and compared them to the gentrifying neighborhoods identified by more detailed research studies (like those I discuss here).[22] *Times* reporters were much more likely to peg gentrification in neighborhoods in Manhattan and adjacent parts of Brooklyn than in the Bronx and Queens. Journalists—or artists, for that matter—tend to see gentrification as it is playing out in their own neighborhoods, and this bias can cause them—and us—to miss important parts of the picture.

Gentrification is also limited to particular areas of even the most economically successful cities. Gentrifying neighborhoods made up slightly more than a quarter of New York City neighborhoods, according to a 2016 study by NYU's Furman Center.[23] The study traced the transformation of fifty-five of the city's neighborhoods between 1990 and 2014. Just fifteen neighborhoods, or 27 percent, qualified as gentrifying (meaning they started off in 1990 with incomes below 40 percent of the median, and experienced rent increases greater than the median neighborhood did). Seven others, or 13 percent, was seen as non-gentrifying, meaning they stayed poor. The largest share of neighborhoods, 60 percent, or thirty-three of them, were categorized as higher-income neighborhoods (with income levels at least 60 percent of the 1990 median)—not necessarily affluent, but consistently middle class. Moreover, the non-gentrifying neighborhoods were often located right next door to the gentrifying ones, especially in Upper Manhattan and parts of Brooklyn—a sign of the juxtaposition of concentrated advantage and disadvantage that defines the city today (see Figure 4.2).

Furthermore, according to the Furman Center study, there was considerable variation in rent increases across New York City's neighborhoods over the past two decades (see Table 4.1). Williamsburg and Greenpoint saw the largest increase—a whopping 79 percent. Rents increased by more than 50 percent in Central Harlem, the Lower East Side, and Chinatown; more than 40

Figure 4.2: Gentrifying and Non-Gentrifying Neighborhoods in New York

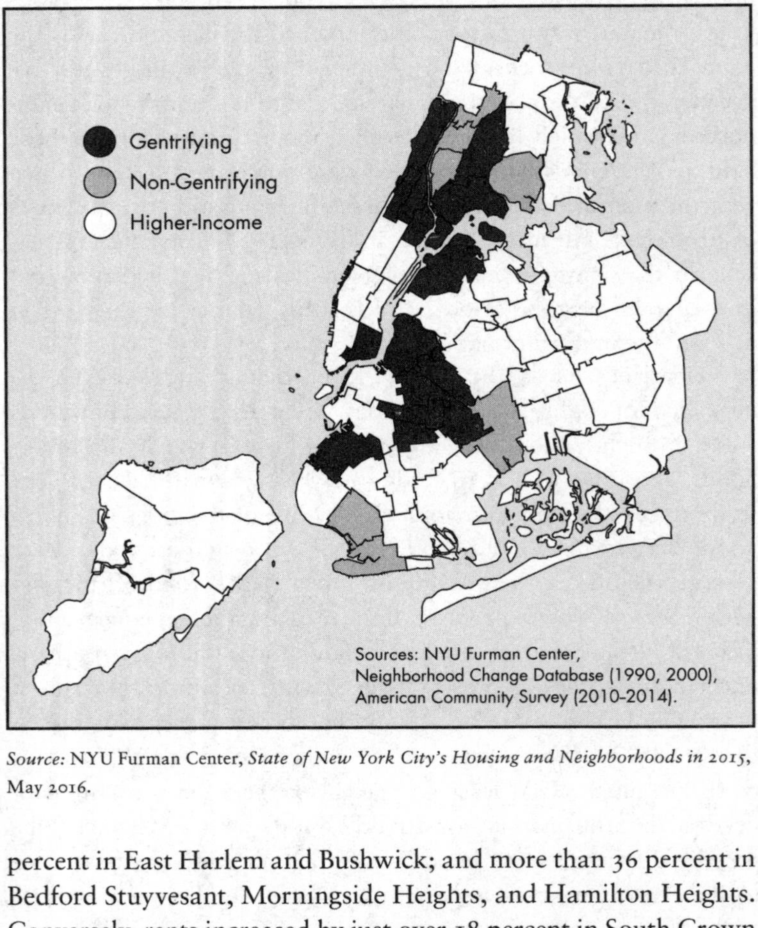
Gentrifying
Non-Gentrifying
Higher-Income
Sources: NYU Furman Center,
Neighborhood Change Database (1990, 2000),
American Community Survey (2010-2014).

Source: NYU Furman Center, *State of New York City's Housing and Neighborhoods in 2015*, May 2016.

percent in East Harlem and Bushwick; and more than 36 percent in Bedford Stuyvesant, Morningside Heights, and Hamilton Heights. Conversely, rents increased by just over 18 percent in South Crown Heights and more than 20 percent in Brownsville and Ocean Hill.

An even more varied pattern of housing values can be seen in Brooklyn, a place whose name has become synonymous with gentrification, as captured in the telling term Brooklynization. Despite the popular perception that Brooklyn has been turned into a playground for hipsters and a breeding ground for young white families, many of the borough's neighborhoods remain poor, with

Table 4.1: Change in Rent in New York City's Gentrifying Neighborhoods

Neighborhood	Percent Change in Average Rent, 1990 to 2010–2014
Williamsburg/Greenpoint	78.7%
Central Harlem	53.2%
Lower East Side/Chinatown	50.3%
Bushwick	44.0%
East Harlem	40.3%
Morningside Heights/Hamilton Heights	36.7%
Bedford Stuyvesant	36.1%
North Crown Heights/Prospect Heights	29.9%
Washington Heights/Inwood	29.3%
Mott Haven/Hunts Point	28.0%
Astoria	27.6%
Sunset Park	23.9%
Morrisania/Belmont	23.5%
Brownsville/Ocean Hill	20.5%
South Crown Heights	18.1%

Source: NYU Furman Center, *State of New York City's Housing and Neighborhoods in 2015,* May 2016.

large numbers of minority residents, and some have seen their housing values decline. Between 2004 and 2014, housing prices increased by a staggering 269 percent in trendy Williamsburg; 126 percent in Fort Greene; and 92 percent in Gowanus, despite its notoriously polluted and flood-prone industrial canal, which has been designated a Superfund site. Housing prices gained 70 percent or more in downtown Brooklyn; in Ditmas Park, a quiet neighborhood of wood-framed Victorians and historic apartment houses; and Crown Heights, the African American and Hasidic neighborhood that was the site of fierce rioting in 1991. And housing prices rose by 69 percent in Boreum Hill; 68 percent in Prospect Lefferts Gardens; 61 percent in the former industrial areas of DUMBO and Sunset Park; and 60 percent in already plush Park Slope with its magnificent townhomes.[24]

On the flip side, housing prices actually fell in other, less advantaged Brooklyn neighborhoods. Prices declined by 30 percent between 2004 and 2014 in Gerritsen Beach, largely on account of the devastation of Hurricane Sandy. They were down by 10 percent in Fort Hamilton, a solidly middle-class neighborhood with limited subway access, and by 12 percent in the working-class neighborhood of Canarsie. Housing prices fell by 8 percent in Flatlands and 27 percent in Remsen Village, both low-income neighborhoods that are poorly served by transit. Where transit connections are poor and other investment is low, gentrification tends not to occur.

R egardless of how extensive gentrification is or where exactly it is occurring, the most heated issues are those relating to who is displaced by it. Lance Freeman, the leading student of gentrification and displacement, has found that gentrification actually displaces far fewer people than is commonly thought. In a 2004 study, Freeman and a colleague found that members of poor households in the gentrifying neighborhoods of New York City were actually less likely than those of poor households in non-gentrifying neighborhoods to move out of their neighborhoods. Of course, this may be because there are fewer poor households in gentrifying neighborhoods. Still, the study found that a neighborhood could shift from a population where 30 percent of its residents were in poverty to one where 12 percent of its residents were in poverty over a time period of about a decade "without any displacement whatsoever." Another of Freeman's studies showed that disadvantaged households in gentrifying neighborhoods were actually 15 percent less likely to move than those in non-gentrifying neighborhoods. In still another study, Freeman found that the probability that any one household in a gentrifying neighborhood would be displaced was a mere 1.3 percent.

Other research that builds on Freeman's by separating the effects of gentrification on homeowners from the effects on renters found that renters in gentrifying neighborhoods faced a 2.6 percent higher risk of displacement (which is about the same as for getting a divorce), but no evidence that gentrification displaced homeowners.[25] The big takeaway from this research is that the direct displacement of people by gentrification is not as big of an issue as it is made out to be, and that it is the wrong lens from which to view the effects of gentrification on poor and disadvantaged urbanites.

Part of the reason is that gentrification tends to take place either in older industrial neighborhoods, where few people live anyway before the gentrification begins, or in working-class districts where homeowners benefit from the rising prices caused by gentrification, and where any renters who are displaced can afford to find comparable housing nearby. Gentrification is much more likely to occur in these two types of neighborhoods than it is in neighborhoods where there is a large concentration of chronic poverty with its concomitant social problems. Ultimately, the focus on direct displacement is something of a red herring, deflecting attention from the bigger ways in which re-urbanization and gentrification hurt the poor and disadvantaged.

The worst consequences for the less advantaged occur not in gentrifying neighborhoods per se but in the far more disadvantaged neighborhoods where the great majority of the poor actually live. The way gentrification hurts the poor in these less advantaged places is through its trickle-down or ripple effects on housing prices. A 2015 study using detailed credit-score data to trace the impact of gentrification in Philadelphia between 2002 and 2014 showed how these trickle-down effects work.[26] Overall, just 15 percent of the city's census tracts experienced gentrification over that period. Like Lance Freeman, the researchers in this study found little evidence that direct displacement was a significant problem. The economic conditions of Philadelphia's gentrifying neighborhoods improved substantially, with household incomes growing by 42 percent over the study period, compared to a 20 percent decline in non-gentrifying neighborhoods. The economic situation of less advantaged residents who remained in these gentrifying neighborhoods improved as well. Residents of gentrifying neighborhoods were not really much more likely to move out of them than the residents of non-gentrifying neighborhoods were to move out of their own neighborhoods.

But the least advantaged and most economically vulnerable residents who, for one reason or another, did move out of gentrifying neighborhoods ended up in higher-poverty neighborhoods with more crime and worse schools. Middle- and working-class residents were able to ride the tide of gentrification and even gain slightly from the improvements that came with it. If they left, they were able to use these gains to buy into decent neighborhoods in the city or in the more affordable parts of the suburbs. Meanwhile, the most vulnerable groups were shunted into the most disadvantaged neighborhoods, where their rent burdens tended to increase. It was ripple effects like these, rather than the direct displacement of individual homeowners or renters, that hit hardest at the urban poor.

Philadelphia's experience is instructive, but the ripple effects of gentrification are magnified in superstar cities and tech hubs, where re-urbanization is happening at a much faster pace and on a larger scale. In New York City, for example, the share of rent-burdened households spending 30 percent or more of their pretax income on rent rose from 41 percent in 2000 to 52 percent in 2014. The share of rent-burdened households in gentrifying neighborhoods increased from 42 percent to 53 percent over the same period. It grew even more, from 46 percent to nearly 60 percent of households, in non-gentrifying neighborhoods, another indication of gentrification's trickle-down effect. And the increase in housing prices hits hardest at the least advantaged households, more than three-quarters of which were rent burdened by 2014.[27]

The threat of displacement itself may be growing in some rapidly gentrifying cities as well. Over a quarter of neighborhoods in San Francisco are at risk for substantial displacement, according to a 2015 study.[28] By 2030, the study predicts, displacement is likely to increase substantially more as the competition for scarce and ever more expensive space continues to accelerate. Even though direct displacement has not been a big problem in the past, it may become one in superstar cities as housing prices rise and more neighborhoods are transformed. As gentrification ramps up, not only will the most vulnerable suffer, but the tensions between local residents and new arrivals will rise.

One thing is for certain: the gentrifiers and the local residents—those coming in and those in danger of being pushed out—have very different perceptions of their neighborhoods and how they are changing. "What do they call Bushwick now? What's the word?" Spike Lee asked the audience that night in February 2014 at the Pratt Institute. "East Williamsburg," was their response. "These real estate motherfuckers are changing names!" he shouted. "How you changin' names?"[29]

The kind of cultural erasure that bothers Lee can be all too real. An ethnographic study of the gentrification of a mainly low-income African American neighborhood in South Philadelphia revealed the very different ways in which long-term residents and newcomers experience gentrification.[30] The study asked residents about how the neighborhood had changed, and specifically, about what they called the neighborhood. Black residents tended to use the neighborhood's older name, South Philly, whereas the white residents used newer names, such as Graduate Hospital, G-Ho, South Rittenhouse, or Southwest Center City. The white residents typically believed the minority portion of the neighborhood was a high-crime zone, when in fact it had lower crime rates than the whiter, more affluent part they lived in. Race was the key factor in the different ways the residents saw and described what was happening to their neighborhood: the differences in how the white and black residents defined the neighborhood held regardless of income level or the number of years the respondents had lived there. "Most whites defined the area as many things, except how minority respondents defined the area," the study's authors noted, adding, "The large and inclusive socially constructed neighborhood was eventually displaced." In other words, the old neighborhood was essentially defined away by its new residents.

The connection between race and gentrification can also be seen in the way people talk about the restaurants they frequent in white and black neighborhoods. Popular restaurants are a common signal of gentrification and neighborhood change. A 2015 study used Yelp restaurant reviews to track the popular perceptions of two gentrifying Brooklyn neighborhoods: Greenpoint, a traditionally Polish neighborhood, and historically black Bedford Stuyvesant, or Bed-Stuy. Greenpoint was seen by Yelp reviewers as a mainstay for authentic ethnic culture, but Bed-Stuy was framed very differently, with Yelp reviewers using terms like "dangerous," "gritty," "sketchy," "hood," and "ghetto" to describe it. They saw new restaurants as a positive force for changing the area, however. As one Yelp reviewer put it, a particular restaurant was "the kind of place Bed-Stuy needs."[31] Such studies illustrate the extent to which the identities of gentrifying neighborhoods are socially constructed and reconstructed, as well as the extent to which race remains a factor in how gentrification is perceived. When it comes to how neighborhoods are defined, the gentrifiers ultimately win out.

Race plays an even larger and more problematic role in determining which neighborhoods are impervious to gentrification and stay chronically poor. The Chicago neighborhoods that saw the greatest economic improvements between 1995 and 2014 were white, and those with the least were black, according to a 2014 study.[32] The study tracked ninety-nine gentrifying and gentrifiable neighborhoods in the city, including twenty-six in which gentrification had begun by 1995, sixteen more that were on the fringes of the process, and another fifty-seven that were adjacent to gentrifying neighborhoods and therefore ripe for change. One of the most intriguing aspects of the study was its use of Google Street View to identify where gentrification had occurred by tracking new building projects, the level of upkeep of older buildings, and other visible signs of neighborhood change. The study found race to be the key factor in determining which neighborhoods gentrified and which did not, after taking into account residents' incomes, education levels, and other factors typically associated with gentrification.

Across the board, the likelihood that a neighborhood would gentrify declined as the proportion of black residents increased. Ultimately, the areas that gentrified were those that were at least 35 percent white and no more than 40 percent black. Neighborhoods with more than 40 percent black residents saw little economic improvement and tended to stay poor. This racial threshold essentially stopped gentrification from spreading. In other words, gentrification remains highly bounded, showing few signs of spilling over into black neighborhoods even when the black neighborhoods are in very close proximity to the gentrified (or gentrifying) neighborhoods. We can all think of obvious exceptions to this rule—traditionally African American neighborhoods like New York's Harlem, Crown Heights, and Bedford Stuyvesant have all experienced intensive gentrification, for example. But the main message of this study, which is applicable in the lion's share of cities, is sobering: the great bulk of poor black neighborhoods remain virtually immune to gentrification, with their residents remaining largely trapped in chronic and persistent poverty.

It is this racially concentrated urban poverty that constitutes the far bigger problem for cities. The overwhelming majority of neighborhoods that were poor in 1970 remained poor thirty years later, according to a study examining all the high-poverty neighborhoods within a ten-mile radius of the urban center in America's fifty-one large metros (those with populations of 1 million people or more). For every census tract that gentrified between 1970 and 2000, ten remained poor and twelve that were once stable slipped into concentrated disadvantage. Very few poor neighborhoods saw any substantial improvement in their economic fortunes over this period. Just 105 census tracts, about 10 percent of the total, saw their poverty rates fall below 15 percent (meaning that a smaller proportion of their residents lived in poverty than was the case for the nation as a whole). Another 1,200 tracts shifted from low poverty (less than 15 percent below the poverty line) to high poverty (more than 30 percent below the poverty line). Even more shockingly, the number of high-poverty tracts tripled.[33] When all is said and done, chronic, concentrated urban poverty is a far bigger problem than gentrification and remains the most troubling issue facing our cities.

G entrification gets a lot of attention, and it is a significant problem in expensive superstar cities and tech hubs. In these places, the pain that gentrification causes is real and needs to be taken seriously. But the even more pressing problem is the much larger number of neighborhoods that it bypasses entirely, those where racially concentrated poverty persists and is deepening.

Rather than kneejerk resistance to change or attacks on new urbanites, the more appropriate response is to assist those who are most vulnerable. It makes little sense to discourage investment in cities and urban neighborhoods, especially in places that desperately need it. Indeed, the real task of urban policy is not to try to stop the market forces that are leading to the economic revitalization of certain urban areas, but to improve the housing options, economic opportunities, and neighborhood conditions of those who are being left behind (topics to which I will return in the last chapter of this book).

Ultimately, gentrification is the specifically urban manifestation of America's new class geography, and it is most visible in the places that have re-urbanized the most and where the competition for urban space is fiercest. America's class divides have been deepening across the board, and they imprint themselves in different ways in different kinds of cities and metro areas. In some places that are experiencing rapid re-urbanization, these divides are increasingly visible between advantaged and disadvantaged areas within the city itself; in others they occur between and across a city and its suburbs. Despite their varied forms, these new divides reflect the growing inequality and economic segregation that are fundamental features of our new class geography. These are the phenomena that lie at the heart of the New Urban Crisis and that are the subjects of the next three chapters of this book. Next, we'll take a close look at the gaping economic inequality that is increasingly becoming baked into the new geography of class in America.

5

THE INEQUALITY OF CITIES

U p until 2012, few people outside of Brooklyn and New York
City's progressive political circles had even heard of Bill de
Blasio. Though he had been elected to the citywide Office of Public Advocate in 2009, he'd spent most of his political career on
the New York City Council representing Brooklyn's 39th District,
which spans mostly upscale Cobble Hill and Park Slope, more
recently gentrifying areas like Carroll Gardens, Gowanus, and
Windsor Terrace, and blue-collar neighborhoods such as Kensington and Borough Park. By 2013, New York's larger-than-life
mayor Michael Bloomberg, the billionaire founder of the media
giant that bears his name, was finishing his third and final term.
De Blasio had thrown his hat in the ring to replace him, but few
imagined that he stood much of a chance. Christine Quinn, the
speaker of the City Council and a Bloomberg ally, was widely understood to be the mayor's chosen heir; most pundits assumed her
election would be a sure thing.[1]

Under Bloomberg's leadership, the city's economy had come
roaring back from the 2008 economic crisis.[2] By 2011, the city had
returned to the peak employment levels it had enjoyed before the
crash, led by strong growth in its creative and tech industries alongside its mainstays of finance, real estate, education, and health
care. The city's hard-hit financial sector, which had lost more than
30,000 jobs in 2008, was on the mend, and bankers and analysts
were again hauling in huge bonuses. Massive construction projects
were under way at Ground Zero in Lower Manhattan, over the

old Hudson Yards just north of Chelsea, along the East River in Williamsburg, in downtown Brooklyn, and elsewhere. The city's high-tech sector, which had been nearly wiped out when the dot-com bubble burst in 2001, was booming again, and to cement its future, the Bloomberg administration had announced a $2 billion initiative to build a two-million-square-foot applied science and engineering campus on Roosevelt Island for Cornell University and Israel's Technion.

The city's streets were cleaner than they'd ever been and teeming with activity. Violent crime was way down, and tourists were pouring in at record rates. Manhattan was even flush with bicycles, thanks in part to its new bike lanes and bike-sharing infrastructure. New York City was winning the worldwide competition for both capital and talent—the key to the city's success, as Bloomberg had put it himself in an op-ed in *The Financial Times*. "A city that wants to attract creators must offer a fertile breeding ground for new ideas and innovations," he'd written. Taking a page from my own creative-class playbook, he'd added: "Economists may not say it this way but the truth of the matter is: being cool counts. When people can find inspiration in a community that also offers great parks, safe streets and extensive mass transit, they vote with their feet."[3]

Bloomberg was as competent and consequential a mayor as New York City had ever had. His final years in office should have been a nonstop victory lap. But something was amiss. For all that the city had prospered since 2002, huge numbers of New Yorkers were feeling anything but flush. The widespread perception instead was that New York had become a place where the rich were getting even richer, while the poor and the working and middle classes were falling further and further behind. By 2013, the top 5 percent of Manhattan households were earning eighty-eight times what the poorest 20 percent did. The city's 400,000 or so millionaires outnumbered the entire populations of New Orleans, Pittsburgh, Cleveland, or Minneapolis. But many more New Yorkers were seeing their living standards eviscerated by a combination of declining real wages and escalating housing prices. In August

2013, a *New York Times* poll found that 55 percent of voters believed that Bloomberg's policies favored the rich. Asked whether New York had become "too expensive for people like you to live in," 85 percent answered yes.[4]

Propelled by the populist backlash to the city's widening economic divide, de Blasio's insurgent campaign put inequality front and center. His mantra, as I noted back in Chapter 1, was that New York had become a "tale of two cities." "Without a dramatic change of direction—an economic policy that combats inequality and rebuilds our middle class—generations to come will see New York as little more than a playground for the rich . . . a gilded city where the privileged few prosper, and millions upon millions of New Yorkers struggle each and every day to keep their heads above water," he declared in a spring 2013 speech that galvanized his candidacy. "History has taught us that no economy—and no city—can thrive in the long-term under such circumstances."[5] To change the city's direction, he promised to raise taxes on the wealthy, establish universal prekindergarten, expand after-school programs, raise the minimum wage, create more living-wage jobs, and build hundreds of thousands of units of affordable housing.

To the shock of pundits and political prognosticators in the city and just about everywhere else, de Blasio won the September 2013 Democratic primary handily, easily defeating Christine Quinn and Bill Thompson, who had run a plausible campaign against Bloomberg in 2009. De Blasio's Republican opponent, Joe Lhota, a former chairman of the Metropolitan Transit Authority, called him an unrepentant socialist whose policies would wreck the city's economy. But the city's voters weren't buying it. De Blasio won the election with a whopping 73 percent of the popular vote, taking even larger majorities of the city's black (96 percent) and Hispanic (87 percent) voters and those who made $50,000 or less (86 percent).[6]

De Blasio's 2013 campaign captured some basic truths of our present moment: Inequality in cities is on the rise; the problem of inequality is a fundamentally urban one; and, in the long run, urban inequality threatens economic growth. Although its precise causes and dynamics vary from city to city, inequality is a major and growing problem in virtually all cities and metropolitan areas. But when its various measures are collated and aggregated, it's clear that economic inequality is most severe in our biggest and most successful cities and metro areas. The larger, denser, and more knowledge-intensive and tech-based a city or metro is, the more unequal it tends to be. Superstar cities and knowledge hubs are not just the theaters where inequality is most on display; their success is inextricably tied to the very clustering of talent and firms that shapes the widening gap between rich and poor.

I nequality in America has risen at a stupefying rate over the past couple of decades. After a long period of moderation spanning roughly the New Deal to the election of Ronald Reagan, income inequality shot up to heights that rivaled that of the Gatsby era of the 1920s. Between 1928, on the eve of the Great Depression, and 1979, the year before Reagan was elected president, the share of income going to the top 1 percent declined in every single US state except Alaska. In 2007, just before the economic crisis, the share of national income that went to the top 1 percent was 23.5 percent, the highest it had been since 1928. Between 1979 and 2007, the 1 percent pocketed more than half (53.5 percent) of the overall increase in income across the United States. Since the economic crisis of 2008, the top 1 percent has captured a staggering 85 percent of all income growth. And as of 2013, the 1 percent was making roughly twenty-five times the average income of the remaining 99 percent nationwide.[7]

The gap between the 1 percent and the rest soared even higher in many metro areas, especially in superstar cities and leading tech hubs. In New York City, for example, the 1 percent hauls in more than forty times the average income of the bottom 99 percent; in Los Angeles, San Francisco, and San Jose, they make about thirty times as much.[8]

The overall level of income inequality in the United States as a whole is bad enough—it is 0.450 on the Gini coefficient index, the standard for measuring income inequality. (Gini coefficient values range from 0 to 1, with 0 indicating zero inequality and 1 indicating the most extreme inequality.) The US value is about the same as Iran's, and worse than Russia's, India's, or Nicaragua's. But within many US cities and metro areas, the Gini coefficient is even worse, rivaling some of the most unequal countries on earth. New York City's inequality is similar to that of Swaziland. Los Angeles's matches up with Sri Lanka's. Boston's and San Francisco's levels of inequality are similar to those of El Salvador and Rwanda, respectively. Miami's is about the same as Zimbabwe's. Of course, the poor in New York are not as bad off as the poor in Swaziland. But the fact of the matter is that the gap between the richest and poorest groups in America's cities is similar to that of some of the most disadvantaged and unequal places in the world. And for a rich country like ours, that is as tragic as it is disturbing (see Table 5.1).[9]

Urban inequality across the United States is growing rapidly. It increased in almost two-thirds of US metro areas—226 out of 356— between 2006 and 2012. And income inequality runs higher within

Table 5.1: The Inequality of US Metros Compared to Countries

Large Metro	Income Inequality	Comparison Country
New York-Northern New Jersey-Long Island, NY-NJ-PA	0.504	Swaziland (0.504)
Miami-Fort Lauderdale-Pompano Beach, FL	0.496	Zimbabwe (0.501)
Los Angeles-Long Beach-Santa Ana, CA	0.485	Sri Lanka (0.490)
Memphis, TN-MS-AR	0.482	Ecuador (0.485)
Houston-Sugar Land-Baytown, TX	0.479	Mexico (0.483)
New Orleans-Metairie-Kenner, LA	0.478	Madagascar (0.474)
Birmingham-Hoover, AL	0.475	China (0.473)
San Francisco-Oakland-Fremont, CA	0.475	El Salvador (0.469)
Boston-Cambridge-Quincy, MA-NH	0.469	Rwanda (0.468)
Chicago-Naperville-Joliet, IL-IN-WI	0.468	Bolivia (0.466)

Source: Martin Prosperity Institute, based on data on income inequality from the US Census for metros and the *CIA Factbook* for nations.

city boundaries than in their broader metro areas. It is higher in the urban cores of New York, LA, and Chicago than in their respective greater metro areas; even higher in the urban centers of Boston and Miami; and higher still in the urban cores of Washington, DC, and Atlanta compared to their respective metro areas.[10]

In some places, income inequality is driven by the rising fortunes of those at the top, while in others it is a product of the

Table 5.2: Cities and Metros with the Greatest Gaps Between Rich and Poor

		Household Income		
Rank	Metro Area	95th percentile	20th percentile	95–20 Ratio
1	Bridgeport-Stamford-Norwalk, CT	$558,970	$31,333	17.8
2	New York-Newark-Jersey City, NY-NJ-PA	$282,359	$23,853	11.8
3	San Francisco-Oakland-Hayward, CA	$353,483	$31,761	11.1
4	New Orleans-Metairie, LA	$196,658	$18,173	10.8
5	McAllen-Edinburg-Mission, TX	$136,570	$12,760	10.7
6	Boston-Cambridge-Newton, MA-NH	$293,653	$27,883	10.5
7	Los Angeles-Long Beach-Anaheim, CA	$243,771	$23,743	10.3
8	Miami-Fort Lauderdale-West Palm Beach, FL	$202,461	$19,775	10.2
9	New Haven-Milford, CT	$221,661	$22,652	9.8
10	Houston-The Woodlands-Sugar Land, TX	$240,711	$24,758	9.7
	City			
1	Boston, MA	$266,224	$14,942	17.8
2	New Orleans, LA	$203,383	$11,466	17.7
3	Atlanta, GA	$281,653	$16,057	17.5
4	Cincinnati, OH	$164,410	$10,454	15.7
5	Providence, RI	$196,691	$12,795	15.4
6	New Haven, CT	$187,984	$12,293	15.3
7	Washington, DC	$320,679	$21,230	15.1
8	Miami, FL	$184,242	$12,262	15.0
9	San Francisco, CA	$383,202	$26,366	14.5
10	New York, NY	$249,609	$17,691	14.1

Source: Alan Berube and Natalie Holmes, "City and Metropolitan Inequality on the Rise, Driven by Declining Incomes," Brookings Institution, Metropolitan Policy Program, January 14, 2016.

sinking economic conditions of those at the bottom. This becomes clear when we look at the metros and cities with the greatest 95–20 ratios, where the incomes of the top 5 percent of households exceed the incomes of the lowest 20 percent by multiples of 10 to 18.[11] As Table 5.2 shows, in Bridgeport-Stamford the top 5 percent rakes in, on average, in excess of $550,000. Income inequality in the superstar cities of New York and Los Angeles and the knowledge hubs of Boston, Washington, DC, and San Francisco is also driven by those at the top. But there are other metros where large 95–20 ratios are driven by the especially low incomes of those at the bottom. Such places include the Sunbelt cities of New Orleans and Miami, with their large service economies and high incidences of racially concentrated poverty.

Wage inequality, which is different from income inequality, provides another lens into urban America's widening economic divide (see Table 5.3). Income inequality takes income from rents and capital at the top of the scale into account, as well as the economic condition of people at the bottom who are unemployed or do not work; wage inequality simply measures the gap between the lowest-paid and the highest-paid workers. Superstar cities and knowledge hubs rank especially high on the wage-inequality metric as a consequence of the high wages paid to techies and knowledge workers. San Jose, in the very heart of Silicon Valley, has the highest level of wage inequality of any large US metro. New York and LA as well as the tech hubs of Austin, San Diego, Raleigh-Cary in North Carolina's Research Triangle, Washington, DC, and San Francisco all number among the top ten large metros on this metric, as well as Dallas and Atlanta.

As with income inequality, one can look at the extremes and compare the gap in wages received by the top 10 percent and the bottom 10 percent of workers, a measure referred to as the 90–10 ratio (see Table 5.4). In the United States as a whole, the top 10 percent of workers make roughly five times as much as the lowest-paid 10 percent.[12] But in superstar cities and knowledge hubs, the gap is much wider. In San Jose, the top 10 percent make over seven times as much as the bottom 10 percent. In New York, San

Table 5.3: Wage Inequality

Large Metro	Wage Inequality
San Jose-Sunnyvale-Santa Clara, CA	0.481
Austin-Round Rock, TX	0.418
New York-Northern New Jersey-Long Island, NY-NJ-PA	0.413
San Diego-Carlsbad-San Marcos, CA	0.409
Los Angeles-Long Beach-Santa Ana, CA	0.409
Raleigh-Cary, NC	0.408
Washington-Arlington-Alexandria, DC-VA-MD-WV	0.407
Dallas-Fort Worth-Arlington, TX	0.406
San Francisco-Oakland-Fremont, CA	0.401
Atlanta-Sandy Springs-Marietta, GA	0.398

Source: Martin Prosperity Institute, based on wage inequality data from the US Department of Labor, Bureau of Labor Statistics.

Francisco, and Washington, DC, they haul in six times as much, and in LA and Boston they make five and a half times as much.

As these patterns of wage inequality and income inequality suggest, economic inequality in America's cities and metro areas varies in its precise nature and causes. Indeed, my colleague Charlotta Mellander and I found that these two types of inequality ultimately stem from different phenomena. Our study took a close look at the different factors that are shaping both wage and income inequality across US metros: (1) globalization and technological change; (2) the enduring legacy of race and concentrated poverty; and (3) the weakening of the post–World War II social compact between business, government, and labor.[13]

Wage inequality stems mainly from factors bolstering the pay of top earners. It is largely the consequence of what economists call skill-biased technical change.[14] Globalization has shifted many manufacturing jobs to lower-wage countries like China; new technologies and increases in productivity have eliminated millions more. With the decline of once middle-class blue-collar jobs, the workforce has bifurcated into a cadre of highly paid knowledge and professional workers and a much larger and lower-paid

Table 5.4: Metros with the Biggest Wage Gaps

Large Metro	90–10 Wage Gap
San Jose-Sunnyvale-Santa Clara, CA	7.19
Washington-Arlington-Alexandria, DC-VA-MD-WV	6.72
San Francisco-Oakland-Fremont, CA	6.17
New York-Northern New Jersey-Long Island, NY-NJ-PA	6.04
Houston-Sugar Land-Baytown, TX	5.54
Boston-Cambridge-Quincy, MA-NH	5.54
Los Angeles-Long Beach-Santa Ana, CA	5.51
San Diego-Carlsbad-San Marcos, CA	5.44
Baltimore-Towson, MA	5.39
Atlanta-Sandy Springs-Marietta, GA	5.31

Source: Martin Prosperity Institute, based on data from the US Department of Labor, Bureau of Labor Statistics.

phalanx of workers in routine service jobs. Wage inequality, we found, is statistically associated with the concentration of college graduates, high-tech industry, and knowledge and professional workers.[15] Little wonder then that wage inequality is particularly high in leading knowledge hubs.

Income inequality is more reflective of long-standing poverty and economic distress at the bottom of the socioeconomic pyramid. William Julius Wilson and other sociologists have long argued that inequality is a product of both poverty and racial disadvantage.[16] Our findings bear this out: income inequality across metro areas is statistically associated with both poverty and race as measured by the African American share of metro population, controlling for other factors.[17] Furthermore, income inequality is lower where the unionized share of the workforce is higher, and higher in places with lower rates of taxation. Our analysis found statistical associations between urban income inequality, the weakening of unions, and the erosion of the systems of progressive taxation that underpin social insurance programs.

In other words, urban economic inequality is at once a product of the winner-take-all excesses at the top of the economic order and of the persistent tragedy at the bottom. It is not only the result of big structural changes in the economy, such as globalization and automation, but also of policy choices—reductions in taxes and welfare benefits, anti-union measures—that have undone the old social compact and eroded the wages of American workers.[18] These choices can be reversed if we choose to do so.

Whatever its precise dynamics, the problem of urban inequality is most acute today in superstar cities and knowledge hubs.[19] To get an overall picture of inequality across metro areas, I combined income and wage inequality into a single measure, the Composite Inequality Index (see Figure 5.1). By this measure, New York, Los Angeles, and San Francisco rank as America's three most unequal large metro areas. Houston is fourth and Charlotte fifth. Philadelphia, Dallas, Boston, Chicago, and Birmingham complete the top ten. All in all, the top ten most unequal large metros include America's five largest metros and seven of its ten largest. If we consider all metros, Bridgeport-Stamford outside of New York is America's most unequal. College towns also number among America's most unequal metros on this metric, thanks to the large wage gaps between well-paid faculty and low-paid service workers and employed students.[20] These include College Station, Texas (home to Texas A&M); Boulder, Colorado (University of Colorado); Gainesville, Florida (University of Florida); Athens, Georgia (University of Georgia); Durham, North Carolina (Duke University); Morgantown, West Virginia (West Virginia University); Charlottesville, Virginia (University of Virginia); State College, Pennsylvania (Pennsylvania State University); and Ann Arbor, Michigan (University of Michigan).

But if college towns reflect the inequalities of their workforces, large, dense, knowledge-based places don't just reflect inequality, they help create it. Economic inequality grows worse as cities and metros grow larger, denser, and more clustered.[21] This, again, is the very nub of the New Urban Crisis—the same factors that drive economic growth also drive inequality.

There's abundant evidence for this connection between inequality and the size of metro areas. Nearly 70 percent of metros with more than 1 million people have a gap between their

Figure 5.1: The Composite Inequality Index

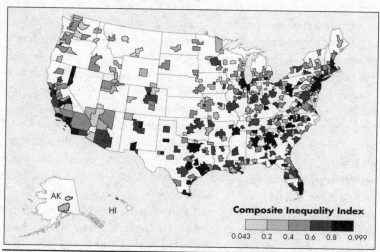

Large Metro	Composite Inequality Index
New York-Northern New Jersey-Long Island, NY-NJ-PA	0.979
Los Angeles-Long Beach-Santa Ana, CA	0.962
San Francisco-Oakland-Fremont, CA	0.919
Houston-Sugar Land-Baytown, TX	0.909
Charlotte-Gastonia-Concord, NC-SC	0.882
Philadelphia-Camden-Wilmington, PA-NJ-DE-MD	0.873
Dallas-Fort Worth-Arlington, TX	0.861
Boston-Cambridge-Quincy, MA-NH	0.858
Chicago-Naperville-Joliet, IL-IN-WI	0.853
Birmingham-Hoover, AL	0.852

Note: The index combines income and wage inequality.

Source: Martin Prosperity Institute, based on wage inequality data from the US Department of Labor, Bureau of Labor Statistics, and income inequality data from the US Census Bureau, American Community Survey.

highest- and lowest-paid workers (based on the 90–10 ratio) that exceeds the national average. This is the case in only 34 percent of metros with between 500,000 and 1 million people; in just 10 percent of metros with between 100,000 and 500,000 people; and in less than 3 percent of metros with fewer than 100,000 people. Two detailed studies by my University of Toronto colleague Nathaniel Baum-Snow also show this connection. One found that the size of metros alone accounted for roughly 25 to 35 percent of the total increase in economic inequality between 1979 and 2004, even after controlling for education, skill levels, industry structure, and other factors. The other, which focused on wage inequality between 1979 and 2007, found that size accounted for one-third of the increase in those years.[22]

Since our largest cities and metro areas are the most liberal politically, it is also the case that our most liberal cities number among the most unequal. This may seem ironic at a time when liberal mayors of big cities, such as Bill de Blasio, are making inequality the centerpiece of their political campaigns. And yet across the United States, inequality is not just a little higher, but substantially higher, in liberal areas than in more conservative ones. All of the twenty-five congressional districts with the highest levels of income inequality were represented by Democrats, according to a 2014 analysis.[23] My own analysis of all 350-plus US metros found wage inequality to be positively correlated with political liberalism and negatively associated with political conservatism.[24] Of course, inequality is not a direct product of liberal political views; rather, liberalism and inequality are simply both attributes of large, dense, knowledge-based metros. Still, as more affluent and more highly educated Americans move back to cities, they help make them less equal.

A high level of income inequality is not just inequitable and unfair, but it can be, and often is, a drag on economic growth. Metros with higher rates of inequality experienced slower overall rates of economic growth, according to a 2009 study that controlled for education, skill levels, and other factors that tend to drive growth across metros.[25] More unequal metros also had significantly shorter spells of growth, according to a separate 2014 study. Tracking some two hundred metros over the period 1990 to 2011, the study found inequality to be the largest and most significant factor in metros having shorter spells of job growth: the higher a metro's level of inequality was, the shorter its growth spell; the lower it was, the longer the growth lasted. More precisely, a 1 percent increase in income inequality brought with it a better than 20 percent chance that a run of job growth would stall.[26]

Furthermore, very few US cities or metro areas have been able to combine high levels of economic growth with low levels of inequality. This troubling finding comes from two 2016 studies. The first compared America's one hundred largest cities on two metrics: their levels of neighborhood inequality (at the ZIP-code level) on the one hand, and, on the other, their levels of prosperity or distress (based on median income, employment growth, education levels, the change in business establishments, and similar factors). It found that just nine of these cities had high levels of prosperity alongside low levels of inequality. And these were all smaller and more sprawling places, such as Scottsdale, Arizona, and Plano, Texas, or college towns, like Madison, Wisconsin, that are relatively affluent and homogeneous to begin with. As Figure 5.2 shows, leading tech hubs like San Francisco and San Jose combine very high levels of prosperity with high levels of inequality, while New York, Los Angeles, Washington, DC, and Boston combine high levels of inequality with somewhat more modest but still relatively high levels of economic prosperity.[27]

The second study, by the Brookings Institution, examined the connection between economic growth and social inclusion (a measure that accounted for the economic condition of the middle class, the extent of poverty, and the divide between the races). In the great majority of metros, increased economic growth did not bring economic improvement for low-wage workers or the poor.[28] Even though it used different metrics and examined cities as opposed to metros, it also found that just nine of the one hundred

Figure 5.2: The Disconnect Between Inequality and Prosperity

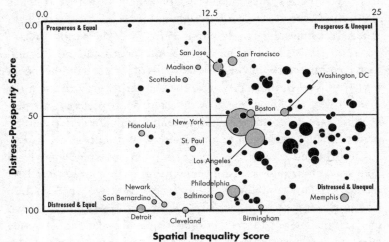

Note: Circle size reflects population.
Source: The 2016 Distressed Communities Index (Washington, DC: Economic Innovation Group, February 2016).

largest US metros saw improvement on social inclusion between 2009 and 2014, even though ninety-five of them experienced economic growth.

If high levels of inequality tend to retard growth, lower levels of it can promote growth. This pattern can be hard to discern across US cities and metros, largely because the level of inequality across the country is so high. But it comes through clearly when we look at the connection between inequality and leading-edge creative economies across countries, many of which have lower levels of inequality than the United States, and some of which have far more developed social welfare states. When my colleagues and I examined the connection between inequality and creative economic strength (based on the Global Creativity Index, a composite metric that captures countries' capabilities in technology, talent, and tolerance) in 139 nations, we arrived at two important conclusions.

Figure 5.3: Inequality Versus Global Creativity

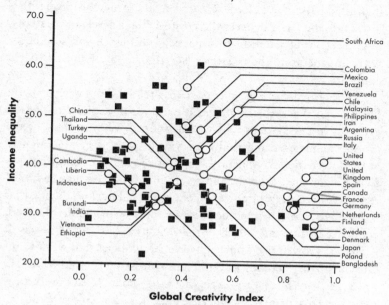

Source: Richard Florida, Charlotta Mellander, and Karen King, *The Global Creativity Index 2015* (Toronto: Martin Prosperity Institute, 2015).

First, more innovative and creative economies actually have lower levels of inequality. This can be seen in Figure 5.3, which compares how countries stack up on income inequality and global creativity. The downward-sloping line indicates the negative correlation between the two.[29]

Second, nations fall into two distinct groups when it comes to the relationship between inequality and the competitiveness of their creative economies. The first group, which lies above the downward-sloping line and includes the United States and the United Kingdom, combines high creativity with high inequality. The second group, which lies below the line and includes Sweden, Finland, and Denmark, combines high creativity with substantially lower inequality. These two groups represent two different paths that nations can take to maximize creativity: the low-road path of the United States, where income inequality is high, or the high-road path of the Nordic countries, where income inequality is low. Only the latter delivers the positives (high levels of creativity, high levels of economic performance, and high living standards) without generating the negatives (severe inequality and all that it entails).

Not only does economic inequality tend to hold back growth, but policies that redistribute wealth and income, like those of the progressive tax systems and well-developed welfare states of the Nordic countries, can actually generate growth. When researchers at the International Monetary Fund looked at the connections between inequality, growth, and redistribution across nations, they reached three very important conclusions. First, countries that redistribute more income have lower rates of inequality. Second, countries with greater levels of redistribution have higher levels of economic growth. And third, government policies that work to reduce inequality actually lead to higher rates of growth.[30] All in all, lower levels of inequality, even when they come from government policies to redistribute income, are good for economic growth.

Inequality is not just an occasional bug of urban economies; it is a fundamental feature of them. It is driven by the same economic motor that powers growth. Just as clustering and growth go together, so do clustering and inequality. Inequality is an ironic and troubling attribute of urban success. But as we have seen, although clustering is necessary for economic growth, inequality is not. Efforts to ameliorate inequality do not necessarily put growth in jeopardy—in fact, they can actually help to spur more growth. The connection between inequality and growth is not preordained. Cities, like nations, have a choice. They can permit the gap between the rich and the poor to grow ever wider, allowing those at the bottom to fall through a porous social safety net; or they can combat inequality through redistribution and other policy mechanisms without sacrificing growth, and in many cases increasing it.

In the last chapter of this book I will have more to say about how cities might achieve both more growth and less inequality, along with a more inclusive and sustainable prosperity. However, there is an even more problematic aspect of urban clustering we must consider first, and it is one of the major obstacles to following that path: the growing problem of economic segregation, or spatial inequality—the separation of the advantaged and the disadvantaged into entirely separate and distinct areas of the city and suburbs. As we will see, this process of economic sorting is even more vexing than inequality per se, as it compounds the advantages available to those at the top while also compounding the adverse circumstances of the less advantaged.

6

THE BIGGER SORT

In April 2015, a few days after a young black man named Freddie Gray died in police custody, the city of Baltimore erupted in rioting. It was eerily reminiscent of what had happened in my hometown of Newark a half-century earlier, when rumors that police had killed a cab driver set off a powderkeg. But whereas Newark had been declining for some time before the riots tipped it over the brink in 1967, Baltimore's economy was on the upswing. The Inner Harbor was a big hit with tourists and convention-goers, and its revitalized neighborhoods, such as Federal Hill, were drawing affluent and educated people back to the city. The city and the surrounding metropolitan area had a substantial share of high-tech industry, fueled by Johns Hopkins University, one of the world's foremost research institutions. Greater Baltimore, in fact, numbered among the nation's top twenty metros for its creative and innovative economy.

But if Baltimore's gentrifying neighborhoods were reviving and thriving, large sections of the city were rife with poverty. Not far from the Inner Harbor, atop a hill overlooking it, stands the Sandtown-Winchester neighborhood where Freddie Gray lived. Many of its row houses are boarded and sealed. There are no corner stores, and the tree boxes along its sidewalks are mostly barren. More than a third of Sandtown-Winchester's households live below the poverty line. Shootings and murders in the neighborhood occur at double the rate for the rest of Baltimore, a city with one of the highest rates in the country for both. Residents of

Sandtown-Winchester could expect to have their lives cut short by six and a half years compared to the average Baltimorean.[1] Freddie Gray's death and the events that followed it showed how Baltimore really is two separate cities—one a thriving city of highly educated, prosperous knowledge workers, the other a sinking city of largely African Americans trapped in persistent poverty.

The problem extends far beyond Baltimore. Despite the economic gains brought about by the back-to-the city movement, concentrated urban poverty is worsening across America's cities and metro areas. On this, the numbers are staggering. By 2014, 14 million Americans lived in concentrated poverty in extremely poor neighborhoods—the highest figure ever recorded and twice as many as in 2000. Two-thirds of the nation's one hundred largest metro areas experienced growth in concentrated poverty between 2005 and 2014.[2] Black Americans were five times more likely than whites to live in extremely poor neighborhoods.

Behind these trends is something even more insidious than rising economic inequality—the deepening sorting and segregation of Americans by income, education, and class. A decade or so ago, journalist Bill Bishop observed that Americans were sorting not just by political beliefs and cultural preferences but also by socioeconomic class—a phenomenon he dubbed "the big sort."[3]

That big sort has become an even bigger sort today, as the locational divide between rich and poor Americans has worsened. Between 1980 and 2010, the income segregation of rich and poor grew in twenty-seven of the nation's thirty largest metros. By 2009, more than 85 percent of the residents of America's cities and metro areas lived in locations that were more economically segregated than they were in 1970. In the forty-plus years spanning 1970 to 2012, the share of American families living in either all-poor or all-rich neighborhoods more than doubled, increasing from roughly 15 percent to nearly 34 percent.[4] In America today, economic inequality is also spatial inequality: rich and poor increasingly occupy entirely different spaces and worlds.

At the center of the bigger sort is the decline of America's once thriving middle class and the sturdy middle-class neighborhoods that literally defined the American Dream. The share of American families living in middle-class neighborhoods fell from nearly two-thirds (65 percent) in 1970 to less than half (40 percent) in 2012. The middle-class share of the population shrank in a whopping 203 of 229 US metros between 2000 and 2014, according to data compiled by the Pew Research Center. The metros where the middle class is smallest reads like a veritable who's who of superstar cities and tech hubs: New York, Los Angeles, San Francisco, San Jose, Washington, DC, and Boston as well as Houston, Miami, New Orleans, Sacramento, and Hartford. According to my own analysis of the Pew data, the metros where the middle class is smallest are denser, more knowledge based, and more diverse—all features of more economically vibrant places. Conversely, the metros where the middle class is largest are whiter, have a larger working class, and have higher levels of political conservatism—all features of economically declining places.[5] Furthermore, the metros that had bigger middle classes in 2000 are the ones that saw the largest middle-class declines by 2014. Distressingly, the middle class is smallest in economically vibrant places and largest in declining ones.

To better understand the full breadth and depth of this ongoing bigger sort, I worked with my colleague Charlotta Mellander to develop a set of indexes to gauge the full extent of America's economic segregation by income, education, and occupational class. Our measures track the geographic separation of these different groups or classes based on their residential locations across 70,000-plus US census tracts. We also developed several composite indexes to track economic segregation overall and the combination of economic segregation and inequality together.[6]

As we will see, while different types of metros suffer in different ways from the various kinds of economic segregation, our overarching analysis reveals a more basic underlying pattern. Across each of these categories of income, education, and occupational segregation, as well as in our composite index, which takes into account their overall and combined effects, economic segregation is greater in bigger, denser metros with large concentrations of high-tech industries, college graduates, and members of the creative class. And, as we will also see, our deepening economic segregation is driven by the clustering together of more advantaged groups, especially the wealthy, who have the resources to isolate and wall themselves off in their own communities.

L et's begin with income segregation, which is the most commonly recognized and studied form of economic segregation. Our measure of income segregation considers the geographic separation of high-income and low-income households (those making more than $200,000 a year and those falling below the federal poverty line).[7]

The pattern is different from that of the geography of inequality that we saw in the previous chapter. The top ten large metros on our overall index of income segregation include Cleveland, Detroit, Milwaukee, Columbus, and Buffalo in the Rustbelt, plus Memphis, Philadelphia, Phoenix, Kansas City, and Nashville (see Table 6.1). Aside from New York, which lies just outside of the top ten on income segregation, superstar cities and tech hubs like LA,

Table 6.1: Income Segregation

Rank	Large Metro	Index	Rank Among All Metros
1	Cleveland-Elyria-Mentor, OH	0.964	2
2	Detroit-Warren-Livonia, MI	0.957	3
3	Memphis, TN-MS-AR	0.948	4
4	Milwaukee-Waukesha-West Allis, WI	0.935	5
5	Columbus, OH	0.912	8
6	Philadelphia-Camden-Wilmington, PA-NJ-DE-MD	0.887	11
7	Phoenix-Mesa-Scottsdale, AZ	0.882	12
8	Buffalo-Niagara Falls, NY	0.864	16
9	Kansas City, MO-KS	0.861	17
10	Nashville-Davidson-Murfreesboro-Franklin, TN	0.858	19

Source: Martin Prosperity Institute, based on data from the US Census.

Boston, DC, and San Francisco have lower levels of income segregation. That said, our broader statistical analysis finds that across all metros, income segregation is closely correlated with their size and density along with their concentrations of high-tech industry and the creative class.[8]

Some 15 percent of Americans—roughly 45 million people— live on household incomes that are below the federal poverty line, and their isolation is increasing. The share of poor families living in poor neighborhoods increased from 8 percent to 18 percent between 1970 and 2009, according to research by Kendra Bischoff and Sean Reardon, two of the nation's leading experts on segregation.[9] As with income segregation, the poor are most highly segregated in Rustbelt metros—Milwaukee, Cleveland, and Detroit—along with Hartford, Philadelphia, and Baltimore in the Northeast corridor spanning Boston, New York, and Washington, DC, Memphis in the Southeast, and Denver in the Southwest (see Table 6.2). But New York ranks sixth; and tech hubs have higher levels of poverty segregation than they do of income segregation. Here again, our broader statistical analysis of all metros indicates that segregation of the poor is correlated with the size and density of metros.[10]

Table 6.2: Segregation of the Poor

Rank	Large Metro	Index	Rank Among All Metros
1	Milwaukee-Waukesha-West Allis, WI	0.478	2
2	Hartford-West Hartford-East Hartford, CT	0.462	6
3	Philadelphia-Camden-Wilmington, PA-NJ-DE-MD	0.455	9
4	Cleveland-Elyria-Mentor, OH	0.435	15
5	Detroit-Warren-Livonia, MI	0.433	16
6	New York-Northern New Jersey-Long Island, NY-NJ-PA	0.428	20
7	Buffalo-Niagara Falls, NY	0.416	28
8	Denver-Aurora, CO	0.413	30
9	Baltimore-Towson, MD	0.413	33
10	Memphis, TN-MS-AR	0.410	34

Source: Martin Prosperity Institute, based on data from the US Census.

The consequences of economic segregation for the poor are devastating. In his classic 1987 book *The Truly Disadvantaged*, sociologist William Julius Wilson documented the deleterious effects of the spatial concentration of poverty, ranging from fewer and lower-quality jobs to less developed economic and professional networks and lower-quality schools, higher crime rates, more problematic peer networks, fewer potential marriageable partners, and far less exposure to positive role models.[11] Those who live in chronically poor neighborhoods not only lack economic resources but are isolated from the social and economic institutions that enable upward economic mobility to take place. These disadvantages effectively keep them stuck in poverty for generations.

The flip side of this is the segregation of the wealthy (households with incomes of $200,000 or more), as shown in Table 6.3. Among large metros, the segregation of the wealthy is highest in older industrial metros—Memphis, Birmingham, Louisville, Cleveland, and Detroit—as well as in Nashville, Columbus, Charlotte, and Miami. But here again, our statistical analysis shows that the segregation of the wealthy is greater in larger, denser metros and those with greater shares of high-tech industry.[12]

Table 6.3: Segregation of the Wealthy

Rank	Large Metro	Index	Rank Among All Metros
1	Memphis, TN-MS-AR	0.582	5
2	Birmingham-Hoover, AL	0.576	8
3	Louisville-Jefferson County, KY-IN	0.575	9
4	San Antonio, TX	0.567	10
5	Cleveland-Elyria-Mentor, OH	0.560	13
6	Detroit-Warren-Livonia, MI	0.552	17
7	Nashville-Davidson-Murfreesboro-Franklin, TN	0.549	23
8	Columbus, OH	0.547	25
9	Charlotte-Gastonia-Concord, NC-SC	0.541	29
10	Miami-Fort Lauderdale-Pompano Beach, FL	0.540	31

Source: Martin Prosperity Institute, based on data from the US Census.

Income segregation is driven by the location of the most advantaged. The wealthy are more segregated than the poor; in fact, they are the most segregated group of any in our analysis.[13] This finding is not surprising: the wealthy have the resources to occupy the locations of their choosing and wall themselves off from other, less advantaged groups. In many ways, it reflects what the political philosopher Michael Sandel dubbed the "skyboxification" of society, where the rich sequester themselves in the equivalent of private luxury skyboxes far away from the crowded bleacher seats where the masses take in the game.[14]

When we look beyond income segregation to other types of segregation by education and occupation, a more complete picture begins to come into focus. Not only do these different kinds of segregation reinforce one another, they are consistently a feature of large, dense, knowledge-based metros.

In addition to segregating by income, people also segregate according to their level of education. Education, or what is sometimes referred to as human capital, plays a substantial role in the economic development of nations.[15] It is a key factor in how much money we make and reinforces and reproduces the advantages that money brings.

People with low levels of education—those who did not complete high school—face substantial obstacles in society. They earn far less than those with college degrees and experience far higher levels of unemployment. The large metros where people who did not complete high school are most segregated include Los Angeles; the tech hubs of Austin, Denver, San Diego, San Francisco, and San Jose; and the Sunbelt metros of Phoenix, Dallas, San Antonio, and Houston (see Table 6.4). New York, Boston, and Washington, DC, also have relatively high levels of educational segregation, although they rank outside the top ten most segregated metros on this measure.

Highly educated people—those who have college educations and advanced degrees—enjoy numerous economic advantages. Their incomes and salaries are much higher and their rate of unemployment is far below the national average. The segregation of

Table 6.4: Segregation of the Less Educated

Rank	Large Metro	Index	Rank Among All Metros
1	Austin-Round Rock, TX	0.451	4
2	Denver-Aurora, CO	0.446	6
3	Los Angeles-Long Beach-Santa Ana, CA	0.442	7
4	Phoenix-Mesa-Scottsdale, AZ	0.428	8
5	Dallas-Fort Worth-Arlington, TX	0.428	9
6	San Diego-Carlsbad-San Marcos, CA	0.412	11
7	San Antonio, TX	0.406	14
8	Houston-Sugar Land-Baytown, TX	0.398	18
9	San Francisco-Oakland-Fremont, CA	0.395	20
10	San Jose-Sunnyvale-Santa Clara, CA	0.393	21

Source: Martin Prosperity Institute, based on data from the US Census.

the college educated is highest in older industrial cities, including Birmingham, Memphis, and Louisville, as well as in the energy hub of Houston. But Los Angeles ranks third, and the list also includes San Antonio, Dallas, Charlotte, and Chicago (see Table 6.5). Across all metros, the segregation of the highly educated is closely correlated with size and density, the concentration of high-tech industry, and the creative class's share of the workforce.[16]

Our overall index of educational segregation compares the segregation of college graduates to those who did not complete high school. Los Angeles tops the list, followed by four Texas metros: Houston, Dallas, San Antonio, and Austin. The tech hubs of San Diego and San Francisco complete the top ten, alongside Chicago, Columbus, and Charlotte (see Table 6.6).

Our lives are shaped not just by the educations we obtain and the incomes we earn, however, but also by the kinds of work we do. Our work generates our income and helps shape our identities. Recall that I separate work into three broad occupational classes: the highly paid creative class, the much lower paid and vulnerable service class, and the shrinking ranks of the working class. When it comes to the segregation of the creative class, the now familiar

Table 6.5: Segregation of College Grads

Rank	Large Metro	Index	Rank Among All Metros
1	Birmingham-Hoover, AL	0.424	6
2	Houston-Sugar Land-Baytown, TX	0.419	7
3	Los Angeles-Long Beach-Santa Ana, CA	0.406	8
4	Columbus, OH	0.403	9
5	Memphis, TN-MS-AR	0.399	11
6	San Antonio, TX	0.395	12
7	Louisville-Jefferson County, KY-IN	0.388	16
8	Dallas-Fort Worth-Arlington, TX	0.386	17
9	Charlotte-Gastonia-Concord, NC-SC	0.384	20
10	Chicago-Naperville-Joliet, IL-IN-WI	0.380	23

Source: Martin Prosperity Institute, based on data from the US Census.

Table 6.6: Educational Segregation

Rank	Large Metro	Index	Rank Among All Metros
1	Los Angeles-Long Beach-Santa Ana, CA	0.982	2
2	Houston-Sugar Land-Baytown, TX	0.968	3
3	Dallas-Fort Worth-Arlington, TX	0.967	4
3	San Antonio, TX	0.967	4
5	Austin-Round Rock, TX	0.955	7
6	San Diego-Carlsbad-San Marcos, CA	0.937	10
7	Chicago-Naperville-Joliet, IL-IN-WI	0.932	11
8	Columbus, OH	0.922	15
9	Charlotte-Gastonia-Concord, NC-SC	0.908	19
10	San Francisco-Oakland-Fremont, CA	0.907	20

Source: Martin Prosperity Institute, based on data from the US Census.

pattern of superstar cities and tech hubs comes through more clearly (see Table 6.7). Los Angeles takes first place, and New York City is fifth. The tech hubs of San Jose, San Francisco, Austin, and San Diego also number among the top ten, along with Chicago, the nation's third-largest metro, and three additional Texas metros: Houston, Dallas, and San Antonio.

The segregation of the service class is also highest in tech hubs and superstar cities (see Table 6.8). San Jose, DC, San Francisco, New York, Boston, San Diego, Austin, and LA all number among the top ten most segregated large metros, along with Philadelphia and Baltimore in the Northeast.

The segregation of the working class, whose ranks of factory, construction, and transportation workers have been declining for decades, is roughly similar to the pattern for the creative class, with superstar cities and tech hubs high on the list, as Table 6.9 shows. Los Angeles ranks as the most segregated large metro on this metric, followed by Austin, Dallas, Washington, DC, Raleigh-Cary in the North Carolina Research Triangle, San Francisco, and San Jose in the top ten, with New York and Boston also pretty far up on the broader list.

Table 6.7: Creative-Class Segregation

Rank	Large Metro	Index	Rank Among All Metros
1	Los Angeles-Long Beach-Santa Ana, CA	0.344	1
2	Houston-Sugar Land-Baytown, TX	0.327	4
3	San Jose-Sunnyvale-Santa Clara, CA	0.310	5
4	San Francisco-Oakland-Fremont, CA	0.301	8
5	New York-Northern New Jersey-Long Island, NY-NJ-PA	0.300	9
6	Dallas-Fort Worth-Arlington, TX	0.294	10
7	Austin-Round Rock-San Marcos, TX	0.284	15
8	San Antonio-New Braunfels, TX	0.284	16
9	San Diego-Carlsbad-San Marcos, CA	0.282	17
10	Chicago-Joliet-Naperville, IL-IN-WI	0.281	18

Source: Martin Prosperity Institute, based on data from the US Census.

Table 6.8: Service-Class Segregation

Rank	Large Metro	Index	Rank Among All Metros
1	San Jose-Sunnyvale-Santa Clara, CA	0.185	6
2	Washington-Arlington-Alexandria, DC-VA-MD-WV	0.181	7
3	San Francisco-Oakland-Fremont, CA	0.178	9
4	New York-Northern New Jersey-Long Island, NY-NJ-PA	0.176	11
5	Boston-Cambridge-Quincy, MA-NH	0.161	18
6	Philadelphia-Camden-Wilmington, PA-NJ-DE-MD	0.158	19
7	Baltimore-Towson, MD	0.154	24
8	San Diego-Carlsbad-San Marcos, CA	0.150	29
9	Austin-Round Rock-San Marcos, TX	0.149	33
10	Los Angeles-Long Beach-Santa Ana, CA	0.142	49

Source: Martin Prosperity Institute, based on data from the US Census.

Table 6.9: Working-Class Segregation

Rank	Large Metro	Index	Rank Among All Metros
1	Los Angeles-Long Beach-Santa Ana, CA	0.330	1
2	Austin-Round Rock-San Marcos, TX	0.321	2
3	Dallas-Fort Worth-Arlington, TX	0.304	6
4	Washington-Arlington-Alexandria, DC-VA-MD-WV	0.303	7
5	Raleigh-Cary, NC	0.301	8
6	San Francisco-Oakland-Fremont, CA	0.300	9
7	San Jose-Sunnyvale-Santa Clara, CA	0.296	12
8	Houston-Sugar Land-Baytown, TX	0.295	13
9	Charlotte-Gastonia-Rock Hill, NC-SC	0.287	17
10	Columbus, OH	0.287	18

Source: Martin Prosperity Institute, based on data from the US Census.

When it comes to overall occupational segregation—based on our composite index for the segregation of all three classes—tech hubs and superstar cities again top the list (see Table 6.10). San Jose is first, San Francisco second, and Washington, DC, third, followed by Austin, LA, and New York, and then Houston, San Diego, San Antonio, and Columbus rounding out the top ten. In all these places, members of the creative class, working class, and service class are least likely to be scattered evenly across the metro area and most likely to live alongside others of the same class.

This pattern of overall occupational segregation is shaped by the location of the creative class—the most advantaged of the three groups. The reason is simple: members of the creative class have more money and therefore the greatest ability to choose where to live. They are choosing the most desirable places, pushing the members of the two less advantaged classes into the spaces that are left over.

The precise dynamics of income, educational, and occupational segregation vary, but they are closely associated with each other

Table 6.10: Overall Occupational Segregation

Rank	Large Metro	Index	Rank Among All Metros
1	San Jose-Sunnyvale-Santa Clara, CA	0.981	2
2	San Francisco-Oakland-Fremont, CA	0.979	3
3	Washington-Arlington-Alexandria, DC-VA-MD-WV	0.971	4
4	Austin-Round Rock, TX	0.956	7
5	Los Angeles-Long Beach-Santa Ana, CA	0.955	8
6	New York-Northern New Jersey-Long Island, NY-NJ-PA	0.953	9
7	Houston-Sugar Land-Baytown, TX	0.936	13
8	San Diego-Carlsbad-San Marcos, CA	0.924	14
9	San Antonio, TX	0.918	15
10	Columbus, OH	0.904	16

Source: Martin Prosperity Institute, based on data from the US Census.

statistically, and when they are measured together, a clear picture of the overall geography of economic segregation across America emerges.[17] This pattern is captured in two broad indexes my team and I developed—one measuring overall economic segregation, the other combining this measure with measures of wage and income inequality. Figure 6.1, the Overall Economic Segregation Index, maps the first of these based on our combined index of the three dimensions of income, educational, and occupational segregation.

As the map displays, overall economic segregation is most intense along the Boston–New York–Washington corridor in the Northeast and around Los Angeles and the San Francisco Bay Area on the West Coast, along with parts of Texas and a few other areas across the nation. The knowledge hub of Austin tops the list of the most economically segregated metros. All six of America's largest metros—New York, LA, Chicago, Dallas, Houston, and Philadelphia—number among the top ten most segregated. The knowledge and tech hubs of DC, San Francisco, and Boston rank high on the list of large metros as well. Across all metros, college towns like Tallahassee, Tucson, and Ann Arbor also rank quite high in overall economic segregation.[18]

Maps and lists are one thing, but a fuller picture of economic segregation comes through in our analysis of the factors that shape it across the board—that is, when we correlate the Overall Economic Segregation Index with data on the key economic and demographic characteristics of metro areas, including their size, density, and concentration of high-tech industry.

For one, economic segregation follows closely from the size of metro areas. The Overall Economic Segregation Index is closely correlated with the size of metros.[19] Indeed, more than two hundred small and medium-sized metros have levels of overall economic segregation that are lower than those of the least-segregated large metros—and the pattern is generally similar for the various individual types of segregation. Figure 6.2 helps us visualize the relationship between metro size (based on population) and economic segregation. The line slopes sharply upward and to the right, indicating a strong positive association between the two.

Figure 6.1: Overall Economic Segregation Index

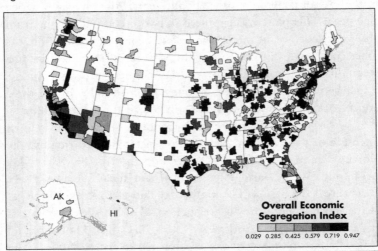

Rank	Most Segregated Large Metros	Overall Economic Segregation Index	Rank Among All Metros
1	Austin-Round Rock, TX	0.925	3
2	Columbus, OH	0.912	4
3	San Antonio, TX	0.903	6
4	Houston-Sugar Land-Baytown, TX	0.903	7
5	Los Angeles-Long Beach-Santa Ana, CA	0.893	10
6	New York-Northern New Jersey-Long Island, NY-NJ-PA	0.889	11
7	Dallas-Fort Worth-Arlington, TX	0.875	12
8	Philadelphia-Camden-Wilmington, PA-NJ-DE-MD	0.873	13
9	Chicago-Naperville-Joliet, IL-IN-WI	0.868	15
10	Memphis, TN-MS-AR	0.867	16

Source: Martin Prosperity Institute, based on data from the US Census.

Figure 6.2: Metro Size and Economic Segregation

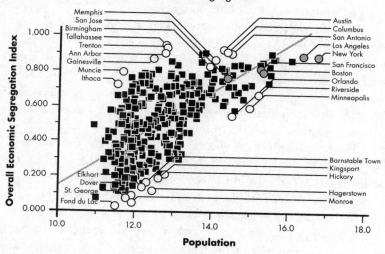

Note: Population values are logged.

Source: Martin Prosperity Institute, based on data from the US Census.

Economic segregation is closely related to density. The Overall Economic Segregation Index is positively correlated with population density. It is also positively correlated with the share of commuters who take mass transit to work, which also reflects the effect of density. Generally speaking, transit is more common in denser metros, while people drive to work alone in more sprawling ones.[20]

Economic segregation is also a feature of wealthier metros: the more affluent the area, the greater the economic segregation, and vice versa. The Overall Economic Segregation Index is positively correlated with both wages and economic output per capita, a basic measure of productivity.[21]

Economic segregation is even more closely associated with key features of knowledge-based metros: high-tech industry, the creative class, and college graduates. The correlations to high-tech industry and the creative class are among the very highest in our analysis. On the flip side, economic segregation is lower in metros

that have more working-class jobs and higher rates of unionization, which tend to bolster blue-collar wages.[22]

Furthermore, economic segregation, like inequality, is connected to the long-standing divisions between conservative and
liberal places. The Overall Economic Segregation Index is positively associated with political liberalism and negatively associated
with political conservatism.[23] Although this correlation reflects the
broader characteristics of large, dense, economically successful
places, it doesn't reduce the irony of the connection.

The next map adds to this big picture. Figure 6.3 shows how
the nation's 350-plus metros stack up on the Segregation-Inequality
Index, a combined measure of economic segregation and both income and wage inequality.[24] Superstar cities and knowledge hubs
rise to the very top of the list. New York is first among large metros, Los Angeles second, Houston third, and San Francisco fourth.
Once again, all six of America's largest metros number among the
top ten of the most segregated and unequal metros with more than
1 million people. Bridgeport-Stamford actually takes first place
when all US metros are taken into account, with college towns,
including College Station, Gainesville, Tallahassee, Durham,
Athens, and Boulder, as well as Trenton (which includes Princeton University), ranking quite highly. The Segregation-Inequality Index is closely associated with the size and density of metros;
their wealth and affluence; and, even more than economic segregation alone, their concentrations of high-tech industry, the creative
class, and college graduates.[25]

Indeed, economic segregation and economic inequality closely
track one another. Metro areas that are high in economic segregation are also high in income inequality, and the connection
between economic segregation and wage inequality is even more
pronounced.[26] This relationship between economic segregation
and inequality can be traced back at least three decades. A detailed 2009 study found that both segregation and inequality grow
alongside the size of metro areas, and that the connection remains
strong even after controlling for the effects of education levels,
race, industry and job structures, and more.[27]

Figure 6.3: The Segregation-Inequality Index

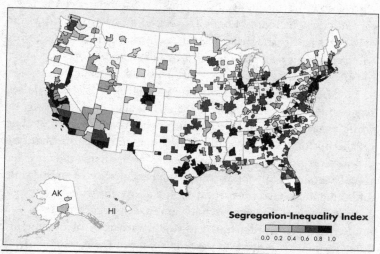

Rank	Large Metro	Segregation-Inequality Index	Rank Among All Metros
1	New York-Northern New Jersey-Long Island, NY-NJ-PA	0.977	2
2	Los Angeles-Long Beach-Santa Ana, CA	0.967	3
3	Houston-Sugar Land-Baytown, TX	0.934	7
4	San Francisco-Oakland-Fremont, CA	0.920	9
5	Philadelphia-Camden-Wilmington, PA-NJ-DE-MD	0.903	12
6	Dallas-Fort Worth-Arlington, TX	0.897	13
7	Charlotte-Gastonia-Concord, NC-SC	0.892	15
8	Chicago-Naperville-Joliet, IL-IN-WI	0.889	17
9	Austin-Round Rock, TX	0.885	18
10	Birmingham-Hoover, AL	0.879	20

Source: Martin Prosperity Institute, based on data from the US Census and the US Department of Labor, Bureau of Labor Statistics.

This pattern is not unique to the United States. Both economic segregation and inequality have grown substantially in many European cities, including London, Stockholm, Madrid, and Milan, over the past decade or so.[28] And, as in the United States, worsening economic segregation in European cities has been driven by the resources and choices of the affluent and advantaged.

The combination of economic inequality and economic segregation is deadly. It reinforces the advantages of those at the top while exacerbating and perpetuating the disadvantages of those on the bottom. Taken together, they shape not just inequality of economic resources, but also a more permanent and dysfunctional inequality of opportunity. Such inequality of opportunity adds an additional 25 percent over and above the general wage gap between college and high school graduates, according to a 2015 study. In other words, our traditional measures of income and wage inequality understate the true extent of the economic divide because they fail to take account of this devastating combination.[29]

Such differences in opportunity compound across generations. It's well known that children from richer households live in wealthier neighborhoods and have access to better schools than children from poorer households. But today, parental income has become a key factor in where many young adults can afford to locate. The exorbitant housing prices in superstar cities and tech hubs mean that more and more young people can't afford to buy a home in them, even if they work in high-paying tech jobs. The only way they can buy into these places—and the professional opportunities they offer—is via the proverbial bank of mom and dad. The ability of adult children to secure the locations that are key to their own life prospects increasingly turns on the wealth of their parents. Those who do not have this advantage can be locked out. Class and location combine to reinforce one another, not just in the present moment but over generations.

The harsh reality in America today is that poor neighborhoods stay poor, and rich neighborhoods stay rich. Segregation tends to lock not just people, but also neighborhoods, into place.

Indeed, 75 percent of the neighborhoods that were poor in 2000 were still poor a decade later; conversely, 80 percent of neighborhoods that were affluent in 1990 were still affluent a full two decades on.[30] Increasingly, our ZIP codes are our destiny.

Economic segregation is not just a class issue: it is inextricably connected to race and to America's long-standing racial divides. I identified a deeply disturbing connection between race and the creative economy in *The Rise of the Creative Class*. Specifically, I found that across metros, the minority or non-white share of the population was negatively correlated with the concentration of high-growth, high-tech firms. More recently, I found black Americans to be sorely underrepresented in the creative class. Blacks hold just 8.5 percent of creative-class jobs, despite making up 12 percent of the population. Whites, in contrast (specifically, non-Hispanic whites), hold almost three-quarters of creative-class jobs (73.8 percent) while making up less than two-thirds of the population (64 percent). Just 28 percent of black workers hold creative-class jobs, compared to 41 percent of white workers. The share of white workers in creative-class jobs exceeds 40 percent in thirty-seven of the fifty-one metros with more than 1 million people, whereas the share of black workers in creative-class jobs exceeds 40 percent in just one large metro. Black workers make up a larger share of the creative-class jobs in larger, denser metros with more college graduates, more high-tech firms, and greater diversity (in terms of immigrants and the gay and lesbian populations), but they lag in such jobs in areas where they make up a large share of the population overall. This is likely because the members of the black creative class are drawn to places with more propulsive economies, with higher-skilled, higher-paying jobs, and with greater overall economic opportunity.[31]

Today, economic segregation remains closely associated with race, even as levels of racial segregation have declined from the staggering levels of a half-century or so ago—that is, before the civil rights movement of the 1960s. Between 1970 and 2010, the racial segregation of blacks declined in all of the nation's eighty-five largest metros, according to a 2012 study by Edward Glaeser and Jacob Vigdor.[32] That said, race and economic segregation continue to be inextricably intertwined. My Overall Economic Segregation Index for metro areas is positively correlated with both the share of population that is black and with the share of population that is Hispanic or Asian. On the flip side, the index is negatively associated with the share of the metro population that is white.[33]

None of this is surprising: race continues to play a substantial role, alongside class, in how people and neighborhoods are divided. What is surprising is that the black creative class appears to have a moderating effect on both economic segregation and inequality. Across US metros, the black creative class is not statistically associated with income inequality, and there is only a modest correlation between the black creative class and economic segregation. This is markedly different from what we find with the white creative class and the creative class as a whole, both of which are positively associated with segregation and inequality.[34] From a policy perspective, these findings suggest that efforts to boost the black creative class may help to combat both inequality and segregation. Such efforts are sorely needed, given the extent to which blacks are underrepresented in the creative class.

Ironically—and troublingly—cities and metro areas can be both more diverse and more segregated at the same time. My own analysis shows that segregation is positively associated with two common measures of diversity: the concentration of gay and lesbian people and the share of the population that is foreign-born.[35] A 2015 analysis by Nate Silver comparing the overall ethnic and racial diversity of the nation's one hundred largest cities to the racial and ethnic segregation of their neighborhoods found segregation to be higher in more racially and ethnically diverse cities.[36]

Ultimately, the one-two punch of race and economic segregation hits hardest at poor African American neighborhoods. Black Americans are much more likely to live in areas of concentrated poverty than their white peers. One in four black Americans lives in a high-poverty neighborhood compared to just one in thirteen whites.[37] Furthermore, our cities are splitting into areas of racially concentrated poverty and racially concentrated affluence. According to a 2015 study of fifteen large US metro areas, Los Angeles had 129 neighborhoods of racially concentrated poverty that were more than 80 percent black and Hispanic, and 12 areas of racially concentrated affluence that were more than 90 percent white. Chicago had 138 neighborhoods of concentrated poverty that were 80 percent black and Hispanic, and 58 neighborhoods of concentrated affluence that were more than 90 percent white. Across all fifteen metros, areas of racially concentrated poverty were more than 75 percent black and Hispanic, while areas of racially concentrated affluence were more than 90 percent white.[38]

Those who grow up in poor black neighborhoods tend to stay in them. Two-thirds of African Americans who were raised in the poorest 25 percent of American neighborhoods are raising their own children in similarly disadvantaged neighborhoods. "Neighborhood inequality is multi-generational, something that is passed down from parents to children in the same way that genetic background and financial wealth are transmitted across generations," is the way sociologist Patrick Sharkey, the author of a major study on racially concentrated poverty, *Stuck in Place*, puts it.[39]

These trends take a toll on middle-class blacks as well, who are much more likely to live in or near high-poverty neighborhoods than their white counterparts. In fact, about half of middle-class African Americans are raised in neighborhoods with poverty rates of 20 percent or more, compared to just 1 percent of their white peers.[40] Even when poor black parents are able to claw their way out of poverty, they, too, often see their children fall back into it.

The economic penalty for growing up in conditions of racially concentrated poverty is considerable. The difference in lifetime earnings between those raised in the richest 20 percent of neighborhoods versus those raised in the bottom 20 percent is about the same as the difference between just completing high school and having a college degree, according to a 2015 study by Douglas Massey and Jonathan Rothwell. When differences in cost of living are taken into account, that difference adds up to nearly $1 million—$910,000, to be exact. Ultimately, the low level of economic mobility of black Americans is a product of their being concentrated and segregated into chronically poor, disadvantaged neighborhoods.[41]

The most damaging consequence of economic and racial segregation is the limit it imposes on the ability of less advantaged Americans to move up the economic ladder. Prospects for upward economic mobility are considerably lower in more segregated, more economically unequal places, according to the highly influential studies of economist Raj Chetty and his collaborators.[42] Children from predominantly black neighborhoods face especially long odds in moving up the economic ladder. Roughly one-fifth of the gap in earnings between blacks and whites as adults is attributable to the counties where they grew up. Racially concentrated disadvantage creates a substantial barrier to economic mobility and the American Dream.

Interestingly enough, the prospects for economic mobility are greatest in New York, Los Angeles, the San Francisco Bay Area, Boston, Greater Washington, DC, and Seattle, all of which rank among the top twenty places for upward mobility, according to Chetty and company's analysis. Even though they are highly segregated and unequal, these metros have more robust economies with larger clusters of high-paying industries and jobs that offer greater avenues for upward mobility. Conversely, the prospects for upward economic mobility are substantially worse in the less populated, more spread out metros, where the disadvantaged tend to be located farther away from jobs and economic opportunity.

But the prospects for economic mobility also vary considerably within as well as across metros. My own experience attests to this. My working-class parents moved from Newark to North Arlington in Bergen County (albeit the most working-class community in that county) when I was two years old and my brother was a newborn. They did so to put us on a path to a better life, as they frequently reminded us as we were growing up. Their intuitive sense of what was best for their kids is borne out by Chetty's empirical research, which finds that children have among the best life prospects if they grow up in Bergen County, and among the worst if they grow up in Newark. My parents also hit the timing right, because the research finds that children whose families make such moves when they are toddlers see the biggest benefits.

In addition to better pathways for upward mobility, larger, denser, more knowledge-based metro areas also offer the poor and disadvantaged better prospects for a long and healthy life. In still another study, Chetty and his collaborators found that the poor live longest in superstar cities and tech hubs like New York, Los Angeles, San Francisco, San Jose, and Boston, and that they face the shortest life expectancies in the Rustbelt metros of Detroit, Gary, Toledo, and Dayton as well as Las Vegas, Tulsa, and Oklahoma City.[43] If we want to help poor and working-class people move up the economic ladder and live longer, healthier lives, it's important to ensure that they are not forced out of the biggest, richest, and most educated cities by their rising housing costs.

That said, providing poor people with the means to move to large cities, or even to better neighborhoods within them—so-called people-based policies—will not somehow magically solve the problem of concentrated poverty. The positive effects of moving decline substantially as kids grow older—and such moves have little impact on teenagers. Race is a factor as well. White and Hispanic kids who move to better neighborhoods have a much better shot at upward economic mobility than black children do.[44] Not to mention the damage that it does to disadvantaged neighborhoods: by siphoning off the people and families with the best chances of success, purely people-based policies can leave those troubled neighborhoods even further behind. As Chapter 10 will show, if we wish to break the cycle of concentrated urban poverty, people-based policies must be combined with place-based policies that bolster neighborhood conditions.

So, what does it all mean?
While the various types of economic segregation are higher in some kinds of metro areas than others—Rustbelt metros suffer

from high levels of income segregation, and Sunbelt metros have high levels of educational segregation, for example—taken as a whole, it becomes clear that economic segregation is worse in larger, denser, more economically successful, and more diverse metros. This finding reflects the central contradiction that sits at the heart of the New Urban Crisis: the places that are the most productive and offer the highest wages, that have the largest concentrations of high-tech industry and the most talented people, that are the densest and offer the most abundant mass transit options, that are the most diverse, and that are the most liberal in their political leanings nonetheless face the harshest levels of economic inequality and economic segregation.

In this chapter and the previous one I have used aggregated data to show the extent of segregation and inequality in America's cities and metro areas and the quintessentially urban factors that are driving them. In the next, I'll use more granular data to visualize and map these divides at the neighborhood level, revealing how our cities and suburbs are splintering into small areas of concentrated advantage and much larger areas of concentrated disadvantage.

7

PATCHWORK METROPOLIS

Amerca's class divides have long been etched into its living patterns. For much of the twentieth century, the rich and the upper middle class lived in verdant suburbs like Boston's Brookline, Detroit's Grosse Pointe, Philadelphia's Bryn Mawr, or Greenwich, Connecticut. The aspiring working and lower middle classes settled in smaller, denser, closer-in suburbs, such as Levittown on Long Island, or North Arlington, New Jersey, where I grew up. The poor and the truly disadvantaged were crammed into inner-city ghettos like Chicago's South Side, or New York's South Bronx, or parts of Newark, not far from where I was born. By the 1970s, it was generally the case that suburbs were predominantly affluent, upwardly mobile, and white, while cities were declining, hollowed out, and increasingly populated by members of minority groups and the poor.

Karl Marx's disciples, following his lead, have long believed that class identity is forged in the workplace—on the factory floor, so to speak. Yet class today in America is not just about the kind of work we do but also about the places in which we live, which shape everything from our access to jobs and economic opportunity to the schools our kids attend, our health and well-being, and our prospects for upward mobility. The intersection of class and location is attracting the attention of commentators from across the ideological spectrum. In his 2012 book, *Coming Apart*, Charles Murray contrasts two different class-based neighborhoods that exemplify the twin poles of America's deepening economic and political divides: the affluent and outward-looking residents of suburban Belmont, Massachusetts, outside of Boston, and the left-behind, inward-looking, and alienated working-class residents of Philadelphia's Fishtown neighborhood. Robert Putnam, in his 2015 book, *Our Kids*, chronicled the decline of his hometown, Port Clinton, Ohio, as a case study on the decline of the middle class and the fading of the American Dream.[1]

America's class geography no longer follows the old pattern of rich suburb and poor city. As we have seen, highly paid knowledge workers, the affluent, and young people have been returning in large numbers to urban centers over the past decade or two, while growing numbers of the poor and disadvantaged are being edged out into the suburbs. This apparent reversal of America's long-established geographic divide is sometimes referred to as a great inversion.[2]

Yet the geography of class in contemporary America is different from what either of those models portray. Our class geography is now being reshaped into a more complex and variegated pattern that I call the Patchwork Metropolis. Although its precise signature varies from place to place, the core feature of this new class geography is a metropolitan landscape that is being split into areas of tightly clustered zones of concentrated advantage and even larger swaths of concentrated disadvantage that crisscross cities and suburbs alike.

In the previous chapter I used aggregated statistics to show how metro areas are becoming more segregated by income, education, and occupational class. In this one, I use more granular data to identify and visualize how these new divides etch themselves within metro areas. In contrast to other frameworks that track the location of different types of economic activity (such as industrial, commercial, and residential uses), or classify people according to their income (grouping them, for instance, as high, middle, and low income), I mapped the residential locations of the three major classes. To do so, my team and I used detailed data to identify the census tracts where each of the three groups we considered— the highly paid creative class, the lower-paid service class, and the shrinking ranks of the working class—form a plurality. We mapped these patterns across roughly a dozen and a half leading metro areas in the United States, Canada, and the United Kingdom, including a mix of city types that ranged from superstar cities and tech hubs to sprawling Sunbelt metros and deindustrializing Rustbelt areas.[3]

Although each and every metro area has its own unique class fingerprint, our maps and analysis show that the Patchwork Metropolis conforms to four broad types.

In the first type, the advantaged creative class effectively recolonizes the urban center while also remaining highly concentrated in the suburbs. The less advantaged service and working classes are pushed into the leftover spaces in the city, and to an even greater extent out into the suburban and exurban fringes. This pattern is evident in superstar cities like New York and London, as well as in knowledge hubs like San Francisco, Boston, and Washington, DC, along with Toronto and Chicago.

In the second type, the creative class remains concentrated in the suburbs with more limited movement back to the urban center. This pattern can be seen in the Sunbelt metros of Atlanta, Dallas, and Houston and in Rustbelt ones like Detroit, Pittsburgh, and Cleveland.

In the third pattern, the entire metropolis is essentially cleaved in two, with the advantaged creative class and the disadvantaged service class occupying entirely separate blocs of territory spanning the urban center and suburbs. Vancouver, Austin, and Philadelphia exemplify this pattern.

The fourth type finds the more affluent creative class occupying an archipelago of small, self-contained clusters surrounded by the less advantaged classes. The pattern is typified by Los Angeles and Miami, where the creative class is strung out along the coastline, with smaller clusters in and around the urban core and around universities and knowledge institutions.

Across each of these types, this new patchwork geography is shaped by the locational prerogatives of the advantaged creative class, whose members are drawn to and cluster around locations depending on four key factors.

The first factor is proximity to the urban core. This back-to-the-city pattern is most intensive in the superstar cities of New York and London and the knowledge hubs of Boston, San Francisco, and Washington, DC. But less intense versions of it can be seen in many cities and metro areas.

The second factor is proximity to transit. Members of the creative class cluster around subway stops and transit lines that allow them to save time and limit long car commutes. This factor is especially important in dense superstar cities and knowledge hubs with expensive housing and extensive transit systems.

The third factor is proximity to major universities and other knowledge-based institutions. Historically, the people who lived near universities—students pursuing their degrees—were relatively transient; they left when they graduated. Caught up by the decline of their cities, by the 1970s and 1980s urban universities like the University of Southern California in Los Angeles, Columbia University in New York, and many others were transformed into walled-off islands. Today, the neighborhoods surrounding urban universities and other similar knowledge-based institutions have become locations of choice for the creative class, even when many who are drawn to them have no specific connection to the university per se.[4]

The fourth factor is proximity to natural amenities. The creative class not only clusters in the most economically functional parts of cities and suburbs but also in their most aesthetically pleasing locations—for example, near parks and other green spaces, near mountains, and especially along coastlines and waterfronts. This pattern is most pronounced in metros like Los Angeles and Miami where the creative class is massed along the coastline, but it can also be seen in the old waterfront industrial districts of other cities, where former factories and warehouses are being repurposed and reused as housing, shops, galleries, and offices for knowledge workers.

In order to fully understand the contours of the Patchwork Metropolis, we need to first look back to the classic theories of urban formation and development, as they provide the foundational building blocks for an understanding of our class geography today.

A s I set about to better understand and map this new class geography, I found myself going back to the pioneering work of the early twentieth-century urbanist Robert Ezra Park and his colleagues at the University of Chicago. Their ideas are so powerful that they continue to shape our thinking about our urban and metropolitan landscape to this day. Even if their models no longer fully capture today's realities, their seminal efforts to outline the shape and form of the early industrial city provide a basic approach that can help us understand the new class geography of our time.[5]

Park's odyssey is so remarkable that it seems the stuff of fiction. He was born in 1864 in Harveyville, Pennsylvania, a small town in the anthracite coal region near Scranton. Park worked as a railroad laborer before attending the University of Minnesota and the University of Michigan. After a stint as a journalist, he returned to academia, earning his master's degree at Harvard under the philosopher William James. He later moved to Germany to study with Georg Simmel, the brilliant sociologist and author of the 1903 classic *The Metropolis and Mental Life*, receiving his PhD from the University of Heidelberg. Park became fascinated and appalled by the problem of race relations, both in Africa (he worked briefly as a press agent for the Congo Reform Association) and in the United States (where he helped found the Committee on Urban Conditions Among Negroes, now the Urban League). He spent ten years at the Tuskegee Institute in Alabama, where he worked with Booker T. Washington on his book *The Man Farthest Down*.

Park ultimately landed at the University of Chicago. With his colleagues and students, he dove into the study of Chicago, with its factories and slaughterhouses and red-light districts, its new skyscrapers, its working-class neighborhoods, its slums, and its rapidly developing areas of suburban affluence. A pioneer in urban ethnography, urban sociology, and urban geography, with a reach that extended into urban economics as well, Park authored studies on homelessness, juvenile delinquency, and high-poverty communities. Chicago became his laboratory.

Like a biologist studying the form and structure of organisms, Park peered inside the structure of the city to identify its basic components and building blocks. For him, the city was much more than a collection of physical attributes, buildings, and transportation arteries; it was a mechanism for organizing and differentiating various types of human activity. "The city is not merely a physical mechanism and an artificial construction," Park wrote in his classic 1925 volume *The City*, coauthored with his colleagues Ernest W. Burgess and Roderick D. McKenzie. "It is involved in the vital processes of the people who compose it, it is a product of nature and particularly of human nature."[6] The city was made up of separate districts and neighborhoods that structured and organized different types of human activity. According to Park, it was "a mosaic of little worlds which touch but do not interpenetrate." To better understand the city and its elemental components, he and his colleagues mapped and diagrammed the locations of business and commerce; factories, warehouses, and other kinds of industrial activity; and the residential areas of the working, middle, and upper classes in and around Chicago.

Their work generated an extraordinarily influential framework for understanding and visualizing the basic structure of the city and metropolis. It described urban areas as taking shape in a series of concentric zones comprised of different types of activity. At the very center of the city—its nucleus, as it were—stood the central business district, with its mix of high-rise office buildings, courthouses and other government facilities, department stores, and key railroad and transit hubs. Surrounding that core was a series of zones radiating outward in successive rings. The ring surrounding the core housed the factories, slaughterhouses, and warehouses of the industrial district, which they famously dubbed "the zone in transition." After that were the working-class residential neighborhoods with their tightly packed jumbles of rooming houses, tenements, saloons, and bathhouses, many of them within

Figure 7.1: Chicago School Models of Cities

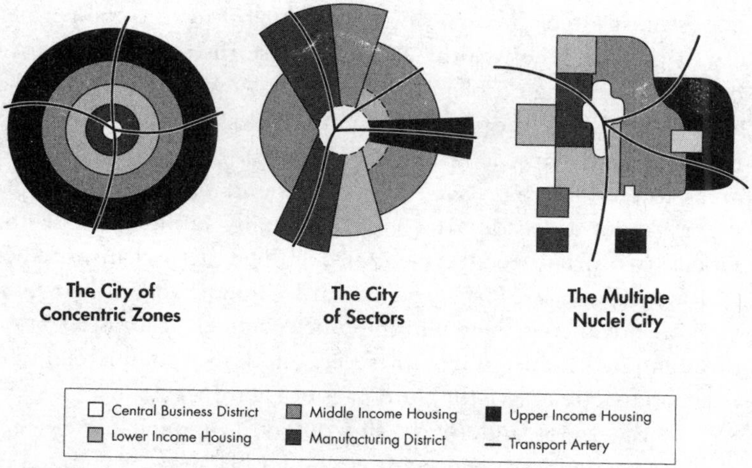

| The City of Concentric Zones | The City of Sectors | The Multiple Nuclei City |

Central Business District ☐ Middle Income Housing ■ Upper Income Housing ■
Lower Income Housing ■ Manufacturing District ■ Transport Artery —

Source: Graphic by Martin Prosperity Institute.

earshot (and smelling distance) of the industrial district. The density of settlement declined with the distance from the urban center. Farther out came the residential districts of the middle and upper classes with their tree-lined streets, larger lots, and bigger houses (see the first part of Figure 7.1).

A decade or so later, Homer Hoyt, an economist who earned his PhD at the University of Chicago, refined and reconfigured that basic model. Instead of forming neat concentric circles, he argued, the metropolis developed in a series of even more distinctly differentiated wedges or sectors along its major transportation arteries (see the second part of Figure 7.1). In a 1939 study of sixty or so US metros for the Federal Housing Administration, he showed how the most advantaged residents of a city shaped its contours by choosing where to live and work. "In considering the growth of a city, the movement of the high rent area is in a certain sense the most important because it tends to pull the growth of the entire city in the same direction," he wrote, dubbing this high-rent sector "the favored quarter." Overwhelmingly and inexorably, the higher-priced neighborhoods were moving outward toward the suburban fringe. "High rent or high grade residential neighborhoods must almost necessarily move outward toward the periphery of the city. The wealthy seldom reverse their steps and move backward into the obsolete houses which they are giving up," he added. "The lure of open fields, golf courses, country clubs, and country estates acts as a magnet to pull high grade residential areas to sections that have free, open country beyond their borders." About a decade after Hoyt originally outlined his sector model, two urban geographers, also trained at the University of Chicago, Chauncy Harris and Edward Ullman, added their own tweaks, advancing their multiple nuclei model of an even more differentiated metropolis with several nodes of commercial and residential activity (see the third part of Figure 7.1).[7]

By the 1960s and 1970s, this outward-oriented pattern became so pronounced that the urban center began to be emptied of many of its core economic functions. In their 1959 study of Greater New York, *Anatomy of a Metropolis*, the economists Edgar Hoover and Raymond Vernon documented what they called the flight from density. Industry and commercial activity, as well as people, they said, were making a trek from the city to the suburbs. This outward shifting of people and jobs reached its pinnacle with the rise of the so-called edge city, in which exurban office parks and malls essentially replicated and replaced the functions of the increasingly deserted and dysfunctional urban center.[8]

By the late 1990s and early 2000s, as we have seen, the shape of our cities and metro areas began to change significantly, as affluent and educated people started returning to the urban cores and poverty began to be pushed outward into the suburbs. This turn of events has brought with it a new and more variegated pattern that has evolved beyond the existing models. Parts of our cities are richer than they were and parts of our suburbs are poorer, but they have not simply changed places. My tour through some of our leading cities will highlight the four basic patterns of the new patchwork geography and the factors that are reshaping our cities and suburbs today.

The first of today's new patterns arises from the back-to-the-city movement of people in superstar cities and tech hubs. As mentioned above, the cities and metros that exemplify this pattern include the superstars of New York and London; the tech hubs of San Francisco, Boston, and Washington, DC; and the revitalized Great Lakes cities of Chicago and Toronto. These cities and metros are larger and denser than most; have high concentrations of the creative class, especially in and around their urban cores; and are comparatively well-served by transit, all of which helps to shape the geographic organization of the major social and economic classes.

In New York City, the creative class has colonized the urban core from the southern tip of the financial district in Manhattan through Tribeca, SoHo, the Village, Chelsea, Midtown, and the Upper East and West Sides (see Figure 7.2). For all the talk of gentrification in Brooklyn, the creative class is confined almost completely to parts of the borough that are adjacent to Lower Manhattan, though it is beginning to stretch out from there. But

Figure 7.2: New York

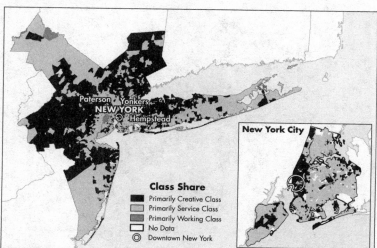

Source: Map by Martin Prosperity Institute, based on data from the US Census.

the creative class is not just concentrated in the city; it is also located in a broad band of suburbs in Long Island, New Jersey, and Westchester County. The service class spans the city and suburbs as well. The Bronx is almost completely service class, with the exception of upscale Riverdale; so is Queens, apart from a few working-class neighborhoods and several small creative-class hubs, such as affluent Forest Hills. The leading service-class locations are all in the outer boroughs and on Long Island. There are just a few plurality working-class locations left in the region, mostly in and around Newark, Elizabeth, Paterson, and Passaic in New Jersey, very close to where I was born and grew up. The extent to which blue-collar neighborhoods have disappeared is startling for a region that still had a huge manufacturing base and extensive working-class neighborhoods just decades ago.

London's creative class is even more tightly concentrated in and around its urban core, making up roughly 80 percent of the residents of inner-city neighborhoods like Kensington, Chelsea,

Figure 7.3: London

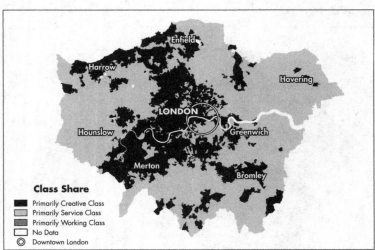

Source: Map by Martin Prosperity Institute, based on data from the United Kingdom, Office for National Statistics, Neighbourhood Statistics and Census Output.

the City of London, Camden, and Parliament Hill (see Figure 7.3). The service class is mostly pushed out to the city's periphery and arrayed in three large areas to the northwest, northeast, and south of the city. There is also a substantial pocket of service-class workers closer to the central core, right below the River Thames. Surprisingly, there is not a single tract in London where the working class makes up a plurality of residents, a development that would have come as quite a shock to Karl Marx, who spent so many decades in the British Museum writing about its plight.

Chicago class geography today bears only a passing resemblance to the one that Park and his colleagues wrote about. As in New York and London, its creative class has poured back into the urban core, repopulating and repurposing its warehouses and factory buildings while bleeding over into adjacent blue-collar neighborhoods, such as Wrigleyville around the Chicago Cubs' Wrigley Field (see Figure 7.4). The creative class is located in many suburbs as well. There is a major creative-class cluster in Hyde Park around the University of Chicago, and the creative class also hugs the lakeshore,

Figure 7.4: Chicago

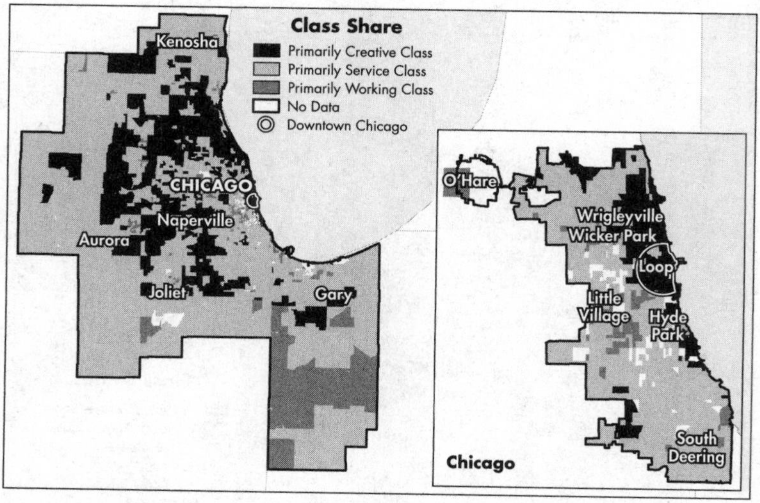

Source: Map by Martin Prosperity Institute, based on data from the US Census.

running from downtown into the suburbs with a substantial cluster in Evanston, where Northwestern University is located. The service class also spans the city and suburbs. Large pockets of disadvantage remain in the city itself. Nine of the metro's ten neighborhoods with the highest service-class concentrations are in Chicago proper. Four are in Englewood, a three-mile-square neighborhood in the southwest that has a poverty rate in excess of 40 percent, more than twice the city's overall rate. The service class is also concentrated in the areas between the urban and suburban creative-class clusters and at the outer fringes of the metro. Few working-class districts remain in this once great industrial city, with the largest blue-collar clusters in relatively far-off Joliet and Gary.

In my adopted hometown of Toronto, the creative class is very tightly concentrated in and around the downtown and urban core, which is home to the University of Toronto, several other colleges and universities, and the major hospitals and medical centers. From there, it radiates outward in a T-shaped pattern along the city's main subway and transit lines (see Figure 7.5). The cross of the T extends farther west and east, across the lakefront and along transit

Figure 7.5: Toronto

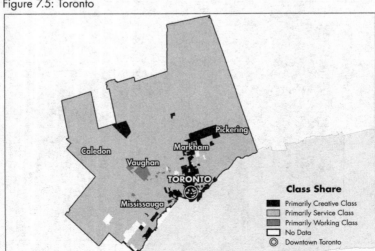

Source: Map by Martin Prosperity Institute, based on data from Statistics Canada.

lines through the rapidly gentrifying Queen West district and then out to the suburbs of Mississauga and the upscale lakefront suburb of Oakville, and finally takes on a more lopsided pattern as it heads north to the suburbs of Markham and Pickering. The service class is pushed out to the peripheries. My map reflects the same general pattern initially identified in a study by my University of Toronto colleague David Hulchanski, which showed Toronto being carved into three separate kinds of areas—a small set of affluent neighborhoods near the urban core and along the major transit lines, a larger set of much poorer neighborhoods away from transit and extending out into the suburbs, and a dwindling set of middle-income neighborhoods.[9] Just a few plurality working-class districts remain, scattered in the suburbs west of the city.

This basic pattern can also be seen in leading tech hubs. San Francisco's creative class, for instance, is thickly clustered across its downtown, the Marina District, the University of San Francisco, the historically upscale neighborhoods of Pacific Heights and Russian Hill, the Haight down to the Castro, and the more recently

Figure 7.6: San Francisco

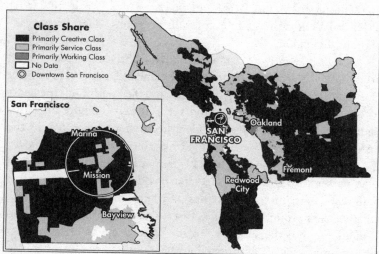

Source: Map by Martin Prosperity Institute, based on data from the US Census.

gentrified tech districts of the Mission and SoMa (see Figure 7.6). But again, the creative class extends far into the suburbs. It occupies large swaths of territory around the University of California in Berkeley, in Marin County in the north, and in the southeast and southwest around Stanford University and Silicon Valley. It is also massively concentrated in the East Bay, which is home to six of the ten neighborhoods with the largest creative-class concentrations in the metro. The neighborhood with the largest creative-class concentration of all is Upper Rockridge in Oakland. But Oakland also has a large population of the less advantaged service class, many of whom live below the poverty line. There, and across the Bay Area, the service class is lodged in between the major creative-class districts and out along the peripheries of the suburbs. In the city of San Francisco itself, the service class clusters at the outskirts of some of the most affluent and advantaged neighborhoods. Despite its increasing affluence, the city remains home to eight of the ten neighborhoods with the highest service-class concentrations in the Bay Area, most of them located in and around downtown. There are also large service-class zones at the far peripheries north of Marin and east of Oakland in a long band running from Oakland to Fremont, in Menlo Park, and in East Palo Alto in the heart of Silicon Valley. Virtually no plurality working-class districts remain in the region.

Boston's creative class is similarly tightly clustered in and around its downtown core, from the Financial District and Faneuil Hall to upscale Beacon Hill and Back Bay; the South End, the heart of the city's gay community; and the Fenway-Kenmore area (see Figure 7.7). Following a pattern identified half a century ago by the historian Sam Bass Warner in his classic book *Streetcar Suburbs*, the metro has been shaped by its transit infrastructure.[10] The Red Line passes through Cambridge and has drawn large numbers of high-tech companies and startups and huge concentrations of the creative class around its stops and stations. The creative class also extends far into the suburbs. To the west, a major creative-class cluster runs outside Cambridge into Belmont and the historical colonial towns of Lexington and Concord and to the upscale suburbs

Figure 7.7: Boston

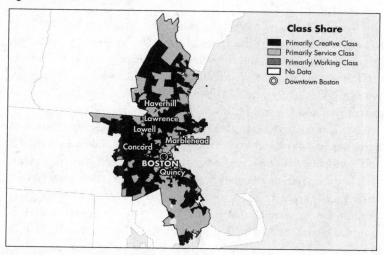

Source: Map by Martin Prosperity Institute, based on data from the US Census.

of Newton, Wellesley, and Sudbury, most of which are connected to the core of the city by transit. Substantial creative-class clusters are also located along the region's famed Route 128 high-tech corridor.[11] Moreover, there are considerable creative-class concentrations in the affluent communities that line the northern coastline, including Manchester-by-the-Sea, Swampscott, and Marblehead. Three of the metro's ten leading creative-class neighborhoods are in Boston proper, and four are in Cambridge. The remaining three are in Newton, an upscale suburb that sits on the Green Line close to Boston College. The service class is concentrated in a tight band outside downtown Boston, continuing north past Marblehead and south to Quincy along the coast, forming two big clusters at the northern and southern fringes of the metro. Nine of the ten most concentrated service-class neighborhoods in the metro are in the city of Boston, mainly in South and East Boston around historically black Roxbury and near Logan Airport. Slightly less than 15 percent of the region's workers belong to the blue-collar working class, well below the national average—and a stark change from the middle of the twentieth century, when Boston was a preeminent manufacturing center.

Washington, DC's, creative class makes up nearly half the metro's workforce, one of the highest levels in the country, spanning large areas of the city and the suburbs (see Figure 7.8). The creative class predominates in the upscale urban neighborhoods of George-town, Cleveland Park, and others in Northwest DC, and around downtown and Capitol Hill, which have seen considerable gentrifi-cation. The creative class also extends into the close-in suburbs of Bethesda in Maryland and Arlington and Alexandria in Virginia and into suburbs even farther out, including Fairfax, Manassas, and Leesburg in northern Virginia and Gaithersburg and Fred-erick in Maryland. Three of the metro's top ten creative-class neighborhoods are located in the District proper—Adams Mor-gan, Cleveland Park, and Lanier Heights. The other seven are in close-in, transit-served suburbs: four are in Arlington, two more are in Bethesda, and one is in Alexandria. The class divide in the

Figure 7.8: Washington, DC

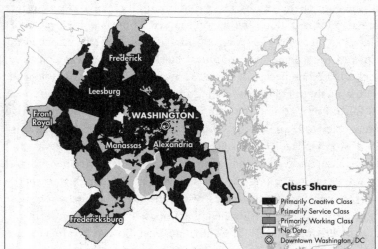

Source: Map by Martin Prosperity Institute, based on data from the US Census.

District of Columbia itself runs across an east/west axis with the creative class concentrated in the northwest and the service class massed in the east. The service class occupies a significant cluster south and east of the District that extends into Prince George's County, Maryland. Seven out of ten of the metro's most concentrated service-class neighborhoods are located in historically African American sections of the District itself, and two more are in Prince George's County, which is almost 65 percent black. Across the region, the service class makes up some 40 percent of the workforce. Greater DC is one of the very few places in America where the service class accounts for a smaller share of the workforce than the creative class.

In the second pattern of the Patchwork Metropolis, the advantaged creative class remains much more concentrated in the suburbs. This suburban pattern is found in two very different types of metros: Sunbelt metros such as Atlanta, Dallas, and Houston, and Rustbelt ones like Detroit and Pittsburgh. In Sunbelt metros, the creative class has long been drawn to upscale suburban areas, and although commutes can be arduous, these places remain far more car-dependent than the metros listed above for the back-to-the-city pattern. In Rustbelt metros, whose urban centers were hollowed out long ago by pervasive white flight, the suburbs have long been the preferred locations for the creative class. In some of these places, including Greater Detroit, older suburbs that developed in the early part of the twentieth century along rivers or rail lines have been able to partially re-create the urban characteristics of walkability and mixed-use shopping, dining, and nightlife districts. Despite their differing economic fortunes, these metros are more spread out, are more car-dependent, and have much less mass transit than the superstar cities and knowledge hubs discussed above. The back-to-the-city movement has also been more limited in these metros than in the cities previously covered, and they have smaller shares of the creative class as well.

Figure 7.9: Atlanta

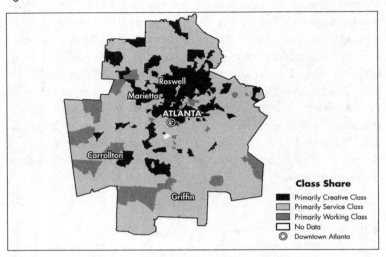

Source: Map by Martin Prosperity Institute, based on data from the US Census.

Atlanta's creative class occupies the areas north and east of the city's core, from downtown through Midtown and Buckhead in the city proper to the upscale suburbs to the north (see Figure 7.9). The southeast is nearly all service class, with just a few creative-class islets. Seven of the region's top ten service-class locations are located within the city limits of Atlanta. Many of these neighborhoods are poor and black. The working class occupies the far corners of the metro.

Dallas's creative class is clustered in its northern suburbs of Plano, Frisco, and Irving, where six of the metro's ten creative-class neighborhoods are located (see Figure 7.10). The region's southern tier is almost entirely service class, interspersed with a few creative-class clusters. Along the Trinity River just south of downtown, there is also a less prominent divide that separates working- and service-class neighborhoods to the west from creative-class enclaves to the east.

Houston's creative class is located in two rings: a large suburban band that loops around the center of the metro from the

Figure 7.10: Dallas–Fort Worth

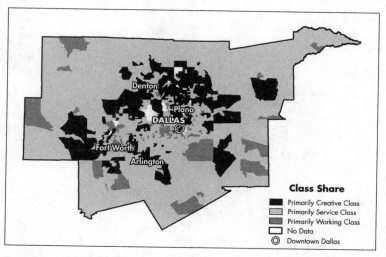

Source: Map by Martin Prosperity Institute, based on data from the US Census.

Woodlands in the north toward Sugar Land in the southwest, and a much smaller cluster around the urban core (see Figure 7.11). That said, nine of the metro's top ten creative-class neighborhoods are in the city proper, with seven of them located in the upscale area around Rice University. The service class is located in two big swaths of territory. The first is between the downtown and inner suburban creative-class cluster. Nine of the ten neighborhoods with the largest service-class concentrations are located in this band. The rest of the service class is pushed much farther out to the far fringes of the metro. Houston's working class is mostly concentrated in districts to the south and north of downtown around the Port of Houston.

Moving from metros in the South to those in the North, we find a similar suburban-centric pattern in hard-hit Rustbelt metros. Sunbelt metros were literally built around highways and sprawl, but Rustbelt metros, after witnessing white flight and seeing their centers hollowed out as a result of it, have not yet experienced enough new urban growth to fill in the downtown areas once again.

Figure 7.11: Houston

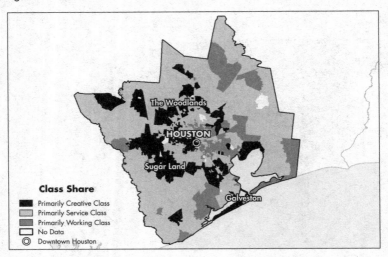

Source: Map by Martin Prosperity Institute, based on data from the US Census.

Detroit's creative class is located in a large wedge of suburbs to the north and west of the city, right over its famed Eight Mile boundary, extending from Ferndale and Royal Oak to upscale Birmingham and the Bloomfields. Each and every one of the metro's top ten creative-class neighborhoods is located in the suburbs (see Figure 7.12). Two are in Birmingham; two are in Bloomfield Township; another is in Bloomfield Hills, home of the Cranbrook Academy; and another is in Troy. Two more are located in Huntington Woods, a lush enclave that hosts a public golf course and the Detroit Zoo; and the last two are in the Grosse Pointes—Grosse Pointe Shores and Grosse Pointe Park—where Gilded Age mansions line the lakeshores.

The region's class divides overlie and underpin its long history of racial cleavage; the city has suffered some of the worst white flight of any major US city. There is, however, a small and growing creative-class hub in the city's urban core: in and around Mies Van der Rohe's Lafayette Park; in Corktown; along the Cass Corridor, where the city's major arts and cultural institutions are located;

Figure 7.12: Detroit

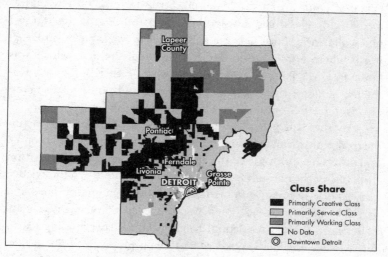

Source: Map by Martin Prosperity Institute, based on data from the US Census.

and in nearby Midtown, the home of Wayne State University. Detroit's downtown has received significant investment, most prominently from billionaire Dan Gilbert, who has acquired millions of square feet of commercial and residential space in many of the city's old landmark buildings. (He famously said that he simply took advantage of the great "skyscraper sale" that occurred after the 2008 crash.)[12] There is another small creative-class cluster along the lakeshore on a narrow strip running north along Jefferson Avenue toward Grosse Pointe, and another to the north in historically upscale Palmer Woods.

The service class is concentrated in the city of Detroit but spans large parts of the suburbs as well. A large sea of disadvantage and despair surrounds a small island of urban revival in the city's center. Decimated by deindustrialization and white flight, the city has lost more than half its population since 1950, and large areas are now virtually abandoned.[13] In 2009, at the height of the recent economic crisis, the city's official unemployment rate neared 30 percent. In the summer of 2013, the city declared bankruptcy. All ten of the region's most concentrated service-class neighborhoods are in the city itself. Strikingly, only a few plurality working-class neighborhoods remain in the city. The largest blue-collar neighborhoods are farther out in the suburbs: in Dearborn, where Ford's headquarters is located; Pontiac, which was home to GM's Pontiac Motor Division and Fisher Body unit; Romulus, home of the GM Romulus engine and power-train plant; and even farther out in Lapeer County close to Flint.

Another Rustbelt city, Pittsburgh, was my base case of postindustrial transformation in *The Rise of the Creative Class*, and I and others have chronicled the ups and downs of its transformation from one of the nation's foremost industrial centers to a knowledge hub.[14] The city's reinvention and revival has been underpinned and driven by its universities. There has long been a large creative-class presence in the old residential neighborhoods surrounding Carnegie Mellon and the University of Pittsburgh, such as Shadyside, Squirrel Hill, and Point Breeze, with their large, historical houses and tree-lined streets (see Figure 7.13). Pittsburgh has also seen a

Figure 7.13: Pittsburgh

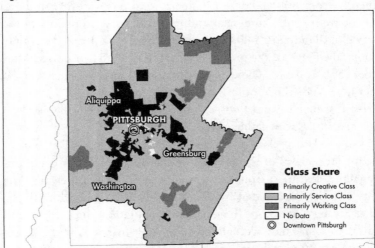

Source: Map by Martin Prosperity Institute, based on data from the US Census.

back-to-the-city movement in its well-preserved downtown core and old warehousing zone, the Strip District, and adjacent neighborhoods. Still, the bulk of the region's creative class remains clustered in its outlying northern, southern, and eastern suburbs. The service class is located both in the less advantaged areas of the city and in the suburban periphery. Working-class neighborhoods are completely gone from the city of steel, pushed into the outskirts of the suburbs and exurbs.

In the third pattern of the Patchwork Metropolis, both the city and the wider metropolis are essentially cut in two, with one side occupied by the advantaged creative class and the other by the less advantaged classes. This model sits somewhere between the first two. The metros that exemplify this pattern have creative-class concentrations that are similar to some of the metros in the first model, but not quite as dense. They have seen more of a back-to-the-city movement than the metros in the second model, but

Figure 7.14: Vancouver

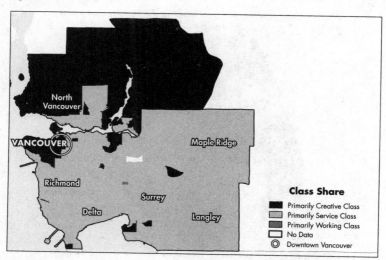

Source: Map by Martin Prosperity Institute, based on data from Statistics Canada.

their creative-class contingents tend to be more suburban than in the first model. As their urban centers have gentrified, these areas have expanded and blended into upscale suburban areas, forming the large, unified creative-class bloc of territory that we see on the maps. Vancouver, Austin, and Philadelphia exemplify this pattern.

Vancouver is starkly divided in two, with the creative class dominating the urban core and the waterfront to the west and in the north around the natural amenities of parks and mountains (see Figure 7.14). Vancouver has seen considerable gentrification of its downtown core through a combination of local demand and a huge influx of foreign, mainly Asian, capital. The service class is pushed almost entirely toward the east and south. There are just a few plurality working-class neighborhoods in the entire region.

Austin is divided east to west (see Figure 7.15). Its creative class is concentrated in a huge wedge to the west that runs from downtown through its high-end suburbs out to Round Rock and in another separate bloc in the far southeastern portion of the metro. Austin's downtown has seen substantial revitalization,

Figure 7.15: Austin

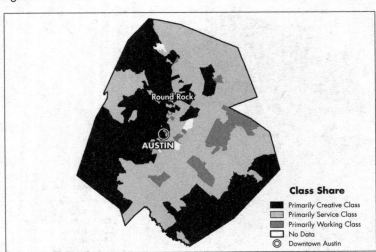

Source: Map by Martin Prosperity Institute, based on data from the US Census.

including the development of large amounts of new housing. The service-class and smaller working-class areas are massed entirely in the more disadvantaged areas of the east.

In Philadelphia, the creative class occupies two distinct blocs in the eastern and western portions of the metro (see Figure 7.16). There are two major creative-class enclaves in the city itself. The first is in its gentrified downtown neighborhoods, including Society Hill and Rittenhouse Square, and more recently in the areas around the University of Pennsylvania. The second is to the west around Chestnut Hill and Roxborough, leafy historical neighborhoods with large houses that are home to St. Joseph's University and Philadelphia University. Philadelphia's service class is located in a band that threads between the two major creative-class blocs, which are separated by the I-95 corridor and the river, and at the peripheries of the metro. Eight of the top ten service-class neighborhoods in the region are in the city proper, most of them in its hard-pressed northern neighborhoods. Just three significant working-class districts remain in the region: in Camden, New

Figure 7.16: Philadelphia

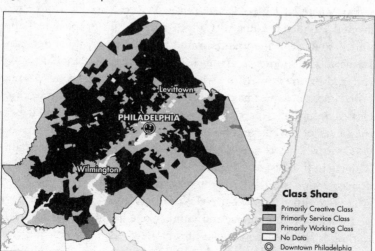

Source: Map by Martin Prosperity Institute, based on data from the US Census.

THE NEW URBAN CRISIS

Jersey, to the east; around Wilmington and Dover, Delaware, to the south; and farther northeast toward Trenton.

In the fourth pattern of the Patchwork Metropolis, the creative class occupies isolated islands or archipelagos that extend across the city and suburbs. The two best examples of this type are Los Angeles and Miami. These are quintessentially postindustrial metros that did not grow up around a historical commercial and industrial center like older northern and Midwestern cities did. Instead, their class geography was shaped around freeways and the car, which produce decentralization. In both, the advantaged creative class is located across the natural amenity of the waterfront, and to a lesser extent clustered around universities, knowledge institutions, and their reviving urban cores.

Los Angeles's creative class is arrayed along its magnificent coastline, stretching from Malibu in the north to Irvine, Laguna Beach, and Dana Point in the south, and expanding significantly eastward in both the north and south (see Figure 7.17). A major creative-class cluster stretches from Hollywood, Bel Air, and Westwood, where UCLA is located, out to Venice; a second can be seen around Pasadena, home to Caltech and the Jet Propulsion Laboratory; and a third is found around the University of California at Irvine in the southeast. A much smaller creative-class cluster has emerged in downtown LA, where artists and creatives have repurposed and reoccupied its old loft buildings. The service and working classes occupy the spaces in between the creative-class islands near the center of the city and fill out a large expanse in the suburbs beyond the urban core and across its farther-out fringes. Between Santa Monica in the west and Pasadena in the east, a massive service-class concentration stretches all the way south to Anaheim and Santa Ana. Two other large service-class clusters appear in LA's northern and northeastern corners, and another one in the inner-city neighborhoods between downtown and Hollywood. LA's working-class neighborhoods are clustered near Burbank, in the south around historically black Compton, and around the huge port of Long Beach.

Figure 7.17: Los Angeles

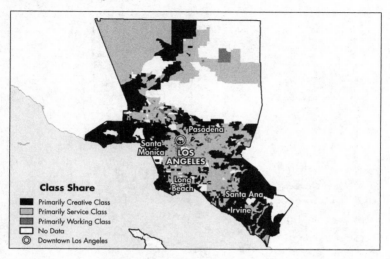

Source: Map by Martin Prosperity Institute, based on data from the US Census.

Miami's creative class stretches out along its Atlantic coastline and bayfront (see Figure 7.18). Six of the region's ten leading
creative-class neighborhoods are along the coast. Three others are
close to universities—the University of Miami in Coral Gables,
Florida Atlantic University in Boca Raton, and Florida International University west of Miami. Five of the top ten creative-class
neighborhoods are located in Miami proper, mainly close to
downtown and on or near the waterfront. (Trendy South Beach
and ultra-wealthy Palm Beach do not register high concentrations
of the creative class, likely because of their high percentages of
nonresident owners of second homes and of retirees who no longer
work.) More than half of the metro's overall workforce is made
up of members of the service class, among the highest levels in
the country. The service class is located in areas off the coast that
surround these creative-class islands. The leading service-class
neighborhoods, where more than 70 percent of residents hold
service-class jobs, are mostly inland. Miami's class geography is
characterized by the juxtaposition of the super-rich stacked along

Figure 7.18: Miami

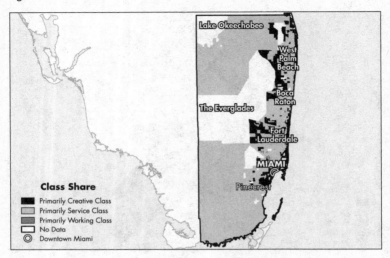

Source: Map by Martin Prosperity Institute, based on data from the US Census.

its coasts and the disadvantage and sinking poverty of many of its interior areas.

We have now seen the four basic patterns of the Patchwork Metropolis across a dozen and a half metros in the United States, the United Kingdom, and Canada. In some metros, the advantaged creative class has poured back into cities in large numbers; in others, this class prefers the suburbs. In some places, the different classes occupy large, distinct blocs of territory; in others, the pattern is more fractured and fragmented. But in each and every case, both the advantaged and the disadvantaged classes are split up across the urban center and suburbs. In stunning contrast to the blue-collar milieu in which I spent my childhood and teenage years, few predominantly working-class districts remain—even in former great industrial cities like Chicago, Boston, Pittsburgh, and Detroit.

This new class geography extends far beyond the cities and metros described here. Across the United States as a whole, the creative class increasingly clusters together in its own enclaves, separate from the less advantaged service and working classes. The full extent of this new class geography comes through in a statistical analysis my team and I conducted of the more than 70,000 census tracts that make up the nation's 350-plus metro areas. We found that the creative class overwhelmingly clusters in tracts that are adjacent to one another and separate from the clusters of the service or working classes. Tracts where the creative class makes up the plurality of residents are negatively correlated both with tracts where the service class is the plurality and with tracts where the working class makes up a plurality of residents. The extent of this geographic divide can be seen across two additional dimensions of class: income and education. The tracts where the creative class makes up a plurality of residents are substantially more affluent and educated; those where the service and working classes form pluralities are far less advantaged. Plurality creative-class tracts are highly correlated with both average income and the share of adults who are college graduates. Conversely, the tracts where the service and working classes make up a plurality of residents are negatively correlated with both. Across the entire United States, the three classes occupy separate and distinct geographic spaces.[15]

Ultimately, the Patchwork Metropolis is shaped by the clustering of the advantaged creative class, whose members occupy the most economically functional and physically desirable locations, leaving the members of less advantaged working and service classes with the places and spaces that are left over. This new geography of class is deeply damaging to our economic and social fabric. As the advantaged groups colonize the best neighborhoods, they gain access to the most economic opportunities, the best schools and libraries, and the best services and amenities—all of which compound their advantages and reinforce their children's prospects for upward mobility. The less advantaged are shunted into neighborhoods with more crime, worse schools, and the dimmest prospects for upward mobility. Simply put, the rich live where they choose, and the poor live where they can.

As we have seen, economic disadvantage now stretches from the urban centers out into the suburbs. Once the axis and anchor of the American Dream, our suburbs are increasingly facing rising poverty, growing inequality, and worsening social problems. In the next chapter, I'll turn to this deepening suburban dimension of the New Urban Crisis.

8

SUBURBAN CRISIS

S ometime in late 1959 or early 1960, right around my second
birthday and about the time my brother Robert was born, my
parents moved us from a rental apartment in Newark to a new
house in the working-class suburb of North Arlington, New Jersey. The house they bought, a small Cape Cod with a postage
stamp of a backyard, cost $15,000 at the time. As my father often
reminded us, the land it sat on had been part of a farm not long
before.

Shortly before our move, Soviet Premier Nikita Khrushchev
and Vice President Richard Nixon had met in a brand-new, fully
furnished kitchen of a model home. Although it looked like one
that could be in any suburb in America, the home was built in
Moscow's Sokolniki Park as part of a cultural exchange program.
On July 24, 1959, while television cameras rolled, the two world
leaders held an impromptu "kitchen debate." "Any steel worker
could buy this house," Nixon pointed out.[1] "They earn $3 an hour.
This house costs about $100 a month to buy on a contract running
25 to 30 years." "In Russia, all you have to do to get a house is to
be born in the Soviet Union," Khrushchev fired back.

The subject soon shifted to global politics and nuclear weap-
ons, but Nixon's words, no less than the house itself, vividly
encapsulated the postwar American Dream: a private home, complete with a television set, dishwasher, clothes washer and dryer,
and a car or two in the driveway, all accessible to members of
the working class like my parents. It was a powerful image, even

if the reality did not always match the dream. In our case, the TV and washing machine broke down frequently, and our car, a 1950-something Chevy with rusted-out holes in the running boards, visited the mechanic on a regular basis. For African Americans and other racial minorities, limited economic opportunity combined with discrimination—in the form of restrictive covenants, exclusionary zoning, and unfair lending practices—kept suburbia out of reach entirely.

Warts and all, my parents never ceased to marvel at the good fortune that had led them to their suburban refuge where they raised their family and spent their entire adult lives. Growing up in North Arlington, I walked to school starting in the first grade, rode my ten-speed bike everywhere, played sandlot baseball and touch football, and started a rock-and-roll band with my brother. At first, we would return to Newark frequently to visit relatives, take music lessons, and shop in the city's still-vibrant downtown. But by the time I reached my teenage years, my relatives had dispersed and many of Newark's downtown department stores had closed, so our trips became less frequent.

By then, suburban malls had opened up in the nearby communities of Woodbridge and Livingston, and industrial parks and office complexes were springing up next to highway interchanges. The same thing was happening all over the country. By the 1970s and 1980s, high-technology industries were thriving in the suburbs outside of Boston, San Francisco, Austin, and Seattle. Many of those bedroom communities developed into full-blown edge cities—places where people lived, worked, and shopped without ever having to visit a real downtown. I didn't set foot in Manhattan until I was in high school, even though it was just a few miles away. America had become a suburban nation, its urban centers in sharp decline.

What a difference today. Affluent, educated, young, childless, white Americans are moving back to cities, while immigrants, minorities, and the poor are heading out to the suburbs. At the same time, blight, poverty, crime, addiction, racial tensions, violence, structural unemployment, and homelessness—all the things that people of my parents' generation thought of as strictly urban problems—have been taking up residence in the suburbs, too.

Once upon a time, the suburbs were places of prosperity, of hope and aspiration. Today, large swaths of them are places of economic decline and distress. As in earlier decades in the cities, in the suburbs today middle-class neighborhoods and communities are being hollowed out. And today's suburbs, like today's cities, have divided into areas of concentrated affluence and concentrated disadvantage.

During the mid-1980s, before anyone thought of the suburbs as being on a downward trajectory, the urban designer David Lewis, a Carnegie Mellon colleague of mine at the time, told me that the future project of suburban renewal would likely make our vast twentieth-century urban renewal efforts look like a walk in the park. Indeed, with their enormous physical footprints, shoddy construction, and hastily put up infrastructure, many of our suburbs are visibly crumbling. Across the nation, hundreds of suburban shopping malls are dead or dying; countless suburban factories, like their urban counterparts a couple of generations ago, have fallen silent. In some suburbs, we are witnessing a decline that is so steep it has been dubbed the onset of "slumburbia."[2]

Incongruous as it might seem, the suburban dimension of the New Urban Crisis may well turn out to be bigger than the urban one, if for no other reason than the fact that more Americans live in suburbs than cities. Suburban populations are hard to quantify precisely, but more than half (53 percent) of Americans say that they live in the suburbs.[3] Just over one in five (21 percent) say they live in rural areas, while just a quarter (26 percent) say they live in urban areas. In fact, 42 percent of Americans who live in cities of 100,000 people or more, up to and including the very largest cities, nonetheless say that they live in a suburb. In the minds of its people, at least, America remains very much a suburban nation.

Many of the places that have the form and layout of classic suburbs actually have larger populations than some of our most well-recognized cities. Mesa, Arizona, for example, which is usually described as a suburb of Phoenix, has a population of about 465,000, which makes it larger than such cities as Atlanta (456,000), Miami (430,000), and Minneapolis (407,000). Bakersfield, California, which many think of as an exurb of LA, has about 369,000 people, more than St. Louis (317,000), Cincinnati (298,000), or Pittsburgh (305,000). Plano, Texas, which is usually considered to be a suburb of Dallas, has 278,000 people, more than Buffalo (259,000).

Members of the privileged elite may be going back to the urban cores, but large majorities of almost everyone else continue to locate in the suburbs. It's mainly college-educated singles, or couples with very young children, who are heading back to cities, while families with kids continue to head to the suburbs, and older Americans, including the younger members of the Baby Boom generation and the nation's seniors, remain in them. At the same time, the less advantaged and the less educated, particularly members of racial and ethnic minority groups, are moving to the suburbs in large numbers, sometimes by choice, but more often because they are being pushed out of the cities and neighborhoods that are being taken over by the new urban elite. Even as high-tech and knowledge jobs are moving back to cities, suburbia remains America's largest source of employment, accounting for more than half (54 percent) of all jobs.[4]

Today's suburbs no longer look much like the lily-white places portrayed on sitcoms like *Leave It to Beaver, The Donna Reed Show,* or *Father Knows Best.* More than half of immigrants now bypass cities altogether and settle directly in the suburbs of larger metros. Whites accounted for just 9 percent of suburban population growth in America's one hundred largest metros between 2000 and 2010; in one-third of those metros, white suburban populations declined.[5]

Not all suburbs are experiencing decline and desolation, of course, any more than all cities are. Many of the immigrants and members of minority groups who are moving to them are no less aspirational than my parents were, and many are more affluent. Although some parts of suburbia are stagnating or declining, there are large areas of affluence and growth. The suburbs are increasingly beset with deep class divisions of their own.

In the postwar years, suburbia's seemingly bottomless demand for durable goods was the greatest driver of the boom economy. But in an era in which clustering is the key driver of innovation, suburban sprawl has come to be a fetter on economic growth. Suburban homeownership drains capital away from other, more productive investments in knowledge, technology, and talent. If the suburbs were once the geographic embodiment of capitalism's deepest promise—the American Dream of upward mobility for all—today they, too, are caught up in the deep contradictions of the New Urban Crisis.

P art of what makes the suburban crisis so painful and wrenching is how utterly unanticipated it was. And yet there's no denying that it's here. Across the United States, more than one in four suburbanites are poor or nearly poor. In fact, the suburbs of America's largest metropolitan areas have more poor people living in them than their inner cities do, and poverty is also growing at a much faster rate in the suburbs. Between 2000 and 2013, the number of people living below the poverty line in American cities increased by 29 percent. During that same period, the ranks of the suburban poor grew by 66 percent. Seventeen million suburbanites lived below the poverty line in 2013, compared to 13.5 million urbanites.[6]

Suburban poverty is a growing problem in metros across the entire nation. In 2000, 29 percent of the New York metro area's poor lived in the suburbs; by 2013, 35 percent did. Over the same period, the suburban share of poverty grew from 44 percent to 50 percent in metropolitan Philadelphia, from 41 percent to 48 percent in Greater Dallas, from 61 percent to 69 percent in the Seattle region, from 52 percent to 59 percent in San Francisco, from 68 percent to 77 percent in St. Louis, from 61 percent to 70 percent in Washington, DC, and from 76 percent to 88 percent in the Atlanta metro. It's happening outside the United States, too. There are more people living in poverty in the suburbs outside of London (1.22 million) than there are in the city itself (1.02 million).[7]

Between 2000 and 2012, the numbers of the suburban poor who lived in neighborhoods of concentrated poverty, where at least 40 percent of residents were below the poverty line, grew by 139 percent. That's triple the growth rate for concentrated poverty populations in the cities. The population in neighborhoods where poverty was merely high—with 20 percent of residents living below the poverty line—grew by 21 percent in cities. In the suburbs, this population more than doubled, growing at a rate of 105 percent. The metro with the largest share of young people who are neither in school nor working isn't the superstar city of New York, the tech hub of San Francisco, or even the hard-hit Rustbelt city of Detroit—it's San Bernardino, in the heart of California's Inland Empire, once seen as the quintessence of the suburban dream.[8]

Some of these new suburban poor were driven out of cities by rising housing prices. But many others had been members of the suburban middle class in good standing until they fell in place, either through job loss or because the value of their homes plummeted in the wake of the 2008 economic crisis.

Meanwhile, some of the advantaged who would have chosen to live in suburbs a couple of decades ago are now moving back to cities. America experienced a large-scale flight from density half a century or so ago; today, we are seeing the beginnings of a flight from suburban sprawl. Not only are suburban populations no longer growing as fast as they were, in many cases they are failing to keep pace with the cities they surround. This marks the end of a trend away from cities and into the suburbs that had held since at least the 1920s.[9]

This flight from sprawl is reflected in the inversion of the value of urban and suburban homes. For years, suburban housing prices consistently exceeded those of the urban center, which in many cases were falling as cities declined. But by the end of 2015, the average value of an urban home exceeded that of the average suburban home by 2 percent—$269,036 compared to $263,987. But this understates the actual gap in the value of urban versus suburban homes, because suburban homes are physically bigger than urban ones. Suburban homes lag behind urban homes by an even greater margin on the more accurate value-per-square-foot basis.

This trend is considerably more pronounced in superstar cities and knowledge hubs where the back-to-the-city movement has been most prominent. In Greater Boston, urban and suburban homes were valued at around $100 per square foot each in 1997. By 2015, urban homes in Boston were worth about $400 per square foot, while suburban homes were worth just $250 per square foot. In Washington, DC, urban and suburban home values were similarly priced at around $100 per square foot in 1997; by 2015, urban values surpassed $300 per square foot, compared to around $225 per square foot for suburban homes. And in San Francisco, urban and suburban homes started off at around $150 per square foot in 1997, but by 2015 urban homes were valued at almost $700 per square foot, as opposed to less than $500 per square foot in the suburbs.[10]

Once areas of safety and serenity, the suburbs today are being hit with rising crime rates as their economies falter and populations shift. The TV series *Breaking Bad* made suburban meth dens as iconic as the urban street corners where drug dealers plied their trade in *The Wire*. The recent opioid epidemic has deep roots in the suburbs. Furthermore, the violent crime rate—which has been declining across the United States—fell three times faster in America's primary cities than it did in their suburbs between 1990 and 2008. Murders actually rose by 16.9 percent in the suburbs between 2001 and 2010, while falling by 16.7 percent in cities.[11] And the suburbs have been the sites of many, if not most, of America's mass shootings, from Columbine to Sandy Hook.

Suburban governments and police departments have been slow to adjust to these new realities. That became agonizingly apparent to the whole world when Ferguson, Missouri, a St. Louis suburb of 21,000, spun out of control in the wake of the police killing of Michael Brown in 2015. Over two-thirds (67 percent) of Ferguson's population is black, but only four of the town's fifty-four police officers were black at the time. Ferguson is hardly a typical case—it had suffered from many local traumas, from a failed airport expansion, in which thousands of homeowners were displaced by eminent domain, to long-standing racial red-lining. But the area's decline was also a product of the broader demographic and economic factors that have buffeted many suburbs across the nation. Ferguson's unemployment rate almost tripled between 2000 and 2014, increasing from under 5 percent to more than 13 percent. Residents with jobs saw their average annual earnings fall by a third during those same years. One in four residents lived below the poverty line by 2015.[12] Ferguson stands not only as a poster child for police abuse, but as a broader symbol of the ongoing decay and distress felt in growing numbers of American suburbs.

The suburban dimension of the New Urban Crisis not only affects those who live there but has broader costs that extend to the US economy as a whole. As well as being energy-inefficient and wasteful, suburban sprawl also limits the mobility of Americans and undermines productivity.

A suburban home was once a cornerstone of the American Dream; now, suburban sprawl has become a key factor holding back Americans' ability to move up the economic ladder. The old saying "drive 'til you qualify" reflects the reality that real estate becomes more affordable in the farthest-out suburbs, but distance levies additional high costs. The rule of thumb is that people should spend roughly 30 percent of their income for housing, but up to 45 percent including transportation. Having multiple cars and keeping them insured, repaired, and fueled up on gas can be an expensive proposition. Living closer to where one works or being able to take public transit can slash those costs considerably. For this reason, a pricier condo or apartment in the urban core or along transit lines can end up being considerably more affordable than a cheaper house in a car-dependent suburb.

Instead of pushing people toward the American Dream, suburbia today actually hinders upward economic mobility. Economic mobility is significantly lower in more spread-out metros today than it is in denser cities. Lower-income workers in suburbia are

farther removed from centers of work and have a harder time finding and getting to jobs than workers who are able to live in a city.
The amount of time that low-income people spend commuting
also plays a substantial role in affecting their odds of moving up
the economic ladder, with low-income people with longer commutes facing lower levels of upward mobility. While it remains
true that persistently poor urban neighborhoods concentrate and
perpetuate a cycle of poverty, poor suburban neighborhoods also
present challenges: they isolate and disconnect their residents both
from jobs and from economic opportunity, and also from the social services that can mitigate poverty's worst effects. Even when
suburbs have social services, the poor are less able to access them
because they are harder to find and harder to reach than urban
social services.[13]

Suburban sprawl is extremely costly to the economy broadly.
Infrastructure and vital local services—such as water and energy—can be 2.5 times more expensive to deliver in the suburbs
than in compact urban centers. A UCLA study found that residents of wealthy Malibu, California (which has an average density
of about 630 people per square mile), use more than ten times as
much energy per person than residents of the working-class suburb of Bell, which has a density of about 14,000 per square mile.
In total, sprawl costs the US economy roughly $600 billion a year
in direct costs related to inefficient land usage and car dependency,
and another $400 billion in indirect costs from traffic congestion,
pollution, and the like, according to a 2015 study from the London School of Economics. The total bill: a whopping $1 trillion a
year.[14]

Long commutes levy additional costs. The average American worker spends nearly an hour (52 minutes) traveling to and
from work each day. That's the equivalent of 9 full 24-hour days a
year. Those who commute 90 minutes each way waste more than
a month (31.3 days). Multiplied by America's 139 million commuters, that's as much as 30 billion hours that could have been spent
doing something more productive. If we could take the 3.6 million Americans who commute 90 minutes each way to work and

shrink their commute to the more typical 30 minutes, the economy would save 1.8 billion hours, or the equivalent of 900,000 full-time jobs.[15]

The broader social costs of sprawl mount even higher when its indirect consequences are factored in. People who live in far-flung suburbs and endure long commutes have higher rates of obesity, diabetes, stress, insomnia, and hypertension, and they are more likely to commit suicide or die in car crashes. All those risks combine to lower their life expectancy by an average of three years. When people were asked to rank their life experiences, commutes came in dead last, after work, child care, and doing chores around the house, according to a study by economists Daniel Kahneman and Alan Krueger.[16]

When we think of commuters, many of us still picture a man in a suit and tie with a briefcase pecking his wife good-bye, or perhaps a high-tech worker in more casual attire zipping down the highway in a sports car. But the real burden of commuting falls heaviest on the poor and the less advantaged. Knowledge workers and professionals, as we have seen, are the people most likely to live near their workplace, or, if not, to have easy access to efficient mass transit. And when they do choose to live in car-based suburbs, they can commute in the comfort and safety of their own cars. The poor and the less advantaged tend to be located farthest away from transit and frequently cannot afford a reliable car. Their suburban commutes are a maze of bus and train rides with multiple transfers, and often include long walks in places with inadequate pedestrian infrastructure.

Besides acting as a drag on economic mobility, efficiency, and productivity, sprawling suburbs are also no longer the job-creation engines they once were. While the suburbs still lead urban centers in their ability to create jobs, that edge is shrinking. Of all of America's 3,000-plus counties, suburban and urban, Kings County, New York—Brooklyn—saw the highest rate of job growth between 2007 and 2015. Between 2007 and 2011, urban centers—areas within a three-mile radius of a city's central business district—added jobs at a faster rate than their suburbs in more than half (21 of 41) of the largest US metros, among them Charlotte, Oklahoma City, Milwaukee, and Indianapolis, as well as New York, San Francisco, and Austin. And although the suburbs are creating jobs at a faster rate than urban centers, those jobs are lower paying, less skilled, and more vulnerable to economic downturns than the knowledge-based and professional jobs that are being created in urban centers. Jobs in urban centers pay 20 percent more than jobs in high-density, more urbanized suburbs, and 37 percent more than jobs in low-density ones.[17]

E ven though there are now more poor people in the suburbs than there are in cities, and the economic prospects of many suburbs are increasingly precarious, large numbers of rich people continue to live in the suburbs, too. Despite the flow of affluent people back into cities, America's very richest neighborhoods are almost all suburban, whether one looks at income levels or housing values.

Table 8.1: America's Richest Neighborhoods Are in the Suburbs

Rank	Neighborhood	City and State	Mean Household Income
1	The Golden Triangle	Greenwich, CT	$614,242
2	Bradley Manor-Longwood	Bethesda, MD	$599,440
3	Potomac Manors	Potomac, MD	$599,331
4	Old Cutler-Hammock Oaks	Coral Gables, FL	$596,851
5	Carderock-The Palisades	Potomac, MD	$595,669
6	East Lake Shore Drive	Chicago, IL	$593,454
7	Swinks Mill-Dominion Reserve	McLean, VA	$562,596
8	Cameo Shores-Highlands	Newport Beach, CA	$554,721
9	Pelican Hill-Pelican Crest	Newport Beach, CA	$549,659
10	Greenhaven	Rye, NY	$540,403

Source: Stephen Higley, "The Higley 1000," Higley1000.com, February 2014, http://higley 1000.com/archives/638.

Nine of the ten richest neighborhoods in America are in the suburbs (see Table 8.1). The cutoff for inclusion in this elite club is $540,000 in annual household income, more than double the threshold for membership in the "one percent."[18] Topping the list is a small area of Greenwich, Connecticut, aptly called the "Golden Triangle," where annual household incomes average more than $600,000. The rest of the list includes elite suburban enclaves outside of Washington, DC, Miami, and Los Angeles. Only one urban neighborhood—Chicago's East Lake Shore Drive—made the list. The wealthiest urban neighborhoods are more diverse than their suburban counterparts, with a much broader range of housing types and income groups, and generally many more renters.

Housing values tell much the same story (see Table 8.2). All but one of the ten priciest ZIP codes in America are in the suburbs—the exception being New York's Tribeca/SoHo.[19] Eight of the ten are in California, including the elite Silicon Valley suburbs of Atherton, Los Altos, and Palo Alto as well as Beverly Hills and Santa Monica, Rancho Santa Fe in San Diego, and Santa Barbara's tony Montecito. The exclusive enclave of Fisher Island, accessible only by boat or ferry, lies in Biscayne Bay just off of Miami Beach.

Table 8.2: America's Priciest Neighborhoods Are in the Suburbs

Zip Code	City/Neighborhood	Region	Median Home Value
94027	Atherton	San Francisco Bay Area	$4,551,333
90210	Beverly Hills	Los Angeles	$3,953,775
90402	Santa Monica	Los Angeles	$2,996,642
33109	Fisher Island	Miami	$2,928,092
94028	Portola Valley	San Francisco Bay Area	$2,916,175
10013	Tribeca/SoHo	New York	$2,912,792
92067	Rancho Santa Fe	San Diego	$2,720,392
94022	Los Altos	San Francisco Bay Area	$2,680,867
93108	Montecito	Santa Barbara	$2,647,517
94301	Palo Alto	San Francisco Bay Area	$2,637,158

Source: Martin Prosperity Institute analysis, based on Zillow Home Value Index for 2014.

When it comes to the most affluent and advantaged places, many of the long-standing distinctions between urban and suburban communities are fading into oblivion. This fact dawned on me at a dinner party several years ago where I witnessed a heated exchange between two couples from Greater New York—one from suburban Fairfield County, the other from Manhattan—regarding which was the better place to live. As they debated, I realized that despite some obvious differences—one couple lived in an apartment and the other in a single-family home, for instance—they enjoyed strangely similar lifestyles in what were once very different kinds of places. They shopped at similar stores, ate in similar restaurants, wore similar clothes, and availed themselves of similar amenities; they even sent their kids to similar schools. Their lives weren't defined by whether they lived in a suburban town or a city, but by their socioeconomic class—and the one that predominated in their particular neighborhoods.

Just as in our cities, some parts of our suburbs are rich, and others are poor. Some are growing quickly, and some are in decline. Growth today is in fact concentrated in dense urban areas and at suburbia's far-flung peripheries. Population growth is occurring fastest in the farthest-out (or "suburbiest") parts of suburbs and in the densest urban neighborhoods, according to an analysis by real estate economist Jed Kolko.[20] It's far less expensive to build on the wide-open, undeveloped land in outlying areas than anywhere else, and it's easier to grow fast when you're starting from nothing. The densest urban places are attracting people and jobs because of their convenience and improved productivity. Meanwhile, the middle of our suburban geography is being hollowed out and squeezed economically: growth is bypassing the older suburban areas that lie between the two poles of urban center and outlying new development.

The stagnation and decline of older suburbs is one of the biggest forces shaping America today. Besides the effect that they are having on individuals and families, on America's neighborhoods and cities, and on the economy of the nation, they are creating an earthquake in our politics.[21]

Suburban distress played a key role in the rise of Donald Trump, who harnessed the simmering anger and resentment of voters in economically distressed working-class suburbs. Trump won the 2016 GOP primary based on his support from whiter, more blue-collar, less educated, and older counties, according to my own analysis. Trump's primary support was concentrated in counties with larger white populations, more blue-collar "old-economy" jobs, larger shares of people who did not graduate from high school, and also the portion of the population living in mobile homes, according to a *New York Times* analysis.[22]

Trump's unpredicted and shocking victory in the general election was a product of the same overlapping class and geographic divides. Along class lines, he drew his support from white, less educated, more religious voters who felt their economic conditions to be worsening. Geographically, his support was concentrated in whiter, less-educated counties with higher levels of economic anxiety and greater concentrations of routine factory and service jobs. Trump took 61 percent of the vote in rural places compared to 33 percent for Clinton. He won 57 percent of the vote in metros with less than 250,000 people, compared to 38 percent for Clinton. He carried 52 percent of the vote in metros with 250,000 and 500,000 people, versus 34 percent for Clinton. All told, he won many more metros than Clinton, 260 to Clinton's 120. However, Clinton captured a greater share of the total metro vote, 51 percent compared to 44 percent for Trump. The average Trump metro was home to just 420,000 people compared to 1.4 million people for the average metro that voted for Clinton.[23]

The suburban dimension of the New Urban Crisis is indeed reshaping our national politics broadly. We're all familiar with the election maps of blue and red states.[24] But what really separates Democratic from Republican places isn't state boundaries, it's population density. Across the past several presidential elections, the Democratic candidates have gotten the bulk of their support from large cities and denser, more highly urbanized areas, while Republican candidates have garnered the preponderance of their votes from low-density suburbs, small metros, and rural areas. In

2008, 2012, and 2016, the Democrats carried the nation's largest metro areas while the Republicans took smaller- and medium-sized metros.[25] Density has become an increasingly significant key fault line in presidential elections. Places tip from red to blue, from Republican to Democrat, when their density reaches about eight hundred people per square mile.[26]

But it's economically squeezed places that lie between the Democratic urban centers and the Republican exurbs that are the real contested terrain of American politics. They are the tipping-point locations on which US presidential elections increasingly turn. Economically distressed suburbs in red states are the ones that swing blue, while economically distressed suburbs in blue states are the ones that swing red, according to research by political scientist Jefferey Sellers. "The most disadvantaged metropolitan communities of the red states have diverged most from the Republican preferences of the wider region," he wrote. "The most disadvantaged communities of the blue states have responded more than other communities there to Republican appeals." Another way to put it is that they are volatile, contrarian, and vote against the status quo. Romney carried them by 2 percentage points in 2012, while Obama won them by a slightly larger margin in 2008.[27] Trump's surprising 2016 victory was a product of his substantial margins in these economically distressed suburbs, especially in the Rustbelt, which allowed him to breach the Democrats' long-held blue wall of Michigan, Wisconsin, and Pennsylvania. These are the same kinds of places that supported the Brexit in the UK and fueled Rob Ford's rise in Toronto. All three provide unmistakable warning signs of the depths of the political disaffection created by the deepening crisis of the suburbs.

When all is said and done, the suburban crisis reflects the end of a long era of cheap growth. Building roads and infrastructure and constructing houses on virgin land was and is an incredibly inexpensive way to provide an American Dream to the masses, certainly when compared to what it costs to build new subway lines, tunnels, and high-rise buildings in mature cities. For much of the 1950s, 1960s, and 1970s, and on into the 1980s and 1990s, suburbanization was the near-perfect complement to America's industrial economy. More than the great mobilization effort of World War II or any of the Keynesian stimulus policies that were applied during the 1930s, it was suburban development that propelled the great golden era of economic growth in the 1950s and 1960s. As working- and middle-class families settled into suburban houses, their purchases of washers, dryers, television sets, living room sofas, carpets, and automobiles stimulated the manufacturing sector that employed so many of them, creating more jobs and still more homebuyers.[28] Suburban sprawl was the key engine of the now fading era of cheap economic growth.

But today, clustering, not dispersal, powers innovation and economic growth. Many people still like living in suburbs, of course, but suburban growth has fallen out of sync with the demands of the urbanized knowledge economy. Too much of our precious national productive capacity and wealth is being squandered on building and maintaining suburban homes with three-car garages, and on the roads and sprawl that support them, rather than being invested in the knowledge, technology, and density that are required for sustainable, high-quality growth. The suburbs aren't going away, but they are no longer the apotheosis of the American Dream and the engine of economic growth.

The solution is much the same for the suburban dimension of the New Urban Crisis as it is for the urban one: more and better urbanism. Overcoming the crisis of the suburbs and restoring their economic prosperity requires that suburbs become denser, greener, more mixed-use, and more connected to urban centers via transit. Before we can turn to specific solutions, however, it's important to understand the fourth and final dimension of the New Urban Crisis, which is playing out in the mega-cities of the most rapidly urbanizing areas of the globe.

9

THE CRISIS OF GLOBAL
URBANIZATION

In May 2014, I addressed a summit of the United Nations Economic and Social Council, the Integration Segment on Sustainable Urbanization. Among the people sharing the dais with me were Joan Clos, the former mayor of Barcelona and the head of UN-Habitat, the UN agency that deals with cities and human settlements, and Anne Hidalgo, the mayor of Paris, who had campaigned on a platform that promised to fight the city's rising inequalities and create more affordable housing. In the gallery were the directors of UN agencies, divisions, and departments that deal with urban affairs and economic and social development, and other leading urbanists.

A month earlier, I had traveled to Medellín, Colombia, for the Seventh World Urban Forum, a meeting that had brought together some 20,000 urbanists, city leaders, and planners from more than 160 countries. The Medellín Declaration, released by the delegates, had made the case that cities and urbanization are key to addressing the great challenges that are threatening our planet.[1] Since returning, I had been thinking and writing nearly non-stop about the issues that had been discussed there.

"Cities are at the very center of the many grand challenges we face—climate change, poverty, job creation, public health, sustainable energy, and inclusive development," I told attendees of the UN summit. "Urbanization promises great things—it has the power to lift living standards, to create economic opportunity, to raise gross domestic product. But left to its own devices, it cannot deliver the goods. My main message is that we have to put cities and sustainable urbanization at the very top of this body's agenda."

At the time of that address, the ideas for this book were beginning to crystallize in my mind. The crisis of global cities and global urbanization, I was starting to see, was a huge dimension of the New Urban Crisis, substantially bigger than the serious urban and suburban challenges in the United States. The coming century will see the greatest wave of urbanization in human history as another 7 or 8 billion people—more than are on the face of the earth today—move to cities, most of them in the poorest reaches of the developing world. More than 60 percent of the urban infrastructure that humans will need in the next half-century is yet to be built. Trillions upon trillions of dollars will be spent building new cities and retrofitting existing ones.

The question is: Will this incredible wave of urbanization bring the growth, progress, and rising living standards that the urban optimists say are coming, or will it generate even greater poverty, deeper economic disparity, and worsening environmental degradation, as the urban pessimists claim?[2] Again, both sides capture important parts of the picture.

Historically, urbanization in the United States and the advanced nations went along with higher rates of economic growth and helped to turn the poor and the struggling working class into a rising middle class. But too many cities in the most rapidly urbanizing parts of the world today are faced with seemingly intractable poverty. For the millions upon millions of people streaming into the burgeoning cities of Southeast Asia, Africa, and other parts of the developing world, there is far too little in the way of economic opportunity. More than 840 million people—roughly one in ten worldwide—are trapped in the impoverished slums of these fast-urbanizing places.[3] The scale of the problem is mind-boggling: The number of people who live in destitute conditions in the world's slums is equivalent to the entire population of the United States and the European Union combined. The "missing middle" that exists between the advantaged cities of the United States, Europe, and Japan and the least advantaged of the Global South makes the divides we face here at home pale by comparison. This is the global dimension of the New Urban Crisis.

Those of us who have the good fortune to live in and around the cities of the world's advanced economies take the benefits of urbanization for granted; they are things that were achieved and consolidated a long time ago. But as urbanization starts up in many other parts of the world, it is proceeding on a scale and at a pace that is unlike any other time in human history. Up until now, the world has completed just one wave of urbanization, that of the developed nations, where 85 percent or more of the population currently lives in urban areas. Two additional waves remain. One is the ongoing urbanization of China, which is accelerating. By 2025, China will have more than two hundred cities with populations of more than 1 million residents. The other, and even bigger, wave will be the coming urbanization of Africa and the rest of Asia.[4]

Today, some 3.5 billion people, roughly half the world's population, live in urban areas. As recently as two hundred years ago, the urban share of the population was only about 3 percent; by 1900, after a century of industrialization, that figure had risen to roughly 15 percent; and by 1950 it had approximately doubled to about 30 percent, or 1 billion people. Over the next century or two, the world's urban population is projected to almost triple, peaking at nearly 10 billion people, 85 percent of a total global population of between 11 and 12 billion. As many as 8.6 billion of those urbanites will live in the cities of the developing world (many of which have yet to be built), while just 1.2 billion or so will occupy the cities of the advanced nations.[5]

To put all this into perspective, consider that in 1800 there was only one city in the world whose population exceeded 1 million—Beijing. By 1900, there were 12. By 1950, the number had increased sevenfold, to 83, and by 2005 it had ballooned to 400. Today, there are more than 500. In 1950, there were only two mega-cities that had more than 10 million people: New York and Tokyo. Today, there are 28, and by 2030, there will be 40 or so. By 2150, according to one plausible projection, the world will have perhaps ten mega-cities with between 50 million and 100 million people, and five more with populations exceeding 100 million. The population of the mega-region that spans Delhi, Kolkata, and Dhaka in India could reach 200 million by that time, making it bigger than all but five nations in the world today.[6]

Profound differences in wealth and productivity divide the less advantaged cities of the developing world from their more affluent counterparts in the advanced nations. One vivid index of these disparities is the number of hours of work it would take an average worker in cities around the world to pay for that paradigmatic commodity of the knowledge economy: an iPhone.[7] In New York City it would have taken an average worker just 24 hours to earn enough money to buy a 16G iPhone 6 in 2015. In developing Mumbai, it would have taken 350 hours. It would have taken 460 hours in Jakarta, and more than 600 hours in Kiev.

A more systematic way to gauge the enormity of the gaps separating the established cities of the advanced world from the rapidly urbanizing cities of the developing world is to compare the amount of economic output generated by each person. Unfortunately, the kinds of statistics that are commonly available for nations—figures that allow us to make apples-to-apples comparisons of their economic situations, wages, incomes, and productivity—are not available for cities and metro areas across the world. While many countries do collect data on cities and metro areas, differences in the ways metros are defined across nations and how economic data is associated with metro areas render it virtually impossible to make meaningful comparisons across national boundaries, even for advanced nations like the United States, Canada, and the countries of Europe. In many of the developing and emerging countries that are urbanizing the fastest, there is no reliable economic data at all. This is a big issue, and as I told the UN summit, it must be remedied before we can ever hope to understand the drivers of successful urbanization.

But there are some ways to work around it. The Brookings Institution has put together a set of estimates for the economic output of the world's three hundred largest cities in its *Global Metro Monitor*, based on data from Oxford Economics and Moody's Analytics.[8] My team and I combined these statistics on economic output with separate data on the populations of these metros to come up with estimates of economic output per person. The data, though not perfect, do provide a rough gauge of the different levels of economic development and productivity across the world's metros. Based on this data, we divided those three hundred metros into four basic groups according to their level of economic development. These four groups range from the most advantaged cities of the West to the most impoverished cities of the Global South.

The first group includes the world's richest and most economically advantaged metros. These are the biggest winners of winner-take-all urbanism, superstar cities like New York, London, Los Angeles, Paris, Singapore, and Hong Kong; knowledge hubs like San Francisco, Boston, and Washington, DC; and a handful of energy-rich places in the advanced developing world. The economic output per person of these places ranges from $45,000 to $94,000. Home to just 4 percent of the world's population, these one hundred or so metros produce roughly 16 percent of all global economic output.

The second group includes relatively well-off cities of the advanced nations, which generate between $30,000 and $45,000 in economic output per person. Among them are Barcelona, Berlin, Copenhagen, Madrid, Melbourne, Miami, Milan, Rome, Seoul, Taipei, Toronto, and Vancouver. These one hundred metros produce 11 percent of the world's economic output, while, again, housing just 4 percent of its population.

The third group is made up of less affluent places where economic output is between $15,000 and $30,000 per person. Among them are struggling industrial cities of the advanced nations, such as Cardiff, Liverpool, and Naples, as well as up-and-coming cities in the developing world like Bangkok, Beijing, Bogotá, Guadalajara, Istanbul, Mexico City, Rio de Janeiro, São Paolo, and Shanghai.

These seventy metros are home to 6 percent of the world's population and produce about 9 percent of global economic output.

The fourth group consists of poorer places that produce just $4,000 to $15,000 in economic output per person. These metros are mainly in the Global South and include some of the world's largest urban areas, including Manila, Jakarta, Cairo, Alexandria, Durban, Medellín, Cali, Mumbai, Kolkata, and Delhi, as well as many poor, urbanizing areas of China. These thirty or so metros are home to roughly 4.3 percent of the world's population yet account for just 3 percent of total global economic output.

The metros in the first three groups certainly have considerable poverty and often huge gaps between the rich and poor, but the fourth group suffers from much higher levels of economic distress and deprivation. About 500 million of the world's slum-dwellers are in South and East Asia; another 200 million are in sub-Saharan Africa; and 110 million more are in Latin America and the Caribbean.[9] With as many as 200,000 people moving into cities every day, the world's slum population is projected to grow to almost 1 billion people by 2020. Large numbers of people in these rapidly urbanizing parts of the world also lack access to basic services like clean water; functional sanitation in the form of flush toilets and sewer or septic systems; or electricity. In Africa, for instance, just slightly more than half (54 percent) of all urbanites have access to the kind of functional sanitation we take for granted in the West. More than two-thirds of urbanites in sub-Saharan Africa lack access to basic electricity. The gap in economic resources and quality of life between the residents of the world's least fortunate places and those in the most fortunate—mostly the Western cities—is truly staggering. For a billion or so urbanites in the developing world, urbanization has been a near total failure.

Far from providing a pathway to economic betterment, many of these slums have become self-reinforcing poverty traps. Teeming with people who are packed into shoddy and inadequate housing and disconnected from economic opportunity, they run the gamut from shantytowns or squatter settlements on the peripheries of cities to crowded inner-city tenements, deteriorating public housing facilities, and poor villages. They tend to be physically isolated, often located at the outskirts of the city, far away from business and economic activity, their residents cut off from the economic mix. In many places, traditional policies and investments have proven largely unable to turn them around. To take just one recent example: in 2009, India announced a large-scale effort to eliminate slums within five years. Barely two years later, leaders conceded that the population of its slums would grow by 12 percent between 2011 and 2017.[10]

There are several reasons for the stubborn persistence of these mega-slums. First, the lion's share of places that are urbanizing most rapidly today are in the poorest and least-developed parts of the world, whereas the places that urbanized a century or so ago were in the richest and most advanced. Second, the world is a much bigger place now, with many more people, and the areas that are urbanizing the most are its largest population centers. Third, a good deal of urbanization is the consequence of people migrating en masse into established cities to escape wars, civil conflicts, extreme violence, or natural disasters.[11] Such massive inflows of people can easily overwhelm a city's ability to effectively absorb them, so tremendous numbers of new migrants end up being packed into rudimentary settlements in mega-slums.

Fourth, globalization itself is a big culprit. The development of vast interconnected systems of global trade has broken apart the historical connection between cities, local agriculture, and local industry that powered the more balanced urban economic development of the past. For much of history, cities provided markets for and consumed the food that local agriculture provided. But with today's vast global food chains, cities no longer depend on the agricultural production of their surrounding hinterlands. People in rapidly urbanizing global cities can be cheaply fed with food imported from other places.[12] Globalization has similarly broken the link between cities and the development of localized manufacturing industries. In the past, cities developed a wide range of basic industrial activities—quarries, brickmaking, lumber yards, food processing, and others—to house, feed, and clothe their people and move them around. In today's globally interconnected economy, all of these things can be inexpensively imported from other parts of the world. Instead of having these activities spread out in cities across the globe, they are concentrated in a much more limited number of places.

As a result, many cities and regions in the developing world are no longer able to build up their economies around the traditional agricultural and industrial activities that spurred local economic development in the past. They have far fewer of the kinds of jobs that can provide pathways for upward mobility and help to raise living standards for the millions upon millions of new urbanites that are streaming into them. When we in the advanced world think about the impacts of globalization, we think about the manufacturing jobs that have been displaced to less expensive foreign factories; but for far too many cities in the developing world, globalization has essentially cut off workers' path to economic development.

The nub of the global urban crisis is this: in the midst of the greatest urban migration in human history, urbanization has ceased to be a reliable engine of progress. For the past couple of centuries in the cities of Western Europe and the United States, economic development and social progress went hand in hand with urbanization. The connection between urbanization and growth has now become much more tenuous, producing a troubling new pattern of "urbanization without growth."[13]

A detailed historical study of the past five centuries of urbanization puts this disconnect into context by tracing the relationship between urbanization and economic development over the past five hundred years. For most of the time between 1500 and the early to mid-twentieth century, the study found, urbanization was only loosely connected to growth. Prior to the great spurt of urbanization that went along with the Industrial Revolution, a tripling of economic output per person was associated with just a 12 percent increase in urbanization. It wasn't until the twentieth century, in fact, that urbanization and economic growth became strongly correlated. By then a tripling of economic output corresponded with a larger increase in urbanization across all nations—20 percent. But this result may have been an artifact of wide-scale industrialization in the advanced nations. During this period, developing and emerging nations remained rural and poor. By 2010, the relationship between urbanization and growth was changing again. Now, poor countries, not rich ones, are experiencing the most rapid urbanization. And the connection between urbanization and growth looks almost like it did in the sixteenth century, with a tripling of economic output per capita associated with just a 13 percent increase in urbanization rates. The key takeaway: we should stop assuming that urbanization and development are inextricably linked. In many of the world's most rapidly urbanizing places, they are not.[14]

Yet, even if urbanization isn't a surefire recipe for prosperity, it is still better than the alternative. For all of their grinding poverty and gaping inequality, the rapidly urbanizing cities of the developing world hold a substantial economic advantage over more rural, outlying areas. The productivity of cities and metro areas, even very poor ones, tends to be considerably greater than that of outlying areas. To investigate this dichotomy, my team and I created a simple measure—an urban productivity ratio—that compares the productivity of a nation's cities to the productivity of its other areas.[15]

The typical large metro in the United States, Europe, or Japan has an urban productivity ratio between 1 and 1.5, indicating productivity on par with or up to 50 percent greater than the productivity of the rest of their respective nations. At 1.6, San Jose—that is, Silicon Valley—has one of the highest urban productivity ratios in the advanced world. London's is 1.5; Boston's and San Francisco's 1.4; New York's 1.3; LA's and Barcelona's 1.2; Tokyo's, Frankfurt's, and Chicago's between 1.1 and 1.2.

The urban productivity ratios for many cities and metro areas in the developing world are considerably higher. More than eighty such metros, including Beijing, Istanbul, Mumbai, São Paolo, and

Shanghai, have ratios showing that their productivity is at least double the productivity of the rest of their respective nations. Roughly fifty of them have ratios showing productivity three to nine times higher in the given city than in the rest of the country in which it is located, and a half-dozen of them, including Manila (13.6), Bangkok (12.6), and Lima (12.6), have ratios showing productivity that is more than ten times greater in the city than in the rest of the country.

But as we've seen, the Brookings *Global Metro Monitor* data cover just the world's three hundred largest metros, which account for less than a third (31 percent) of the world's population. Although traditional data of the sort that Brookings used are not available for many other places, it's possible to put together some rough estimates for a larger number of cities, including the poorest and most rapidly urbanizing. Working with Tim Gulden, a computational geographer now at the Rand Corporation, I developed a proxy measure for economic activity and urban productivity for every city and metro across the world using the nighttime lights that are tracked in satellite images by the National Aeronautics and Space Administration (NASA) and other scientific agencies.[16] Combining this light-emissions metric, which we dubbed light-related regional product, with population statistics, we were able to develop urban productivity ratios comparing the productivity of cities and metro areas to national averages (including the metro area in question). Figure 9.1 maps the results. Notice the larger circles, which indicate higher urban productivity ratios, in Africa, Southeast Asia, and other rapidly urbanizing parts of the planet.

In all, we found more than 125 cities across the developing world that had urban productivity ratios of 3 or above. Forty of these, mainly in Asia and Africa, had ratios that were greater than 5. And seven of them—again in Asia and Africa—had urban productivity more than 10 times greater than their respective national averages. Not all cities in the developing world have such high comparative productivity, but only a very few are significantly less productive than their nations as a whole. Even in the poorest and least-developed places on earth, urban centers offer a better

Figure 9.1: The Urban Productivity Advantage

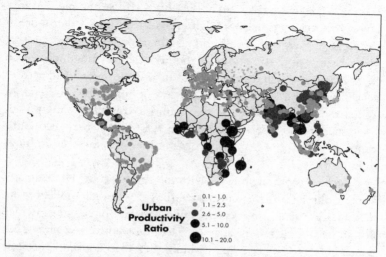

Source: Map by Martin Prosperity Institute, based on data from Joseph Parilla, Jesus Leal Trujillo, Alan Berube, and Tao Ran, *Global Metro Monitor*, Brookings Institution, 2015, www.brookings.edu/research/reports2/2015/01/22-global-metro-monitor, and nighttime light emissions from Richard Florida, Charlotta Mellander, and Tim Gulden, "Global Metropolis: Assessing Economic Activity in Urban Centers Based on Nighttime Satellite Images," *Professional Geographer* 64, no. 2 (2010): 178–187.

way of life than the countryside. Skeptics might counter that this advantage reveals the poverty of these developing countries more than it testifies to the productivity of their cities. But the broad pattern still reflects the basic fact that urbanization, warts and all, is better than the alternative.

But how can we further boost the productivity of these places, and, still more importantly, how can we reconnect the growth rates of their urban populations to a rise in living standards?

The answer lies in helping them to further their own development by unleashing the energy and talent of the people who are clustering in their cities. "To seek the 'causes' of poverty is an intellectual dead end because poverty has no causes. Only prosperity has causes," Jane Jacobs wrote. "The great cold of poverty and economic stagnation is merely the absence of economic development."[17] Poverty occurs in the absence of institutions that unleash the creative energy of people and neighborhoods, or, even more so, when there are dysfunctional structures that stymie and squelch it. Prosperity, in contrast, arises from institutions and structures that harness and leverage these clusters of human creative energy. When the residents of poor communities are able to apply their own energy and talent and develop their skills, their economic conditions and those of their communities are much more likely to improve.

Back in 1972, in an essay with the curious title "Housing as a Verb," John F.C. Turner contrasted the conventional model of top-down government projects that build housing for the poor (which he dubbed "housing as a noun") to more bottom-up efforts in which poor residents essentially build their own housing ("housing as a verb").[18] The first model sequesters the poor, isolating them from economic opportunity and further concentrating poverty, and has generated failure after failure. But in the second model, the poor cluster in the places where they want to be (or need to be)—near the sites of economic opportunity.

Journalist Doug Saunders makes a similar point, highlighting the propulsive role played by what he calls "arrival cities," which he describes as places that essentially build the skills and capabilities of new arrivals from the rural countryside. One such place, which he describes, is Liu Gong Li, an impoverished, formerly agricultural village on the outskirts of Chongqing, a large city of 10 million people in the center of China. By the late 1990s and early 2000s, people began pouring in from the surrounding countryside to gain access to jobs and economic opportunity. With limited jobs available, they began to create their own informal businesses and build their own houses, few of which were actually legal. Today, Saunders points out, Liu Gong Li is a vibrant economic cluster of 120,000 people that has been fully absorbed by the city of Chongqing itself. Although Liu Gong Li looks like a burgeoning slum on the outside, with improvised buildings and raw sewage and garbage in its streets, it is also a cauldron of entrepreneurial activity, filled with small shops and factories where new migrants make textiles, plastics, wood products, and even computer-milled motorcycle parts. It's the kind of place, as one of its residents told Saunders, "where you can turn your grandchildren into successful people if you can find the right way to make a living."[19]

A growing body of research documents the potential of such bottom-up approaches to boost the development of very poor places. The anthropologist Janice Perlman has tracked the progress of Rio de Janeiro's favelas, some 1,200 communities that are home to 1.4 million people, over roughly a half-century, from the 1960s to now.[20] Although favelas are often viewed as permanent poverty traps, Perlman's research shows that they can be vehicles for improving the lives of their residents. By the early 2000s, about half of the grandchildren of the people she originally interviewed back in the 1960s lived in higher-quality housing than their grandparents. Some of them rented, and some of them owned their homes, but the great majority had electricity and running water and indoor toilets, and many of them also had air conditioners, washing machines, and even flat-screen televisions. The favela families also saw impressive gains in education across generations. Three-quarters of the fathers and more than nine-tenths of the mothers of the people she interviewed in the 1960s could not read or write. But by 2000, illiteracy had dropped to just 6 percent among their children, and all of the grandchildren could read and write. Many of the grandchildren of the original favela residents had completed high school, and a considerable number of them had gone on to college. Instead of being condemned to poverty and destitution, favela residents essentially developed themselves and their communities.

A separate study by researchers at the Santa Fe Institute and Slum Dwellers International, the latter a network of organizations in rapidly urbanizing places, provides more general evidence of the efficacy of this bottom-up approach. Residents of slum communities across emerging economies were asked to log their daily activities, initially on traditional paper surveys and more recently on mobile devices. It found that while poor people in poor neighborhoods possessed the underlying talent required for development, their ability to use their talent was stymied by the burdens of their day-to-day lives. Lacking the kinds of basic infrastructure and division of labor we take for granted in the advanced world, they were forced to spend the majority of their time taking care of life's immediate necessities: fetching their own water, bartering for and preparing their food, and traveling long distances by foot or rudimentary forms of transportation. This left them scant time to devote to the things that bring greater development—the further enhancement of their own skills and the broader development of their communities. The way to break this cycle and improve the productivity of slums, the study concluded, is to enable the urban poor to use their time more productively.[21] In Colombia, numerous people told me the story of the great cyclist Nairo Quintana, who had honed his climbing abilities by riding ten miles up and down mountains on a cheap bike to get to and from school. Of course, he was an exception that proved a rule—most people can't turn the time that they spend on basic needs to such spectacular account.

Another study of entrepreneurs in poor areas of Panama found that they were also stymied by a lack of time and resources. Many of their business ideas were quite creative, but, the study found, they did not have the financial resources that would allow them to tweak and refine their plans to make them more effective, or the time to wait for markets to develop more fully. This is troubling, because entrepreneurship and self-employment are important alternatives to traditional forms of employment in parts of the world where conventional jobs are scarce and the poor face considerable discrimination in getting them.[22]

Time after time, we see that what the poor in rudimentary settlements lack is not skills or creativity but the time and the resources to put them to better account. Ultimately, what these places are missing, and need, is the basic infrastructure that enables people and communities to leverage and scale up their capabilities and efforts.

Compounding all of this, the poor in many rapidly urbanizing cities can be trapped in a kind of sprawl that isolates them and cuts them off from broader economic opportunity. Many of the poor who are pouring out of rural areas and into these expanding cities, especially in Africa, are often shunted into slums and makeshift settlements at their peripheries, far away from the opportunities that the urban center affords. While many cities in the developing world are quite dense—Cairo, Delhi, Kolkata, Manila, and Mumbai come to mind—the world's fastest-growing cities are sprawling outwardly more quickly than Western cities are. In the two and a half decades spanning 1990 and 2015, the overall urban population of the developing countries doubled, but the amount of land those new urbanites took up grew three and a half times, according to research by my NYU colleague Shlomo Angel. The density of these cities actually declined by a whopping 52.5 percent over this same period. If the future rate of expansion remains the same, the land consumed by these cities will grow another four times over between now and 2050.[23]

Connectivity is a key element of the solution. The simple addition of basic infrastructure, such as paved roads or rudimentary transit, can help improve access to opportunity and enlarge the size of urban markets. Squatter settlements and residential areas take up a lot of space—the size of the average city block, so to speak, is far greater in them than in more advanced cities. And not nearly enough land is allocated to streets. In Dhaka, a city of 7 million people in Bangladesh, for example, streets take up just 12 percent of the land, far less than in advanced cities.

Functional streets are a critical ingredient for the economic transformation and upgrading of global slums. Not only do they allow residents to get around, they enable the provision of other forms of much-needed physical infrastructure—water and sewage lines and electric power lines, for example. Just as importantly, streets provide the connective fiber that links the slums and their residents to a host of existing urban advantages. A 2014 report by

UN-Habitat notes that "streets trigger economic activity, attracting shops, services and increased residents' identity with their place
of residence, bringing an enhanced sense of security and orderly
development."[24] Formal street addresses help turn illegal squatter
shelters into legal housing and functional neighborhoods. This improvement, in turn, enables more commerce and more mobility,
as now houses can be bought and sold. As neighborhoods become
better connected, isolated poverty traps can be transformed into
pathways for economic opportunity and more fully integrated into
the economic life of the city.

Transit can be an even more powerful way to generate connectivity and link people to economic opportunity. In Addis Ababa,
a city of 3.5 million people in Ethiopia, the addition of a light-rail
system opened up opportunities for slum-dwellers, promoted density and economic development around rail stops, and reduced the
dependence of the city's growing middle class on cars.[25]

It need not be traditional rail transit, either. Connectivity can
be accomplished in other, less expensive ways tailored to local
conditions. When my Creative Class Group colleagues and I developed the inaugural Philips Livable City Awards, one of our three
winners in 2011 was a small shade stand that functions as a shel-
ter from the hot sun or pouring rain. But more than that, it was a
way of organizing and structuring stops for the jitneys and simple
buses that residents could use to get around in Kampala, Uganda,
and other rapidly expanding African cities.

I saw a couple of other ingenious solutions for local connectivity during my visit to Medellín. Not long ago, the city was one
of the most violent and lawless in the world, overrun by drug
kingpin Pablo Escobar and his notorious Medellín Cartel. Communa 13, Medellín's poorest neighborhood—and one of its most
notorious—was cut off from the center of the city, and hence from
employment and educational opportunities, by its elevation. Its
12,000 residents had to negotiate vertiginous paths and stairways,
the equivalent of a twenty-eight-story building, to get into or out
of the neighborhood. Residents of other hillside barrios spent as

much as four hours a day traveling in buses between their homes and their jobs. Then the city government installed a set of outdoor escalators to connect Communa 13 to the rest of the city. Gondolas—hanging cable cars—were used to connect other slums to urban centers. With the support of local government, community groups worked to reclaim the areas around the escalators and gondola stops as vibrant public spaces, and commercial activity and needed social and public services developed around them. These small improvements helped turn isolated, persistently poor slums into safer, more functional, more economically interconnected communities. In 2012, Medellín was named Innovative City of the Year by the Urban Land Institute, Citibank, and the *Wall Street Journal*.[26]

The moral of the story: strategic investments in basic infrastructure can help connect slum-dwellers to jobs; leverage their talent and productive capabilities and enable them to become more fully engaged; and, ultimately, turn the vicious cycle of urban isolation and poverty into a virtuous circle of urban progress.

The new urbanites of global cities and their local neighborhoods and governments can do a lot to spur growth and development, but they cannot do it all on their own. International development policy must put cities and city-building at its core. Cities, not nations, after all, are the basic source of economic and social progress. In 2015, the United Nations took a step in the right direction when it named "inclusive, safe, resilient and sustainable" cities as one of its seventeen new sustainable development goals.[27] It's an important start, but the scale of the problem requires far more. Global urbanization is the grandest of all the grand challenges the world faces, impinging upon and in many ways subsuming the great crises and challenges of climate change, energy use, poverty, and economic opportunity. We won't be able to solve any of them unless we learn to build more productive, more prosperous, more sustainable, and more inclusive cities.

What's needed is not just money, but know-how, information, and data. It's hard to believe, but in contrast to almost any other field, from medicine and law to engineering and business, there is very little systematic training to equip mayors and city-builders with the knowledge and tools they need to develop their communities and cities. Even harder to believe is that they (and we) must do much of this work without enough information: lacking even basic data to track and monitor the progress of cities and metros around the world, it is impossible even to begin to identify what works and what does not. Having reliable, consistent, and fully comparable datasets would make an enormous difference in efforts to reconnect urbanization to rising living standards.

Here, the field of urbanism can learn a lot from the field of medicine. Over the past century or so, teaching hospitals were developed to link medicine more closely to scientific research and to develop state-of-the-art clinical protocols for doctors, medical professionals, and public health officials. Doctors are trained in biology, physiology, anatomy, and other facets of medical science in school, and they receive intensive on-the-job training as interns and attend conferences on an ongoing basis. New drugs and medical interventions are subjected to scientifically based research and clinical trials, and new knowledge is disseminated quickly and efficiently through a network of global medical and public health institutions. Similar kinds of global institutions are required to train city-builders; an analogous laboratory-to-bedside process is needed to get basic data and state-of-the-art knowledge on best practices into the hands of mayors, community developers, and urban leaders across the world.

Over the course of the next century, we will spend more money on building and rebuilding cities than we have spent over the entire span of human history until now. But cities cannot offer humanity a viable future unless they receive the attention they deserve—and the investments and resources that they desperately require.

It is critical that we get this right.

10

URBANISM FOR ALL

When was the last time you heard a national politician talk thoughtfully about cities and urban policy or make them an integral part of his or her agenda? Former president Barack Obama grew up in cities and clearly cares deeply about them, but even his administration failed to make any substantial moves on urban policy. The 2016 Democratic primary featured two former mayors, Bernie Sanders from Burlington, Vermont, and Martin O'Malley from Baltimore; and a third, former Richmond mayor Tim Kaine, eventually joined the Democratic ticket as Hillary Clinton's running mate. Aside from O'Malley's invocations of urban policy, which I helped craft, cities and urban policy were rarely, if ever, mentioned during the 2016 primaries or presidential campaign. The last time we had a serious national conversation about cities was back in the 1960s and 1970s, during the old urban crisis, when some cities exploded in riots and others teetered on fiscal collapse. When Donald Trump and other leading conservative politicians talk about cities, it is typically to point to so-called liberal failures to solve chronic urban poverty and crime. The closest we get to a conversation about actual urban policy today is when politicians call for greater investments in urban infrastructure as a way to stimulate economic growth.[1]

The disconnect between the vital economic role of cities and our policymakers' neglect of them could not be more palpable or troubling. As this book has shown, our ability to innovate and grow the economy depends on the clustering of talent, companies, and other economic assets in cities. Our cities and metro areas are our premier platforms for technological innovation and wealth creation, as well as for social progress and the fostering of open-mindedness, progressive values, and political freedom. They are our best laboratories for devising and testing new strategies for spurring innovation, creating high-paying jobs, and raising living standards.

But as this book has also shown, our cities and urban areas face deep challenges that threaten our entire way of life. The very same clustering force that generates economic and social progress also divides us. Winner-take-all urbanism means that a few big winners capture a disproportionate share of the spoils of innovation and economic growth, while many more places stagnate or fall further behind. As more and more middle-class neighborhoods fade, our cities, suburbs, and nation as a whole are splintering into a patchwork of concentrated advantage and concentrated disadvantage.

The New Urban Crisis is much more than an isolated crisis of superstar cities and tech hubs; it is the central crisis of today's urbanized knowledge capitalism. Its effects are being felt all across the entire United States, from superstar cities and tech hubs to the former industrial powerhouses of the Rustbelt and the sprawling metropolises of the Sunbelt. Figure 10.1 illustrates its extent, showing how America's metros stack up on the New Urban Crisis Index. While no single measure can capture its full breadth, this composite index gauges four of its key elements: economic segregation, wage inequality, income inequality, and housing unaffordability.

On the one hand, the crisis is most acute precisely where we've come to expect, in our two largest superstar cities and our leading tech hubs: Los Angeles ranks first among large metros; New York is second; and San Francisco third. The tech hubs of San Diego, Boston, and Austin also rank among the top ten most seriously affected large metros. My broader statistical analysis reinforces this basic pattern. The New Urban Crisis Index is positively and significantly correlated with the size and density of metros, their concentrations of high-tech industry, their shares of creative-class

Figure 10.1: The New Urban Crisis Index

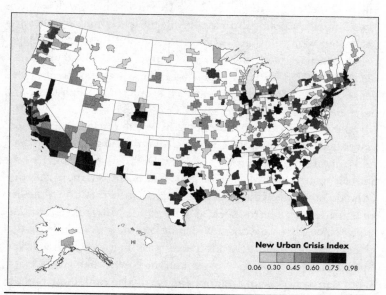

Rank	Large Metro	New Urban Crisis Index	Overall Rank
1	Los Angeles-Long Beach-Santa Ana, CA	0.972	2
2	New York-Northern New Jersey-Long Island, NY-NJ-PA	0.967	3
3	San Francisco-Oakland-Fremont, CA	0.922	6
4	San Diego-Carlsbad-San Marcos, CA	0.884	10
5	Chicago-Naperville-Joliet, IL-IN-WI	0.878	12
6	Miami-Fort Lauderdale-Pompano Beach, FL	0.875	14
7	Boston-Cambridge-Quincy, MA-NH	0.874	15
8	Philadelphia-Camden-Wilmington, PA-NJ-DE-MD	0.852	18
9	Austin-Round Rock, TX	0.845	20
10	Memphis, TN-MS-AR	0.842	21

Source: Martin Prosperity Institute, based on data from the US Census and the US Department of Labor, Bureau of Labor Statistics.

workers and college graduates, and their levels of economic out-put, income, and wages. The New Urban Crisis also closely fol-lows America's political divide, being positively and significantly associated with the share of votes for Clinton in 2016 and nega-tively associated with the share of Trump votes. Once again, we see that the New Urban Crisis is a fundamental feature of larger, denser, richer, more liberal, more educated, more high-tech, and more creative-class metro areas.[2]

But, on the other hand, the crisis is being felt in many more places across America: in Chicago, Miami, and Memphis, which rank among the top ten on the New Urban Crisis Index; in the Sunbelt metros of Dallas, Houston, Charlotte, Atlanta, Phoenix, Orlando, and Nashville, which fall just a bit further down the list; and in Rustbelt metros such as Cleveland, Milwaukee, and De-troit, which also rank high. Widening our view to include smaller places, the Bridgeport-Stamford-Norwalk metro outside of New York takes the top position overall on the New Urban Crisis Index; Santa Barbara, Fresno, Trenton, and Reno also rank quite high, as do an array of smaller college towns.

The breadth of the New Urban Crisis helps us understand why economic anxiety in America continues to mount. The middle class has been eviscerated amid the collapse of the suburban growth model that once fueled the American Dream. The poor and dis-advantaged truly are falling further and further behind the rest of society. But even the affluent third of society who are thriving eco-nomically don't feel as prosperous as they did in the past, because they live in expensive cities where securing their own, and their children's, futures is growing more costly and increasingly difficult.

Indeed, the New Urban Crisis is a big part of the reason why the economy has been unable to recover fully from the economic crisis and remains mired in what some call "secular stagnation." That concept was originally used to describe the economic malaise of the Great Depression, when the economy was unable to gener-ate the innovation, economic growth, and jobs required to raise living standards. Today, former treasury secretary Larry Summers believes we are stuck in a new era of stagnation, with the ongoing economic recovery operating in a lower gear than it could be, and failing to generate enough of the higher-paying jobs needed to restore the broad middle class.[3]

Summers, along with Nobel Prize–winning economist Paul Krugman and many others, believes that the best way out of this economic malaise is for government to stimulate the economy by spending more money on infrastructure. This idea would seem to have historical precedent on its side.[4] In the nineteenth century, canals and railroads unified and expanded the nation and powered economic growth and innovation. By the late nineteenth and early twentieth centuries, streetcars and subways were providing a fresh boost to cities, helping them grow and house larger populations. In the mid-twentieth century, massive investments in roads and highways, combined with generous subsidies for homeownership, propelled mass suburbanization and the prolonged era of economic growth that went with it.

But if spending more money on roads and bridges may help provide short-term economic stimulus today, it will do little to generate sustained economic growth. What we need is not a random menu of shovel-ready projects, but strategic investments in the kinds of infrastructure that can underpin more clustered and concentrated urban development. For infrastructure to really put the economy back on its feet, it must be part of a broader strategy for clustered, urbanized growth.

The New Urban Crisis is a significant turning point in American history. In many ways, it marks the final closing of the vast American frontier. "Since the days when the fleet of Columbus sailed into the waters of the New World," Frederick Jackson Turner declared in his famous 1893 speech before the American Historical Association, "the people of the United States have taken their tone from the incessant expansion which has not only been open but has even been forced upon them." America's western frontier had finally closed, he said, and the nation's foundational epoch had come to an end. As it turned out, he spoke too soon. For the next century, the "crabgrass frontier" of the suburbs, in the historian Kenneth Jackson's memorable phrase, became America's new axis of growth.[5] The New Urban Crisis signals the end of this long epoch of cheap outward-oriented growth.

Now, for the first time in American history, outward expansion is no longer a reliable path to sustained economic growth. Restoring our economy today will turn on our ability to generate more clustered and dense growth in our cities and suburbs. Making this re-urbanization shift will be expensive, certainly when compared with the previous eras of cheap outward growth. Creating the density required for urban clustering, building the transit and other infrastructure that can undergird such urban development, rebuilding our suburbs in denser fashion, and providing affordable housing at the scale that is needed will cost a good deal more than laying down roads and highways and throwing up single-family homes in the suburbs.

Besides being costly, such re-urbanization runs counter to America's deeply ingrained anti-urban bias, which harkens all the way back to Thomas Jefferson's pastoralist vision. That bias remains deeply institutionalized in the structures of our state legislatures and Congress, which give disproportionate power to suburban and rural areas and their residents.[6] It is further attenuated by the long-running conservative conviction that cities are elitist, wasteful, libertine, overrun with crime, and part and parcel of our social unraveling and economic decay. And it is reinforced by the perplexing reality that the traditional American Dream of an affordable home is more achievable in sprawling conservative areas of the country than in dense, knowledge-based liberal ones (as of 2015, housing costs were almost twice as high in deep-blue markets than in red-state ones, $227 versus $119 per square foot).[7]

Summoning up the political will to face up to the New Urban Crisis will be no easy thing. And it will be ever more difficult with Donald Trump as president and the Republicans in control of both houses of Congress. But it is a necessary watershed moment in America's development, on which our future will turn.

S o, what can we do to overcome this New Urban Crisis and put our economy and society back on track?

I am far from the first person to try to identify solutions to the problems and challenges facing our cities. But just as our understanding of the New Urban Crisis has been partial and incomplete, the strategies and solutions that have been proposed for it have been too limited and ad hoc to cope with the depth and scope of its challenges. It is true, as many have said, that we have to overcome the backward-looking NIMBY impulses, or what I prefer to call the New Urban Luddism, that hold back the urban density and clustering that innovation and economic progress require. Of course, it's time to reform the overly restrictive zoning and building codes that limit density. And there can be no doubt that cities and their mayors need more power to run their cities. But as necessary as these things are, even if we do all of them, they will still be insufficient. To address the full sweep of the New Urban Crisis, we will have to do much, much more.

To solve a crisis this deep and systemic, we must put cities and urbanism at the very center of our agenda for economic prosperity. As I noted at the outset of this book, if our crisis is urban, so is its solution. If we are to again enjoy a widely shared and sustainable prosperity, we must become a more fully and fairly urbanized nation. The scale of investment that is required is daunting, but it is not unprecedented. The good news is that we can make significant gains by using resources that are already at our disposal. Our new strategy for a more productive urbanism for all can take shape around seven pillars. I discuss each of them below.

MAKE CLUSTERING WORK FOR US AND NOT AGAINST US

T he clustering force is the key driver of economic growth, and it is absolutely critical that we effectively harness it to create the broadest possible economic and social benefits. As we have seen, the crux of the problem here revolves around the urban land nexus: land is scarce precisely where it is needed the most. We can't make more land, but we can develop the land we have more intensively and efficiently.

A growing chorus of so-called market urbanists argues that the best way to do this is by eliminating the restrictive zoning and building codes that limit the market's ability to build as needed. They make an important point: zoning and building codes do need to be liberalized and modernized. We can no longer allow NIM-BYs and New Urban Luddites to stand in the way of the dense, clustered development our cities and our economy need.

But land use deregulation by itself—though a necessary part of the solution to the New Urban Crisis—is insufficient to address the full breadth of the problem. While it will result in new housing being built and in increased density, the high costs of urban land combined with the high cost of high-rise construction, mean it is likely to mainly add more expensive luxury towers and that it will do little to provide the kinds of affordable housing our cities really need. Even the free-market economist Tyler Cowen has a certain skepticism toward this approach: "More stuff will be built, urban output will expand, land still will be the scarce factor, and by the end of the process rents still will be high," he wrote. "If we deregulate building, landowners will capture a big chunk of the benefits."[8] As a result, very little of the benefit will end up trickling down to those who need it most.

There's another reason to be skeptical. Houston—the paragon of sprawling Sunbelt development, the archetypal expansive metro where developers can build what and where they want unencumbered by zoning or land use restrictions—consistently ranks alongside New York, Los Angeles, and San Francisco on my indicators of inequality, segregation, and the New Urban Crisis. Greater Houston ranks eleventh among the large metros on my New Urban Crisis Index. It ranks fourth among the large metros on my Overall Economic Segregation Index, and fourth among the large metros on the Composite Inequality Index, with only New York, Los Angeles, and San Francisco ranking higher. And Houston ranks third of the large metros on the Segregation-Inequality Index, behind New York and LA. Even though Houston's housing is more affordable than New York's, LA's, or San Francisco's, it is rather expensive compared to that of most other metros, and Houston suffers from among the highest levels of inequality and segregation in the country.

The New Urban Crisis is not just a crisis of a select group of superstar cities and tech hubs, it is a feature of larger, denser, more affluent metros across the board. Deregulating land use, and making superstar cities and tech hubs look more like Houston, will not be nearly enough to save our cities from the New Urban Crisis.

Furthermore, such radical deregulation of land use and housing potentially runs the risk of killing off the proverbial goose that lays the golden egg. Urban economies are powered not by extreme residential density and huge towers, but by the mid-rise, mixed-used density that promotes mixing and interaction. As I mentioned back in Chapter 2, the world's most innovative places are not the skyscraper districts and vertical sprawl of Hong Kong or Singapore, but the former industrial neighborhoods of New York, San Francisco, and London, which are filled with mid-rise buildings, factory and warehouse lofts, and the occasional high-rise, arrayed along streets that enable constant mixing and interaction to take place. As Jane Jacobs warned long ago, "In the absence of a pedestrian scale, density can be big trouble."[9]

Extreme land use deregulation may well end up damaging our most innovative urban districts by encouraging too much vertical sprawl and turning them into deadened condo canyons. It is precisely these kinds of mixed-use neighborhoods that are in short supply, because we effectively stopped building them during the suburban era. Every time we kill one off, we lose an irreplaceable asset for innovation.

Although we certainly need to eliminate backward-looking regulations, we must also take care not to undermine our most precious and unique urban ecosystems. To accomplish this, we need to reform urban land use regimes to ensure that they have the flexibility required for the urbanized knowledge economy and are able to channel development in ways that enhance, and do not undermine, the creative, innovative, and productive capacities of urban economies.

The most effective approach to spurring denser and more clustered development is to switch from our current local reliance on the property tax to a land value tax. Whereas the property tax taxes land and the structures on top of it, a land value tax taxes the underlying value of the land itself. In this way, it creates significant incentives for property owners to put that land to its most intensive use. The basic idea goes back to David Ricardo, who developed influential theories of free trade and comparative advantage in the early eighteenth century. Ricardo saw the unearned income that comes from land as pure waste.

The most influential proponent of the land value tax was the late nineteenth-century economist Henry George. In his book *Progress and Poverty*, he argued that such a tax would not only make more effective use of land, but also raise wages, reduce inequality, and generate greater productivity. The basic premise is that the less developed land is, the higher it is taxed. George in fact suggested that undeveloped land be taxed at a rate of 100 percent, minus the improvements made to it. Absent such improvements, he argued, all of the land's value should return to the public commons. In today's cities, property owners who use their land for, say, undeveloped surface parking lots would be taxed at a very high rate. A small apartment building would be taxed at a lower rate, and a larger one at an even lower rate. This system would provide greater incentives to put land in high-priced urban centers to its most efficient and productive use, increasing density and clustering.[10]

Furthermore, under the current property tax system, landlords and property owners not only have disincentives to add density and further develop their properties, but they are able to reap extraordinary rewards, or rents, by simply profiting from the increase in property values that is created by neighborhood upgrading and the ongoing appreciation of real estate values. The High Line Park in New York, for instance, created a huge increase in the land value of surrounding property, which generated windfalls for real estate developers, but little if any of those gains were returned to the park or the broader community. The same is true on a smaller scale in virtually every urban neighborhood that is seeing an influx of new residents, new restaurants and cafés, new and better schools, or reductions in crime. A land value tax can help ensure that those benefits are shared more broadly by the public, because the rise in the value of the land that occurs through these broader neighborhood improvements is also captured by the tax and returned to the public, where it can potentially be used to invest in needed services and help close economic gaps in the community.

Another intriguing idea involves using local tax policy to essentially co-opt NIMBY opposition to new development. The basic idea, referred to as tax increment local transfers, is to allow the residents of neighborhoods to share in the tax revenues that come from new development—for example, by rebating and reducing their own property taxes over a period of time.[11]

As politically difficult as it might seem to change local tax structures in these ways, the land value tax is attracting broad support from a wide array of economists and urbanists on both sides of the aisle. It is a move that would encourage more building where it is needed, increase density and clustering, and help to make both our cities and the economy stronger.

INVEST IN THE INFRASTRUCTURE FOR DENSITY AND GROWTH

Infrastructure is an important, and necessary, piece of the puzzle. If well planned and invested in strategically, it can help expand the scale of clustered development, the number of places that can support clustered development, and the connections between outlying areas and existing clustered development close to the urban center.

Infrastructure is certainly the topic du jour among politicians of all stripes, including Donald Trump who has called for substantial investments in it to stimulate the economy. The administration of Justin Trudeau in Canada is doing just this, making a huge financial commitment to infrastructure to spur economic growth and create better jobs. But a menu of random projects won't do the trick, and pouring money into more roads and bridges will only hold us back. What we need are strategic investments in the kind of infrastructure that will push us closer together, as opposed to spreading us apart, and that will strengthen and reinforce urban density and clustering that power economic growth. That means shifting infrastructure investment away from roads and highways that spread us out and toward mass transit that helps cluster people and economic activity closer together.

The United States invests shockingly little in mass transit. Much of the transit we do have in cities like New York is a legacy good, often more than a century old. (The extensive transit systems of New York and London were mainly developed before the advent of the automobile.) In fact, the scarcity of such transit-served locations is the reason that land and housing around subway and transit stops has become so expensive. Research shows that transit-served neighborhoods provide better access to jobs and improve residents' chances for upward mobility. Expanding transit will increase the number of these locations and enable greater numbers of people, especially less advantaged people, to gain access to them.

Of course, transit works best in already dense places, such as New York City, San Francisco, Chicago, Boston, and Washington, DC. Although such cities already have transit, they could use still more of it, especially to connect outlying areas to their urban centers and reduce congestion and reliance on cars.

Transit is also needed in more sprawling metros, particularly those that have grown increasingly large and congested. As we saw back in Chapter 2, the development of metro areas faces a geographic limit as they grow larger. When metro areas reach a threshold of 5 or 6 million people, cars and roads are no longer a very effective way to move people around. The United States has quite a few metro areas that are roughly this size—for example, the Bay Area, Greater Washington, DC, Boston, Philadelphia, Houston, Dallas, Atlanta, and Miami. These metro areas are already at or near their outward limit for geographic expansion based on the car. It is increasingly difficult, if not impossible, to add sufficient housing through further outward expansion. Increasing density in the urban center, and especially in the suburbs, is the only way sustainable growth can be achieved. Investing in transit and reducing reliance on the car is a key mechanism for generating denser, more clustered development in both central and outlying areas. One bright spot of the 2016 election was that voters in many states and localities across the nation voted to increase expenditures for transit.

Transit infrastructure can also help expand the outward reach of metros. Over the course of the twentieth century, the introduction of each new form of transportation—the streetcar, subways, and the car—expanded the commuting zone for workers, allowing cities and metro areas to expand outwardly. Better, faster transit, including high-speed rail in some places, could vastly expand the commuting zones and labor sheds of today's metro areas, allowing workers to commute from homes in more affordable places to jobs in more productive ones.

Not everyone who works in a superstar city or leading knowledge hub has to live in one. The study I discussed in Chapter 2 that showed how much our land use restrictions cost the US economy also noted that effective transit can do more to solve the problem simply by allowing workers to commute from more affordable outlying areas to the urban center. Transit and high-speed rail, in particular, can help expand the functional labor markets of these places "overnight," as the researchers put it, without needing to deal with their onerous land use restrictions, and potentially without even having to add any new housing in these cities and metro areas at all.[12]

High-speed rail can even help to link separate metros together in larger and more formidable mega-regions.[13] This has already happened in some parts of the country without the benefit of high-speed rail, namely, the so-called Amtrak Corridor running between Boston, New York, Philadelphia, Baltimore, and Washington, DC, an area with a population of more than 50 million people and economic output north of $2 trillion. The United States has roughly a dozen such mega-regions. Across the Great Lakes, there is the cluster of Midwestern cities that takes in Chicago, Detroit, and Pittsburgh, and the cluster that connects Buffalo and Rochester to Toronto and its surrounding areas. In the South, there is Miami-Tampa-Orlando, the area that stretches from Atlanta to Charlotte, and the Texas Triangle of Houston, Dallas, and Austin. California has mega-regions in the south around Los Angeles and north around San Francisco; the Pacific Northwest has Cascadia, which takes in Seattle, Portland, and Vancouver.

High-speed rail can better connect metros to one another by dramatically reducing the time it takes to move between them. True high-speed rail (traveling at speeds like France's TGV or Japan's Shinkansen) could reduce the travel time between New York and Boston, or New York and Washington, DC, to less than ninety minutes, and between Dallas and Houston, or Dallas and Austin, to about the same; trips from LA to San Francisco, or Pittsburgh to Chicago, would shrink to a more manageable two and a half hours.[14] This could substantially expand the functional labor markets of these places, enlarge their economies, and bolster their overall economic competitiveness.

Private-sector investment is already taking on some of this. A group of private investors has partially resuscitated the high-speed connection between Miami and Tampa that Florida's governor opted not to support. But the most effective way to fund new transit and high-speed rail is to redirect a larger share of the gas tax toward such projects.

It is time to level the playing field for mass transit by reducing the outright subsidy we give to the car in the form of roads and highways. Cities in other parts of the world, including London, have begun to institute congestion charges, which make drivers pay for their use of busy roads to help alleviate traffic, sprawl, and pollution. New developments like self-driving cars, electric vehicles, and on-demand digital delivery systems, such as Uber and Lyft, will certainly play a big role in the city of the future. But we still need mass transit to provide the connective fiber that will increase clustering and enable the development of a larger number of dense, mixed-use clustered neighborhoods that are affordable to more people. Ultimately, this is not about choosing one form of transportation over another. It's about ensuring we have the infrastructure that can move people around efficiently, create the density and housing affordability we need, and, most of all, help to spur overall economic growth.

BUILD MORE AFFORDABLE RENTAL HOUSING

Affordable housing is the third key element that we must address if we are to overcome the New Urban Crisis. In our most expensive cities, housing has become unaffordable for all but the top one-third of society's most advantaged people. Essential service providers, including police and firefighters, teachers and hospital workers, and restaurant and retail workers, are being pushed farther and farther away from urban centers and other key centers of economic activity. In some of these places, it is becoming so hard to attract workers for these functions that large-scale commercial developers are calling for "urban workforce housing" to ensure their cities have the workers they need to operate. The lack of affordable housing in these places is starting to hinder their ability to reproduce themselves and keep their economies running.

The problem of housing affordability may be most acute in superstar cities and tech hubs, but it extends far beyond them. Too many Americans across the country, especially low-income renters, are spending too much of their incomes for housing. And our housing system is strongly oriented toward single-family housing in sprawling suburbs and against the more affordable, clustered rental housing that urbanized knowledge capitalism requires.

A big part of the problem is US housing policy itself. Designed to stimulate suburbanization, our current housing policy massively subsidizes homeowners. The federal government provides an estimated $200 billion in annual subsidies for homeownership via tax deductions for mortgage interest. When the indirect costs are accounted for, the subsidy may run as high as $600 billion, four to twelve times as much as the nation spends on housing assistance to those in need ($46 billion a year).[15] The top 20 percent of income earners gain 75 percent of these benefits, and the top 1 percent hauls in 15 percent. These policies badly distort the housing market, causing it to produce too much spread-out single-family housing and not enough clustered rental housing.

The shift from single-family suburban homes to multifamily rental housing, which I have referred to as the great housing reset, is already under way, despite these distortions. Homeownership has declined substantially from its peak of the mid-1960s, and it is headed even lower.[16] Over the past decade or so, more Americans—especially those in high-priced superstar cities and knowledge hubs—have become renters. The number of renter households increased by 9 million between 2005 and 2015, the largest one-decade increase on record. By the end of that period, 43 million Americans were renters, and the share of renters had grown from 31 percent to 37 percent of the population. More than seven in ten Millennials between the ages of eighteen and thirty-four are renters, as are more than half the residents of New York, LA, and San Francisco.[17]

Renting is more closely aligned with the needs of the urbanized knowledge-based economy than homeownership. Renters are more likely to live close to work or use transit to get to their jobs, while suburban homeowners are more likely to commute long distances in their cars. Metro areas with higher levels of renters have higher levels of innovation; greater concentrations of high-tech firms; higher shares of college graduates and the creative class; and higher wages, incomes, and productivity, while metro areas with higher levels of homeownership are less innovative, less productive, and less diverse, on average, and have smaller shares of highly educated and skilled talent.[18] Building more rental housing and less single-family housing is in sync with and reinforces the urban clustering that stimulates innovation and economic growth.

Still, too many renters are seriously burdened by their housing costs, many of them caught in a death spiral of rising rents and declining incomes. Average rents increased by more than 22 percent between 2006 and 2014, while average incomes declined by nearly 6 percent. The number of renters paying 30 percent or more of their income for rent (which is considered the threshold for being cost-burdened) soared from 14.8 million in 2001 to 21.3 million in 2014, while the number who devoted more than half of their income to rent grew from 7.5 million to 11.4 million. The situation of low-income renters (those with incomes below $15,000) is substantially worse—nearly three-quarters of them (72 percent) devote more than half of their incomes to rent. For the lowest-income households, the share of income spent on rent increased from an already whopping 55.7 percent in 2006 to a staggering 62.5 percent by 2014.

It's time to redirect federal housing subsidies away from affluent homeowners to the less advantaged renters who really need them. Doing so will help create demand for rental units, stimulate more construction of apartment buildings, and generate more clustered development. Continuing unfair subsidies to single-family homeowners only encourages sprawl, which undermines the density and clustering that drive growth while adding substantial other costs to our economy.

These measures, along with rational reform of land use restrictions and investments in transit, will help spur the construction of more clustered and affordable condos and rental apartments. But it still will not be enough to make housing affordable for less advantaged groups, especially in expensive superstar cities. Not surprisingly, a 2016 study of the San Francisco Bay Area found that a combination of building more private-market-rate housing and more subsidized housing is required to address the region's housing affordability challenge.[19]

There has been no shortage of proposed solutions for providing more affordable housing for those truly in need. They include expanding rent control, building more publicly subsidized housing, and making use of so-called inclusionary zoning, that is, mandating that developers construct affordable housing units in exchange for being able to build bigger, taller, high-end projects. While the aims of such policies are admirable, they can be costly and inefficient. Rent control discourages landlords from improving their properties, and it can be gamed. Inclusionary zoning works best in expensive superstar-city real estate markets where developers have incentives to build affordable units in exchange for the ability to build taller buildings. But in other types of cities, these policies can cause developers to build less than they otherwise might. And while larger-scale reforms—such as liberalizing outmoded zoning and building codes, replacing the property tax with a land value tax, or expanding transit—will increase the overall supply of housing, they are not likely to provide nearly enough truly affordable units for those who need them the most: service workers, the less advantaged, and the poor.

The most effective way to help those who are truly in need is to raise their incomes, either by creating better jobs (the subject of the next section), or by providing direct public support in the form of housing vouchers—or, even better, through more broad-based initiatives, such as a negative income tax that provides a basic minimum income (which I will discuss in the section following the next one).

TURN LOW-WAGE SERVICE JOBS INTO MIDDLE-CLASS WORK

Increasing density, investing in transit, and building more affordable housing all at once is a tall order, but even doing all of that will not be enough to tackle the full breadth of the New Urban Crisis. Right now, our economy simply does not have enough high-paying jobs to support a new middle class. We need large numbers of better jobs with higher wages to help lift people out of poverty and enable them to afford better housing. Some will say that Trump and the Republicans are in the way here, but a lot can be done on this front by states and cities and the private sector.

The strategies that politicians typically offer up for rebuilding the middle class will not even come close to solving the problem. Many, most notably Trump himself, like to talk about bringing middle-class manufacturing jobs back to America, for instance. But only 20 percent of Americans do blue-collar work of any sort today, and that includes huge numbers of construction and transportation workers. Just 6 percent of workers actually make things in factories. Even if we were able to bring large numbers of manufacturing jobs back, and even if the much-publicized successes with advanced and so-called artisanal manufacturing continue apace, these new jobs will still amount to just a drop in the bucket. In today's global, tech-driven economy, manufacturing will never be the economic force and the backbone of the middle class that it once was.

Another commonly proposed solution is to get more people to earn college degrees: the basic idea here being, quite correctly, that higher levels of education bring higher wages and salaries. Although encouraging more people to get college degrees is desirable, it will not rebuild the middle class to anywhere near what it was before. There are simply not enough knowledge jobs to go around. And only about a third of our workforce have high-paying knowledge, professional, and creative-class jobs.

As we have seen, the largest and fastest-growing segment of our economy is the low-paid service sector, where more than 60 million American workers, making up more than 45 percent of our national workforce, toil in low-skilled, low-wage, precarious high-turnover jobs. Add in those who work only occasionally in the informal economy, and those who are underemployed, unemployed, or out of the labor force altogether, and as many as two-thirds of all working-age Americans are being left behind. If we want to build a new middle class, we have no choice but to turn the tens of millions of low-paid service jobs we are stuck with into higher-paying jobs.

Transforming low-paid service jobs into middle-class work is not nearly as outlandish a proposition as it may seem at first glance. In fact, it's analogous to how we turned the low-paying manufacturing jobs of the late nineteenth and early twentieth centuries into the family-supporting blue-collar jobs of the 1950s and 1960s. Henry Ford's insight—that assembly-line workers should be paid enough to buy the cars they were making—gets to the nub of the matter.

As my father liked to remind me, he left school at age thirteen to work in a factory. It took the work of nine family members—his father and mother, his six brothers and sisters, and him—to generate enough income to support the family. But when he came back after serving in World War II and took up work in the same factory, his old job paid enough to allow him to support a wife and kids, buy a house, and put my brother and me through Catholic school and college. His job, like millions of others, had been transformed by New Deal policies and programs that helped to boost the pay of manufacturing workers—including the Wagner Act of 1935, which gave workers the right to form unions and bargain collectively for higher wages, as well as the Social Security Act, which was passed in the same year and other social-welfare programs that established a rudimentary social safety net. As a society, America created policies and institutions that turned manufacturing jobs from low-paid work to higher-paid middle-class work. We need to do the same for the millions upon millions of service workers who occupy the lower rungs of the economic ladder today.

A good place to start is by lifting the wage floor. The Obama administration took steps in that direction in 2014, when, via an executive order, the minimum wage for federal contractors was lifted to $10.10. It was a start, but not nearly enough to make a difference in expensive superstar cities and knowledge hubs. But it is states and cities that are taking the lead on raising the minimum wage. Growing numbers of them across the country are raising the minimum wage on their own—and not just progressive cities like Los Angeles, New York, and Seattle. In the 2014 midterm elections, four solidly red states—Alaska, Arkansas, Nebraska, and South Dakota—voted to increase their minimum wages to levels that are some of the highest in the nation when living costs are taken into account.

Conservatives will raise the usual objection that lifting the minimum wage will drive up prices and force more people out of work than it will help. But setting the minimum wage at roughly 50 percent of the prevailing median wage would have no such ill effects, according to recent research.[20] And it's worth remembering that the federal minimum wage effectively stood at 55 percent of the median wage back in 1968.

Given the tremendous variations in housing costs across the country, it is important that the minimum wage reflect the local cost of living. Just as we typically index policies to the rate of inflation, we need to index the minimum wage to take geographic differences in living costs into account.[21] If we set it to 50 percent of the prevailing local median wage, the minimum wage would vary from state to state, or even from metro to metro or city to city, ranging from a high of around $15 an hour in San Jose and DC to roughly $14 in San Francisco, about $13 in Boston, New York, and Seattle, and around $9.50 in less expensive metros such as Las Vegas, Louisville, Memphis, Miami, Nashville, New Orleans, Orlando, San Antonio, and Tampa.

We will still need a concerted effort to turn the large number of low-wage service jobs into family-supporting jobs. Higher pay is not just an increased cost—it can be a path to increased productivity and profit. Poorly paid, poorly treated workers are unmotivated, demoralized, and disengaged. Low-paying companies experience costly turnover. Workers who are paid better and treated better are more motivated and more engaged and can become a useful source of innovation and productivity improvement. The world's leading manufacturing companies long ago realized that paying workers better and engaging them more fully in their work pays huge dividends in the form of the shop-floor innovations that make factories more productive.[22]

There is substantial evidence that paying better wages to service workers would do much the same for companies in the service sector as it did for manufacturing firms. Many of the most successful retail and hospitality companies of the past couple of decades—Trader Joe's, Costco, Zara, Whole Foods, Four Seasons, and others—pay their workers substantially more than minimum wage and substantially more than their competitors as part of a broader "good jobs strategy" to generate higher levels of engagement, drive innovation, limit turnover, and achieve better customer service.[23] Upgrading low-wage service jobs would create other additional benefits for workers, companies, and the economy as a whole. More engaged workers would boost company productivity and profits. Millions upon millions of better-paid service workers would add considerably to demand. And improving the performance of the service companies in the aggregate would add to the productivity and efficiency of the economy broadly.

Higher-paying service jobs can also promote creativity and innovation in less direct ways. One of the best critiques of my own theory of the creative class came from a member of Austin's creative class, who showed that a key element of that city's high-powered creative economy was its high-paying service jobs. He pointed out that the locally headquartered Whole Foods provided a large number of flexible, high-paying day jobs for local artists and other creatives, which added up to substantially more support to Austin's creative economy than the artistic and cultural initiatives of local government and local private foundations combined.[24] Better-paying service jobs can boost the creative economy by helping its participants cover the rent.

Upgrading service jobs is not necessarily an area that calls for direct government intervention. Part of the problem is that too many firms fail to recognize that they can actually improve their productivity and profits by upgrading service jobs. To help spur this, government can support initiatives that help disseminate best practices throughout the economy, as it did through its agricultural and manufacturing extension programs and through award programs recognizing accomplishments in the private sector (for example, the Malcolm Baldridge Award for Quality).

Ultimately, creating a new middle class will mean that many of us will have to pay a bit more for services. But again, the New Deal era can serve as an example. After the Great Depression, we built a middle class by collectively paying a premium for our cars and appliances. If we were willing to pay premiums for such durable goods to help underwrite the middle class of my parents' day, then surely we can pay living wages to the people who take care of our children and elderly and provide us with vital services to create a new middle class today.

TACKLE POVERTY BY INVESTING IN PEOPLE AND PLACES

Perhaps the most troubling and disturbing aspect of the New Urban Crisis is the spread of persistent, concentrated poverty across both our cities and suburbs. To overcome the crisis, we must address it head-on.

Our current approaches to combating poverty can be divided into two basic categories: people-based approaches that provide resources to poor families or help them move to new and better neighborhoods, and place-based approaches that attempt to improve the conditions of disadvantaged neighborhoods by investing in schools, providing needed social services, and reducing crime and violence. We need to do both.

We've already seen how moving families from disadvantaged to more advantaged neighborhoods with better schools can dramatically improve the fortunes of poor children. But obviously, not everyone who lives in an area of persistent poverty will be able to move to new neighborhoods with better schools and more opportunity. Many will be missed, not enough will be given the opportunity to move, and some will prefer to stay where their families and friends are. And moving only the best-performing kids or those from the most motivated families will end up draining the top talent out of the least-advantaged neighborhoods, further concentrating poverty among those left behind.

Overcoming decades upon decades of persistent poverty also requires comprehensive and coordinated place-based investments in disadvantaged neighborhoods. Robert Sampson, who is perhaps the nation's leading expert on concentrated poverty, has called for "affirmative action for neighborhoods" to ensure that each and every neighborhood offers its residents access to economic opportunity and upward mobility. As he aptly put it, "what poor residents seem to want most is not to move but simply to have their communities revitalized."[25] To be effective, these place-based investments cannot be eked out piecemeal; they must span the full gamut of essential social and economic services, from education and economic opportunity to efforts to reduce crime and violence and more.

Above all, overcoming persistent poverty means tackling the problems of urban schools. Far too many disadvantaged neighborhoods are served by underfunded schools that fail to provide students with the skills and capabilities they need to thrive in the knowledge economy, and where dropout rates remain distressingly high. Since education is the key avenue for upward mobility, underperforming schools trap families and children in an intergenerational cycle of poverty. The situation in much of the rest of the advanced world is different. In Toronto, where I live, all children have access to a decent education that is funded by their province. Although US schools receive state and federal funding, they mainly rely on local property taxes, which accounts for the wide variation in school quality. And of course affluent people in urban areas can bypass the public school system entirely by sending their kids to private schools. America's terribly unequal access to education is among the gravest injustices in our society.

It's not just good schools that are missing from poor neighborhoods: children from poor neighborhoods are behind before they even get to kindergarten. More early childhood development programs would help give kids a boost before they get to school. Such programs are in line with a long American tradition of expanding public investments in education to spur economic development. The development of mass public education in the late nineteenth and early twentieth centuries, and the dramatic expansion of college and university training after World War II, promoted economic growth and helped to spur the development of a stable middle class.[26] Investing more in early childhood development, especially in chronically poor neighborhoods, will increase overall human capital and add to the economy again today.

Fundamentally, poverty is the absence of money. Providing every person with a guaranteed minimum income or universal basic income is the most straightforward way to combat it; and the most efficacious way to do that is through a negative income tax, which essentially returns money to the poor so that they can cover their basic needs. Such an approach is a more cost-effective and less bureaucratically cumbersome way of mitigating poverty than providing myriad direct-assistance programs for housing, food, child support, and the like.

A common criticism is that a basic income program like this would encourage slackers and slacking. But a negative income tax is designed to encourage work and entrepreneurial effort; the amount of government support declines as incomes go up. The idea is not nearly as radical as it may seem. A negative income tax almost became US policy during the Nixon administration. A number of nations already use it, and many more are considering it today. The basic approach was introduced by the conservative economist Milton Friedman and his liberal counterpart James Tobin, and it has been endorsed by a wide array of economists on the left and right. More recently, the idea has been picked up by a growing number of Silicon Valley entrepreneurs who see it as the most effective way to combat poverty.[27]

Besides its obvious impact on poverty, a negative income tax would have numerous other benefits. It would provide a mechanism to pay those who perform essential nonpaid work, such as raising children or taking care of sick relatives. Such a guaranteed minimum income could also function as low-cost seed capital by giving people enough money to cover the bills while they develop and launch new businesses.[28] This type of income redistribution could ultimately help limit inequality and boost economic growth, as we saw in Chapter 5.

A negative income tax, combined with a geographically indexed minimum wage and other measures I have outlined here, can begin to form the broad architecture of a new social safety net that can help to mitigate the inequities of the urbanized knowledge economy. Still, it is important to remember that there are long lags between the emergence of new economic structures and systems and the social welfare institutions and policies that are needed to reduce their inequities and enable the development of a broad middle class. It took the better part of a century, from the mid-nineteenth century to the mid-twentieth, to develop the old social safety net of the industrial age. That safety net, which was put in place at the time of the New Deal to address the inequities of the old industrial economy, is not up to the challenges of winner-take-all urbanism, geographic inequality, and concentrated urban and suburban poverty. It is time to put a new social safety net in place that can address the worsening inequities of today's urbanized capitalism.

LEAD A GLOBAL EFFORT TO BUILD PROSPEROUS CITIES

Although we may lack the political will, America has the economic resources to pursue these first five pillars. But as we have seen, the New Urban Crisis does not simply end at America's borders; it also affects a billion or more people in the rapidly urbanizing cities of the developing world, where its problems are often amplified. Historically, our urban policy has had a largely domestic focus, but it is time for it to take on a more global dimension. The sixth pillar is for the United States to lead a broader global effort to build stronger, more resilient cities in rapidly urbanizing parts of the world.

America has much to gain from linking a comprehensive urban policy to its foreign and international development policies. From a purely selfish point of view, building stronger cities around the world with a larger middle class would open up new markets for American businesses. More importantly, developing stronger and more resilient cities in chronically unstable parts of the world would help further key diplomatic, military, and humanitarian goals, such as fighting against terrorism and the burgeoning refugee crisis.

Not only do more stable cities lead to greater economic development and rising living standards, but they are the key to creating a safer, more tolerant, and less violent world. Indeed, the failed states that are the breeding grounds for global terrorism are among the least urbanized places in the world.[29] And military intervention, by its very nature, tends to damage and destroy large cities and disperse populations, leading to a vicious cycle of less urbanization and greater instability. Building stronger cities in these fragile and broken places will make the world more secure.

The United States should also consider underwriting and assisting in the development of refugee cities that could take advantage of the skills and talents of the displaced. This would be a more effective way to address the worldwide refugee crisis than what we are doing now—providing aid for woefully inadequate refugee camps—and it would also be less expensive and enable people to stay closer to home, where they would prefer to be.[30]

There is much to be gained from shifting the focus of America's foreign and international development policies from nation-building to city-building. Helping developing nations create denser, cleaner, more energy-efficient, and more productive cities will help mitigate poverty, enhance global stability, and create a stronger global middle class. It will contribute to America's soft power by establishing critical new relationships with the mayors and other urban leaders who steward the increasingly important power centers of the global economy.

EMPOWER CITIES AND COMMUNITIES

For most of the time that I was writing this book, I envisioned a new Democratic administration that would undertake the deep and sustained investments that are required to usher in this new urbanism for all. In earlier versions, I made a sweeping case for transforming and expanding the Department of Housing and Urban Development into a broader Department of Cities and Urban Development that could coordinate the wide range of existing and future federal initiatives that have a bearing on cities and urban regions. I developed a detailed proposal for a new Council of Cities, comparable to the National Security Council or the Council of Economic Advisers, to advise the president on issues of urban policy. I argued for a new partnership between the national government and the cities in which federal investments would flow to mayors and local officials who know best how to use those funds to strengthen their economies and address their unique problems and challenges.

Then the unthinkable happened, and Donald Trump was elected president. Nothing remotely like what I envisioned and hoped for is likely to happen now with Trump in office and the

Republicans in control of both houses of Congress. We may see some of the investment in infrastructure that Trump promised during his campaign, but that is more likely to be random spending on roads and bridges than the strategic expenditures on transit, energy efficiency, and affordable housing that are required for a more sustainable and inclusive urbanism. Local governments, foundations, and nonprofit organizations will have their hands full trying to fill in the gaps as the Republican majority inevitably cuts back the already meager federal spending on transit, affordable housing, and social services.

If Trump really does build his border wall and make good on his promise to keep out immigrants, he may well undermine the very font of energy and diversity that built America in the first place, shifting new clusters of talent and innovation to other cities in other nations. The geographical and cultural divides that the New Urban Crisis has etched into our landscape are deep, and some may be permanently unbridgeable. And our newly elected government will only make them worse.

When it comes to broad urban policy and investment, the United States will fall further behind other nations. Canada's Liberal government is working to connect infrastructure investment to city-building and is developing a new strategy for affordable housing and urban development (involving me and other leading urbanists). Australia's conservative leadership created a new minister of cities and the built environment to coordinate urban development at the national level.

However, even with a Trump victory and Republican control of the federal government, there are still things that can be accomplished. The most important thing we can do is to help cities and communities get the increased control they need to build their economies and address the challenges of the New Urban Crisis. The United Kingdom is making headway here, forging a new partnership between cities and the national government that is backed by leaders on both the right and the left, including former prime minister David Cameron and former Labour Party leader Ed Miliband, who has also called for creating a new Senate of Cities. In

2015, a blue-ribbon panel of British business leaders, policymakers, economists, and urbanists outlined four key steps to empower cities, including shifting decision-making authority from the national government to cities and metropolitan areas; giving cities greater tax and fiscal authority; placing city leaders on national representative bodies and giving them a permanent seat on the national cabinet; and creating new mechanisms to coordinate major investments in infrastructure, talent, and economic development across metro areas.[31]

It is time for American mayors and community leaders to press for a similar devolution of power that will enable them to better steward and govern their own communities and address their own unique sets of problems as they see fit. Such a strategy recognizes both the advantages that come from local innovation and problem solving and the substantial variation in local capabilities and needs.

Indeed, the geographic divides that separate cities, suburbs, and rural places may already be too deep for a national consensus around urban issues. And, no top-down, one-size-fits-all strategy can address the very different needs and desires of those who live in the dense, expensive, blue-state cities and urban areas and those who live in more sprawling, car-oriented, red-state locations. Cities, suburbs, exurbs, and rural towns are very different kinds of places with very different needs. Just as the minimum wage should be geographically indexed to local costs and conditions, urban policies are best tailored to local conditions and local needs. When it comes to infrastructure, for example, dense cities and metros need transit; more spread-out places need better roads and bridges. Empowering cities, suburbs, and communities of all kinds to better address their own needs and solve their own problems is the seventh pillar of a new urban agenda.

Local officials tend to be more pragmatic than partisan. When I travel across the country, I can hardly tell whether the mayors and local leaders I meet with are Republicans, Democrats, or independents: their economic and community development agendas are driven by local needs rather than partisan ideology. The local level can best understand its own economic conditions and social needs and is best positioned to constructively address them. As the political scientist, Benjamin Barber, author of *If Mayors Ruled the World*, points out, this can be done by enabling cities and local governments to keep more of the tax revenues they ship off to the federal government.[32]

A bipartisan movement of mayors calling for this is likely to find many allies in Washington, on both sides of the aisle. America has a huge institutional advantage in its historically flexible system of federalism, which can balance and rebalance power among the federal government, states, and cities. During the New Deal, Franklin D. Roosevelt forged a new kind of partnership between the federal government and the cities. It's time to do so again, but this time to tip the balance of power toward local empowerment and control.

The present moment affords a real opportunity to recast urban governance in ways that enable local leaders to more effectively tackle the challenges and problems facing urban and metropolitan areas. Some issues require broader coverage than can be provided by our existing system of fragmented municipal governments. In these cases, the scope of authority and span of control can be tailored to the scale of the issue at hand. Transit and transportation investments, for example, could be overseen by the networks of cities and suburbs that make up metropolitan areas, or even the groups of metropolitan areas that make up mega-regions.

If mayors and local leaders seize the initiative and press hard for such a devolution of power today, they will be in an even stronger position when the pendulum swings back in the other direction and America is once again ready to invest in rebuilding its cities and suburbs.

I can't tell you how depressing it's been for me to contemplate a future in which the affordable housing and transit that we so badly need do not get built, where the causes of concentrated poverty remain unaddressed, and where our socioeconomic classes harden into castes. But then I remembered what I have learned from the great cycles of urban decline and rebirth that I have witnessed over the course of my life. This is not the first time the nation-state has turned its back on cities. Despite everything that has happened over the long sweep of history, cities remain our greatest engines of innovation, economic growth, diversity, tolerance, and social progress. They will continue to shape the forward march of civilization.

The New Urban Crisis is a historical watershed. How we respond to it will determine whether our cities, suburbs, and nation will successfully forge a new era of sustainable and inclusive prosperity, or fall victim to our growing inequities and divides.

One thing is certain: if we do nothing, today's urban crisis will only worsen and deepen. The gap between the winners of winner-take-all urbanism and the rest will widen. Our superstar cities and tech hubs will become so expensive that they will turn into gilded and gated communities, their innovative and creative sparks will eventually fade, and they will price out the essential service workers needed to keep their economies running. Older industrial cities will have less of a chance for revival. Sunbelt cities will continue to delude themselves that sprawl equals growth. Our suburbs will grow poorer, more economically distressed, and more unequal. More middle-class neighborhoods will disappear, and our nation will further divide into walled-off enclaves for the rich and larger and larger areas of urban and suburban decay. The poor and disadvantaged will be trapped into ever-expanding areas of concentrated economic and social distress. The rapidly urbanizing cities of the world will experience even more urbanization without growth, and as many as a billion or more new urbanites will remain trapped in slums, squalor, and chronic poverty.

We will not put our economy back on track; we will not spur a new round of innovation; we will not generate the jobs and economic opportunity we need; and we will not close our worsening economic divides, unless and until we come to grips with the New Urban Crisis—the central crisis of our time.

I remain cautiously and realistically optimistic that we can solve this crisis for a basic reason. Despite the backlash that put

Donald Trump in office, our cities remain our best vehicles for identifying and solving our deepest social and economic problems. Even as the urban revival has wrought these challenges, it also makes it much harder to sweep them under the proverbial rug. For most of the twentieth century, the affluent could wall themselves off in pristine suburbs, commuting in air-conditioned trains or in their own cars to their protected office towers. Today, all of our urban dysfunctions are out in plain view. Even as parts of our cities become colonized by the affluent and the educated, those cities remain diverse by ethnicity, race, and class. Mayors, urban leaders, and city residents are being forced to confront their cities' economic and social problems and the conflicts they bring.

Ultimately, the only way forward for our economy and society is more, not less, urbanism. Our clustering together in communities has driven each step of human progress. Now more than ever, we have the basic logic of urban-led growth on our side. Yet, history does not always progress in a simple linear fashion. We may move backward before we can go forward again. There are typically long lags between the emergence of a new economic order and the establishment of institutions and policies that stabilize them and spread their benefits to larger segments of the population. Our last great golden age—the rise of the large middle class during the 1950s—was the culmination of a century's worth of effort and struggle after the initial rise of industrial capitalism. Ultimately, the path to renewed economic progress and prosperity will turn on our cities and the rise of a better, more inclusive urbanism.

Such a new and better urbanism is indeed possible, but it won't create itself. Do we want the divides and contradictions of winner-take-all urbanism, or the promise of a fuller and fairer urbanism for all?

This is the defining issue—and struggle—of our time.

EPILOGUE TO THE
PAPERBACK EDITION

A colleague who heard me speak shortly after *The New Urban Crisis* was published in hardcover approached me at a follow-up event a few months later: "You seem a lot more optimistic than you did the last time I saw you," he remarked. "What happened?" Taken aback, I hesitated for a moment before venturing an answer. Then all at once it struck me. "You're right," I blurted out. "It's because I've been traveling and visiting cities all across the US and Canada." I'd been amazed at how willing people had been to take ownership of their role in the New Urban Crisis, and how ready they were to devise new strategies to come to grips with it.[1]

Everywhere I went, I saw downtown areas and urban districts that had been transformed, not just in superstar cities like New York and San Francisco, but in places like Philadelphia, Chicago, Detroit, Houston, and Atlanta, and in smaller cities like Columbus, Indianapolis, Milwaukee, Pittsburgh, and Minneapolis–St. Paul. Walking their streets, I saw vibrant neighborhoods filled with newly repurposed loft developments, boutique hotels, art galleries, theaters, cafés, restaurants, and diverse groups of people, where two decades ago there was the legacy of urban decline. I knew well that these changes had brought new challenges, but even so, I couldn't help thinking, "Hmmm . . . this creative class thing worked."

It didn't happen by magic. It took two or more decades of hard and persistent work by a whole range of stakeholders and citizens—not just mayors and city councils, but real estate developers, universities, medical centers, chambers of commerce, economic and community development groups, neighborhood associations, and residents, all of them putting their shoulders to the wheel, determined to make their cities and neighborhoods into better, more livable places. These groups worked hard to turn their cities and neighborhoods around. Now they are ready to take the next step, to create a more sustainable kind of urbanism that spreads its benefits more broadly—what I've called an urbanism for all. Everywhere I went, I heard the same refrain: "The urban revival we hoped for has created an even bigger set of problems. We want to be part of the solution."

With this book I set out not just to outline the dimensions of the New Urban Crisis, but to shift the narrative of urban economic development. Just as *The Rise of the Creative Class* created a narrative that helped spur the myriad local actions that led to the urban revival, my objective with this book was to push the prevailing narrative about urban development toward a more inclusive paradigm—in short, to make equity a principal concern of economic development.

Now it was happening in real time, right before my eyes. As one senior economic development professional put it to me after hearing me speak, "For too long we've emphasized economic growth, and that has helped accentuate many of the problems we now face. Our profession is called economic *development*, and that's what we should emphasize—not just growth, but the full development of our people, neighborhoods, and communities." This shift will take time. Just as it took the better part of two decades to turn cities around, the shift to more inclusive urbanism will also likely take a decade or more to gather steam. But I am convinced that the shift has already begun.

After more than a year of Trump and Trumpism, I am more convinced than ever that neither the federal government nor most states will offer to help our cities and metropolitan areas. But the truth is, the past two Democratic administrations didn't help much either. If they weren't actively hostile to cities, their urban agendas were far from robust. It wasn't the federal government that created the urban revival, but cities and local actors themselves.

A more inclusive urbanism similarly depends on the actions of local city-builders—businesses, universities, labor organizations, neighborhood groups, civic activists, and residents. Although local governments must lead, they do not have the resources to underwrite inclusive prosperity. As the largest economic entities in their cities, so-called anchor institutions, which played an outsized role in urban revitalization, can also play a substantial role in ensuring that our cities and metropolitan areas are more inclusive and equitable. Typically, the term anchor institutions or anchors refers to medical centers and universities, so-called meds and eds. But real estate developers can be anchors as well, especially the companies that are creating huge new neighborhoods, such as the Hudson Yards in New York and Boston's Seaport Innovation District. While these developments risk becoming isolated pockets of wealth, amplifying inequality in their surrounding neighborhoods and alienating long-term residents, they also have the potential to foster diversity and community engagement.

Large corporations can be urban anchor institutions, too, especially leading high-tech companies, which are increasingly drawn to cities and downtown areas. At least two of the five tech corporations that together constitute the world's most valuable companies, Amazon and Google, have massive presences in urban cores. Amazon's footprint in Seattle is huge, and it will be equally so in whichever city is selected to host its second headquarters. Forty thousand people work on Amazon's campus of more than 8 million square feet (making it three times the size of the Empire State Building), which accounts for nearly 20 percent of all the office space in Seattle. While Google maintains its large suburban office complex—the "Googleplex"—in suburban Silicon Valley, it also has a major presence in New York City, where more than 3,000 employees work in the renovated Port Authority building in Chelsea. And, in early 2018, the company paid $2.4 billion for the nearby Chelsea Market, which currently houses a popular food court and market as well as offices. The company has also proposed building an estimated 870,000-square-foot tech complex in Central London for another 4,000 employees, and it is in negotiations with the city of San Jose to acquire a parcel of city-owned land around the downtown Diridon Station transit hub that would accommodate some 20,000 employees.

Sadly, those tech companies do not see themselves as urban anchor institutions, but as mobile actors that can extract value from places and then move on. Amazon's auction for its second headquarters, which has pitted more than one hundred communities against each other in a contest to see who can give the most away, is perhaps the most blatant and disturbing example of this kind of extractive orientation. I've spoken and written about it. In January 2018, I even led an open letter, signed by more than 10,000 citizens and 100 or so leading urbanists and economists, urging the political leaders of the finalist cities for Amazon's second headquarters to stop throwing large amounts of tax incentives at Amazon. Rather than subsidize one of the biggest, fastest growing, and most successful large corporations in the world, the letter noted, cities should instead compete on their merits.

Indeed, it is instructive to compare Amazon's piece contrasting its behavior toward its hometown of Seattle to the way the Prudential insurance company has stuck with and invested in my childhood hometown of Newark, New Jersey.[2] Founded in Newark in 1875 as the Widows and Orphans Friendly Society, Prudential stayed in Newark when my family and many others moved out to the suburbs in the early 1960s. The company remained even after the city exploded into riots a few years later. It was there when the factory where my father worked, Victory Optical, in Newark's Ironbound Section, was shuttered, a victim of deindustrialization. It stayed when Newark's political leaders were indicted and jailed on corruption charges. And it was there in the early 1980s, when I went to work as a summer intern for the Newark office of the Department of Housing and Urban Development, which was located in the Gateway Towers adjacent to Prudential's old headquarters building.

Prudential didn't just stay in Newark, but actively invested in it. Back in the Great Depression, Prudential invested in affordable housing. In 1976, when Newark was at its nadir, Prudential launched a multibillion-dollar program to work with public, private, and nonprofit partners to promote financial and social mobility for underserved populations, concentrating on housing, health, energy, and jobs. One of the very few professional people I got to meet as a boy growing up in the blue-collar suburb of North Arlington was an executive at Prudential. He started dating, and later married, the daughter of our next-door neighbors, Ernie and Eleanor Fetti. Eleanor worked in the Hahne and Company department store in Newark and would sometimes take the bus into the city with my mother, also named Eleanor, who worked in the advertising department of the *Newark Star-Ledger*. For my parents, my relatives, and their circle of friends, "The Pru," as they called it, seemed to be the one small ray of hope left for their hometown.

In the late 1990s, when I was spending a sabbatical year at Harvard and the Massachusetts Institute of Technology, a very plugged-in colleague told me about Amazon, a pioneering "dot .com" where you could buy books online. Before Amazon came to be, I had spent hours in local bookstores to build my library on urbanism. With Amazon, I could search for the latest books or even find rare, out-of-print volumes with just the click of a mouse. When I was researching and writing *The Rise of the Creative Class*, Amazon seemed the very paragon of a creative "new economy" company. Its original headquarters was housed in a repurposed hospital building in downtown Seattle, a place teeming with bike lanes and coffee bars. Later it moved to the city's South Lake Union District, the epitome of urban corporate cool.

Seattle's new urban crisis of mounting inequality, increasingly unaffordable housing, and relentless congestion are markedly different from Newark's old urban crisis, but it threatens the city's future just the same. Seattle's problems have been exacerbated by Amazon's stratospheric growth, and the company could, and probably should, play a role in solving them, instead of just looking for another place to grow. Amazon's second headquarters may eventually ease some of the pressure on Seattle's housing market and transportation systems, but it will not absolve the company

THE NEW URBAN CRISIS

of its ethical responsibility to invest in a better Seattle. And it will almost certainly bring the same kinds of problems to its new city that Seattle is struggling with now. It is essential for Amazon to remember that cities are not just platforms for doing business. Their unique attributes are critical to the growth and success of Amazon and other businesses.

Prudential understood this about Newark—even in an era when many people questioned whether cities had lost their core economic functions. And the company still understands it today. In 2017, Prudential opened a new twenty-story tower in the city's reviving downtown. It helped to restore the long-abandoned Hahne building, where Mrs. Fetti used to work and where my family once bought our clothes. The landmark building will house apartments—a significant share of them priced for affordability—as well as a Whole Foods Market, bookstore, destination restaurant, and facilities for my alma mater, Rutgers University. When it comes to the importance of place and community, there is a lot that Amazon can learn from the company that stayed and helped to rebuild its hometown when most everybody else chose to move away.

Anchor institutions have been key drivers of both the urban revival and the New Urban Crisis. But, they can, and should, be part of the solution. Indeed, there is a great deal they can do to support the agenda I outline in Chapter 10—in particular, by acting in three specific areas.[3]

The first is housing. Already, cities across the country and the world are using inclusionary zoning to require real estate developers to build affordable as well as luxury housing. Mayor Bill de Blasio of New York has made affordable housing a focus of his administration, pledging to build and preserve 200,000 housing units over the next ten years. Seattle's Housing Affordability and Livability Agenda (HALA) aims to build 20,000 affordable units for low- and moderate-income residents in the coming decade as part of a larger equity strategy.

But anchor institutions can and should do more. Universities like New York University and Stanford University, for instance, have long provided subsidized housing for their faculties, either by constructing it themselves or providing mortgage assistance and rental supplements to access private housing. But providing housing to well-paid faculty contributes to deepening urban inequality. As part of a larger move towards more inclusive development, universities, medical centers, and other urban anchors should provide workforce housing to their service workers and engage in broader partnerships to provide affordable housing to neighborhood residents. In partnership with Johns Hopkins University, the East Baltimore Development Initiative, for example, has constructed housing for lower-income families and seniors as well as graduate students in Eager Park. The Weinland Park Collaborative in Columbus, Ohio, enlisted the help of local anchor institutions to offer $3,000 in down-payment assistance to Ohio State University employees who purchased homes in the University District. In West Philadelphia, the University of Pennsylvania, Drexel University, and the University City Science Center have undertaken substantial efforts to create affordable housing for neighborhood residents and university workers, as well as faculty and staff, while investing in other community assets. The University of Pennsylvania has developed a housing assistance program that offers employees forgivable loans and mortgage financing options with discounted closing costs. Together, the West Philadelphia Initiatives (WPIs) have also focused on supporting local businesses, engaging in commercial development, and investing in public education by launching a new neighborhood-based public K-8 school. These efforts appear to have significantly improved the West Philadelphia neighborhood from 1990 to 2010 without spurring gentrification, according to a recent study.[4]

High-tech companies and real estate developers can also provide workforce housing for their service workers and affordable housing for neighborhood residents. In Seattle, Amazon has offered to donate 47,000 square feet of office space to house more than 200 members of the city's homeless population each night. That should just be the beginning. Cities and local governments should mandate the inclusion of workforce and affordable housing in development projects.

The second area where anchors have a role to play is in upgrading low-wage service jobs into viable middle-class careers. Large high-tech companies are some of the biggest employers in their communities, and they are world leaders when it comes to retaining and motivating knowledge workers—not only through their high salaries, but also by offering perks like food, recreational amenities, spaces to relax and convene, and on-site day-care centers and health-care resources. But these companies also employ large numbers of low-wage service workers, and contract work out to thousands upon thousands more, who do not receive comparable benefits, if any. Instead of contracting out this work, the SAS Institute in North Carolina's Research Triangle hires its cafeteria workers and groundskeepers directly, providing them with jobs that have the potential to become family-supporting careers. By nurturing relationships between its developers, customers, creative workers, and support staff, SAS has managed to limit its turnover rate to between 2 and 5 percent.[5] It's time for big tech companies to swear off the use of low-paid contract labor and commit to paying all of their workers family-supporting wages.

Real estate developers can also play a role here by choosing tenants strategically. Instead of slotting the trendiest retail boutique or hippest café into their new developments, they can select corporate and commercial tenants who treat their service workers fairly, pay them a living wage, and involve them in job upgrading.

Anchor institutions can also make sustained investments in community assets. Instead of setting up self-contained, gated campuses for themselves or shuttling their workers in private buses, they should invest alongside communities to develop shared public goods like transit, schools, parks, and more. When real estate developers profit from building near public parks and open spaces, they should make contributions to ensure that the entire community benefits. Sharing even a small fraction of the tremendous profits created by locating next to public assets can make an enormous difference. The High Line park in New York has, for example, been a magnet for high-end development. Now its leaders are pushing to make it a model for more inclusive development by establishing mentorship programs and encouraging local businesses to employ neighborhood residents.

As some of the biggest stakeholders in our cities, anchor institutions have a lot to contribute and a lot to gain from inclusive development—and they have the most to lose from local backlash. Local governments and city leaders should work to organize and activate them, perhaps holding them to an "anchors' pledge" to provide affordable and workforce housing, upgrade low-wage service jobs, and invest in public goods. They should also utilize community benefits agreements to codify a clear set of objectives and standards that urban anchor institutions must meet in these three areas.[6]

E ven as we pursue this agenda in the short term, we must also look ahead to the long-term goal of giving cities and their leaders the power to solve their own problems. The key is to devolve economic and fiscal power from the federal to the local level of government. One-size-fits-all strategies simply cannot meet the demands of a nation as geographically, culturally, and economically divided as ours has become, and whose economic policies, including those needed to spur a more inclusive prosperity, work best when tailored to local conditions. As I've traveled the country talking about the New Urban Crisis, I've grown even more convinced of the need to devolve power to our cities.

Toward the end of this book, I cited Benjamin Barber's call to empower and enable cities. Barber, who died in early 2017, was one of our sharpest and most prescient political thinkers. In his classic 1992 *Atlantic* essay "Jihad vs. McWorld," he anticipated both the immiserating effects of corporate globalism and the rise of backlash populism. His later book, *If Mayors Ruled the World*, and his final book, *Cool Cities*, proposed that global cities were our last great hope for progressive and democratic governance.[7] Today, Barber's Global Parliament of Mayors, which he founded in 2016, promotes collective urban decision-making across national borders, addressing critical issues such as climate change, refugee crises, pandemic disease, inequality, and terrorism.[8]

In my last conversation with Barber, he told me that cities were not just the locus of civil resistance in the Trump era, but an institutional counterbalance to national authority. "There is an institutional and constitutional haven for resistance, defined by cities, which have resources, money, citizens, and the power to do something," he said, adding: "It's the confrontation of power with power—of national power with urban power." When I asked him what would happen if Trump followed through on his pledge to withhold federal subsidies from sanctuary cities, Barber offered a truly radical urbanist idea: "If that happens, cities ought to begin to withhold their taxes."

This may seem like an extremist vision, but, fascinatingly enough, similar arguments for a devolution of power are being made on the right. In his book *The Fractured Republic*, Yuval Levin of *The National Review* argued for subsidiarity, the basic notion—which incidentally originated with the Catholic Church—that political, social, and economic issues are best handled at the local level.[9]

More than two decades ago, the economist Alice Rivlin of the Brookings Institution made a powerful case for devolving education, housing, transportation, social services, and economic development programs from the national government to the states, whose leaders, she said, were closest to the conditions on the ground.[10] Today, as conservative national and state governments increasingly clash with progressive cities, a better case can be made for devolving their power even further.

This is backed by a massive amount of research from the Organisation for Economic Co-operation and Development (OECD), whose members are the world's thirty-five most highly-developed countries, showing that decentralized local government is more effective and efficient than centralized control.[11] Indeed, the local level—not the nation-state—is our most powerful source of innovation, economic growth, and social progress.

Back in the early 1990s, when so many business and policy pundits were touting the superiority of Japanese and Korean economic and industrial policies, one of my Asian graduate students at the time set me straight. "That sort of top-down industrial policy works great when you make the right calls, but when you don't, it fails," he told me. "In the US, you have hundreds if not thousands of local economic policies that act to spur competition and innovation."

While top-down national governance tends to impose one set of choices on all of us, localism respects our differences and allows people to choose the kinds of communities that reflect their values. A half-century ago, the economist Charles Tiebout argued that "we vote with our feet," essentially selecting the communities that best serve our wants and needs.[12]

Competition between places for people, business, and investment keeps things honest. Local autonomy allows people to choose the kinds of communities that reflect their values. Local government and local governance are also more democratic than their centralized counterparts, according to Jenna Bednar, a political theorist at the University of Michigan, whose research focuses on the political effectiveness of decentralization.[13]

When it comes to local politics, there is generally a greater willingness to reach across the aisle in the name of reason. Mayors are pragmatic, not partisan or ideological. Their policies are a reflection of what they feel will best serve the needs of local residents. It's little wonder that local government has emerged as a grounding political force at a time when trust in the federal government has reached a historic low. Between 66 percent and 75 percent of Americans express trust in their local government, compared to just 55 to 65 percent for state governments and around 20 to 33 percent for the federal government, according to surveys by Pew and Gallup.[14]

Still, some argue that devolution would worsen our existing divides by consolidating economic advantage in already-advantaged places. But devolution will give places the resources they need to invest in and magnify their competitive strengths. According to the foremost students of the subject, it will encourage specialization and competition that will ultimately lead to more of a race to the top than the bottom.[15]

Indeed, the devolution of power is more likely over time to favor more progressive outcomes. History has shown that local policies are the ones that generate forward movement on a myriad of social issues, pioneering rights for women, minorities, gays and lesbians, and other groups long before such changes were ratified by the federal government.[16]

Another criticism of devolution is that it can place too much power in the hands of mayors and local leaders, who may be ineffective, dysfunctional, or corrupt. Perhaps the classic example is former Toronto mayor Rob Ford, whose anti-urban agenda and Trump-like vendetta against downtown liberals and elites resulted in a seriously dysfunctional municipal government. I can live with that. Unlike Donald Trump, Rob Ford didn't have access to the nuclear codes.

Why would a country of 350-million-plus people, 50 states, 350-plus metro areas, 3,000-plus counties, and thousands and thousands of cities and communities choose to vest so much power in one person and one office? If there was any doubt about it before, we now know for certain that our current governance system, with its concentration of humongous power in a unitary executive, is vulnerable to catastrophic failure.

Ultimately, devolution is not simply a matter of taking power from the federal government and handing it over to cities. It means making the best use of the complex vertical separation of powers between the federal, state, and local levels. It means using subsidiarity to find the best possible alignment between economic issues or policy areas and the appropriate level of government and scale of governance that is required to address it. Transit and transportation investments, for example, could be overseen by the networks of cities and suburbs that make up metropolitan areas, or even the groups of metropolitan areas that form megaregions. Housing investments, whether publicly funded or channeled through public-private partnerships, can be tailored to local conditions—detached houses and garden apartments for more spread-out places, and high-rise rentals for denser and more urban locations.

Still, some may ask: How can this possibly occur? In our

era of a strong centralized administrative state, an imperial presidency, and hyperpartisanship, with both parties thinking they can impose their solutions and strategies on the other, what set of forces could possibly enable such a devolution of power? Intellectually, you can see the possibility in the convergence of thinking by those on the left and the right. Pragmatically, you can see it in the burgeoning movement of local leaders to combat Trumpism on issues such as climate change. In the summer of 2017, the mayors of more than 250 cities representing more than 50 million Americans; 9 states, including New York, California, Washington, Connecticut, Virginia, and Massachusetts; 100 businesses; and 80 universities formed a coalition to adopt and uphold the Paris climate accords. Just as Trump has brought together the nations of Europe, he is also bringing together cities and mayors. In my lifetime as an urbanist, I have never seen anything galvanize a bipartisan coalition of cities and mayors like this.

In this kind of situation, one can even imagine a bipartisan ticket of state and local leaders emerging, not just to challenge Trump, but to address and overcome the current partisan divide. John Kasich, the Republican governor of Ohio, and John Hickenlooper, the Democratic governor of Colorado, have been working together to address pressing national problems, inspiring wishful talk among the punditry of a future bipartisan presidential ticket. One could also envision a bipartisan ticket of two mayors—a Democrat, like Mitch Landrieu of New Orleans or Eric Garcetti of Los Angeles, and a Republican, such as Mick Cornett of Oklahoma City—who could run on a platform of making America truly great by limiting and shrinking the power of the federal government while empowering local communities to do what they think is best.

While these scenarios may seem far-fetched, neither is as mind-boggling as the idea of Donald Trump becoming president. In times of discontent, political realignments can happen quickly. Local communities and their residents have ceded power to the national government for too long, and it has consistently failed to meet their needs. They need to take it back, so they can tackle the opportunities and challenges they face from the ground up.

Publishing a book, it has been said, is a little like attending your own funeral. You learn a lot about your ideas, and yourself. Getting out of the confines of your office and sharing your thoughts in public helps make them clearer. And reading reviews and engaging with critics forces you to think even more deeply about what you've written and what you wanted to say.

The best and most thoughtful reviewers actually engage with your ideas. The worst set up strawmen of their own creation and argue with them. A number of critics have suggested that this book is my *mea culpa* for getting the urban revival wrong. That's simply not so: This book is no apology. It is an extension of my life's work on the centrality of place to capitalist development. If anything, my mistake was that I sorely underestimated and underpredicted the strength, depth, velocity, and ferocity of the urban revival, and the unintended and unexpected consequences that came with it. Indeed, this book identifies and deepens our understanding of the role of urban clustering in shaping the central contradiction of late capitalism: that the very same force that drives talented people to locate and concentrate in cities, and that forms the basic engine of innovation and economic progress, also carves deep divides into our cities and society as a whole. This growing spatial inequality, in turn, creates the conditions for a populist backlash that can threaten the engine of economic advancement and perhaps even the basic norms of democracy itself.

The New Urban Crisis is not a break with my work since *The Rise of the Creative Class* but a continuation of it. Through it all, I have attempted to marry Jane Jacobs's ideas on the centrality of cities with Karl Marx's theories of class and Joseph Schumpeter's theories of creative destruction and disruptive innovation.[17] My interest in redefining Marx's basic categories of class to better reflect the new knowledge economy dates all the way back to my earliest work as an undergraduate and graduate student in the late 1970s and 1980s. During this time I was influenced by the economic sociologist Erik Olin Wright's work on new class locations, Daniel Bell's theories of postindustrialism and the rise of a new scientific, technical, and managerial class, and Peter Drucker's writing on the knowledge economy.[18] But my thinking was most strongly shaped by Marx's own theory of the role of social or collective knowledge in *The Grundrisse*, where he wrote that "nature builds no machines, no locomotives, railways, electric telegraphs, self-acting mules etc. These are products of human industry; natural material transformed into organs of the human will over nature, or of human participation in nature. They are organs of the human brain, created by the human hand; the power of knowledge, objectified. The development of fixed capital indicates to what degree general social knowledge has become a direct force of production."[19]

Building on that basic insight, *The Rise of the Creative Class* used occupational data to identify two new classes: the creative class and the service class. As I defined it, the creative class is made up of workers whose use of their intellectual or mental labor defines their relationship to the means of production. The even larger and more rapidly rising service class is engaged in the production of routine services such as food preparation, office work, retail labor, and health care. These two classes were much larger than the working class, Marx's famed proletariat of manual workers, which had shrunk to just 20 percent of the workforce, with just 6 percent engaged in direct production in factories, while agricultural workers made up less than 2 percent of the workforce. Of course, I reiterated that the fundamental division between the capitalist class, which owns, and the other classes—the traditional working class, the creative class, and the service class—all of which work, remains.

But I was not naïve about the real economic divides between these three subordinate classes. Indeed, I noted that growing divides between the creative class and the working and service classes were responsible for the mounting inequality within and between cities. In a 2003 essay in *The Washington Monthly*, I pointed to the widening gaps between knowledge-based and industrial and rural regions, and the growing pay disparities between creative-class workers and service and blue-collar workers. Cities and metro areas with the largest shares of the creative class,

I found, were the most unequal. In my book, *The Flight of the Creative Class*, I argued that overcoming this growing class divide and creating a more inclusive economy should become a focus of progressive politics.[20]

All the while, I put cities and place at the very center of my analysis. I had long been frustrated by what I saw as a limiting factor in the fields of urban planning and economic and urban geography, which tended to see place and geography simply as containers for the locations of firms, firm networks, and industrial clusters. Urban places, I wrote, were supplanting factories and industrial corporations as the basic organizing platform of knowledge-based capitalism.

Here again, my research followed a long trajectory. My earlier work during the 1980s and 1990s, undertaken with Martin Kenney, drew on Marx, Schumpeter, and the regulation school of political economy to chart the shift from older Fordist mass-production capitalism to newer emergent and alternative spatial forms, such as the geographically concentrated social structures of innovation of high-tech complexes like Silicon Valley, and the geographically organized supplier networks of Japanese capitalism, which more fully tapped and harnessed the knowledge and intelligence of their shop-floor workers.[21] Influenced by the conversation about so-called learning economies, I identified a shift from the older industrial region to a new type of learning region, organized around universities, knowledge institutions, and human capital.[22] But I did not stop there: in *The Rise of the Creative Class* I argued that place had come to supplant the factory floor as the central arena of class conflict.

The New Urban Crisis brings my work on cities and urbanism full circle. My early work as a graduate student, and later as a young professor, examined the old urban crisis of the 1960s and 1970s as an outgrowth of the broader capitalist crisis, and saw suburbs and suburban growth as re-creating the conditions for capitalist development, very much in line with the Marxist geographer David Harvey's notion of the spatial fix.[23]

Today, the urban revival has accelerated to such a point that it has become a fetter on the further growth of capitalism. The clustering and cramming of people and economic activity into small slivers of space drives real estate prices into the stratosphere, forming the land nexus that shapes the fundamental contradiction of late capitalism.

Once again, the means of production—in this case the ultra-valuable urban land on which the clustering necessary for capitalist development takes place—is in the hands of an ultra-privileged rentier class that abuses its advantages. The self-interested actions of the owners of this land—whom I dub the "New Urban Luddites"—limit further clustering and therefore further innovation and economic progress. At the same time, it shapes the growing spatial inequality, which sows the seeds of the reactionary populist backlash.

Ultimately, the New Urban Crisis is not just a crisis of cities but a crisis of the postindustrial knowledge economy writ large. We've reached a critical juncture in the historical trajectory of urbanism and capitalism. We cannot afford to abandon urbanism, which remains the engine of economic and social progress. The only way forward is to create a fairer, better, and more progressive urbanism for all of us.

APPENDIX

This Appendix provides the details for the major variables and statistical analyses used in this book, as well as the full rankings of US metros on three major indexes: the New Urban Crisis Index, the Segregation-Inequality Index, and the Overall Economic Segregation Index.

KEY INDEXES AND MEASURES

The definitions and sources for the key variables and indexes used are as follows.

Class

Creative class: The creative class is made up of workers in occupations spanning computer science and mathematics; architecture and engineering; the life, physical, and social sciences; the arts, design, music, entertainment, sports, and media; management, business, and finance; and law, health care, education, and training.

Working class: The working class consists of workers in blue-collar occupations, including factory production; extraction, installation, maintenance, and repair; production, transportation, and material moving; and construction.

Service class: The service class consists of workers in routine service jobs, including food preparation and other food-service-related occupations; building and grounds cleaning and maintenance; personal care and service; low-end sales; office and administrative support; and community and social services and protective services.

The data for the three major classes are from the US Department of Labor, Bureau of Labor Statistics (BLS), 2010.

Inequality

Income inequality: Income inequality is based on the conventional measure of the Gini coefficient and is from the US Census Bureau's American Community Survey (ACS) for 2010.

Wage inequality: This measure concerns the wage gap between creative-, working-, and service-class workers and is calculated based on the Theil index, which is a commonly used metric for measuring wage inequality.[1] The data are from the BLS's information for 2010.

Composite Inequality Index: This index combines the above measures of income and wage inequality weighted equally into a single index.

Economic Segregation

Chapter 6 employs two types of measures for economic segregation.

Specific Economic Segregation Indexes

There are seven individual indexes for specific types of economic segregation. These indexes track segregation across more than 70,000 census tracts for all US metros. Each index is calculated based on the Dissimilarity Index, which compares distribution of a selected group of people in a location with all others in that location.[2] The more evenly distributed a group is compared to the rest of the population, the lower the level of segregation. The Dissimilarity Index, D, is expressed as:

$$D = \frac{1}{2}\sum_{i=1}^{n} \left| \frac{x_i}{X} - \frac{y_i}{Y} \right|$$

where x_i is the number of individuals in our selected group in tract i, X is the number in the selected group in the metropolitan area, y_i is the number of "others" in the census tract, and Y is the corresponding number in the metropolitan area. The number of census tracts in the metropolitan area is represented by n, and D gives a value for the extent to which our selected group is differently distributed across census tracts within the metropolitan area compared to all others. D ranges from 0 to 1, where 0 denotes minimum segregation (or complete integration) and 1 reflects maximum segregation. These indexes are absolute measures of segregation, where higher values reflect higher levels of segregation. The data reflect the residential location of the various groups and are from the 2010 ACS.

Segregation of the Poor: Measures the residential segregation of households below the federally defined poverty level.

Segregation of the Wealthy: Measures the residential segregation of households with incomes of $200,000 or more.

Segregation of the Less Educated: Measures the residential segregation of adults who did not earn a high school degree.

Segregation of College Graduates: Measures the residential segregation of adults who are college graduates.

Creative-Class Segregation: Measures the residential segregation of the creative class.

Service-Class Segregation: Measures the residential segregation of the service class.

Working-Class Segregation: Measures the residential segregation of the working class.

Composite Segregation Indexes

There are also four composite indexes for broader categories of economic segregation. These are relative measures, where higher values indicate higher levels of economic segregation compared to other metros.

Income Segregation: Combines the segregation of the rich and poor into an index of overall income segregation.

Educational Segregation: Combines the measures of segregation of college graduates and segregation of the less educated (those who did not complete high school) into an index of overall educational segregation.

Occupational Segregation: Combines the measures of creative-class segregation, working-class segregation, and service-class segregation into an index of overall occupational segregation.

Overall Economic Segregation Index: Combines the seven specific economic segregation indexes, equally weighted, into a single composite index of overall economic segregation.

Other Composite Indexes

There are two broader composite indexes. These are relative measures, where higher scores reflect higher levels compared to other metros.

Segregation-Inequality Index: This index combines the Overall Economic Segregation Index with wage inequality and income inequality data to produce a composite measure of inequality and segregation. Each measure is equally weighted.

New Urban Crisis Index: This index combines four measures into an overall index: wage inequality, income inequality, the Overall Economic Segregation Index, and housing unaffordability, based on the ratio of housing costs to income. Each measure is equally weighted.

Other Variables

Other key variables used in various statistical analyses presented in the book include:

Income per capita: Average income per capita, from the ACS.

Wages: Average wages, from the BLS.

Economic output per person: Based on gross regional product per capita, from the US Department of Commerce's Bureau of Economic Analysis (BEA).

College graduates: The share of adults with a college degree or higher, from the ACS.

High-tech industry: Based on the Milken Institute's Tech-Pole Index, which compares a metro's share of high-tech industry output to the nation's as a whole.[3] The data are from the US Department of Commerce's County Business Patterns.

Specific creative-class occupations: We also break out specific subgroups of creative-class occupations, including science and technology; business and management; arts, culture, and media; and education and medical occupations, or eds and meds.

Venture capital investment: The amount of venture capital invested into high-tech startups. These data are from Thomson Reuters analyses for 2013.

Unionization: The share of the employed workers who are union members.[4]

Median housing costs: Money spent on median monthly housing costs, from the ACS.

Housing costs as a share of income: Money spent on housing costs as a share of household income, from the ACS.

Population size: Metro population, from the ACS.

Density: Population-weighted density based on distance from the city center or city hall, from US Census data.[5]

Transit: The share of the population using public transportation to get to work, from the ACS.

Drive to work alone: The share of commuters who drive to work alone, from the ACS.

Bike to work: The share of commuters who bike to work, from the ACS.

Walk to work: The share of commuters who walk to work, from the ACS.

Race and ethnicity: The share of the population that is white, black, Asian, or Hispanic, from the ACS.

Foreign-born: The percentage of the population that is foreign-born, from the ACS.

Gay and Lesbian index: A location quotient for the concentration of gay and lesbian households, from the ACS.

Liberal or conservative: We use several measures based on the votes for the Republican and Democratic candidates for president at the state and metro levels in the 2008, 2012, and 2016 elections.[6]

Appendix Table 1: Correlations for Venture Capital Investment

Variable	Correlation
High-tech industry	0.70**
Wages	0.60**
Population-weighted density	0.55**
Business and management occupations	0.52**
College grads	0.50**
Creative class	0.50**
Income per capita	0.50**
Arts, culture, and media occupations	0.47**
Foreign-born	0.46**
Gay and lesbian	0.46**
Science and tech occupations	0.44**
Innovation	0.43**
Liberal	0.41**
Density	0.38**
Bike to work	0.19*
Eds and meds occupations	-0.13
Conservative	-0.43**
Drive alone to work	-0.45**

Note: One asterisk indicates statistical significance at the 5 percent level; two indicate statistical significance at the 1 percent level.
Source: Analysis by Charlotta Mellander, based on data from Thomson Reuters, US Census, and US Department of Labor, Bureau of Labor Statistics.

Appendix Table 2: Correlations for Gentrification

Variable	Correlation with Gentrification
Wages	0.62**
Income	0.61**
Commuters who use transit	0.61**
Population	0.59**
High-tech industry	0.58**
Creative class	0.55**
Monthly housing costs	0.53**
College grads	0.51**
Gay and lesbian	0.47**
Median cost of rent	0.47**
Density	0.44**
Median price of housing	0.40**
Walk to work	0.36**
Bike to work	0.35*
Wage inequality	0.33*
Science and technology workers	0.32*
Service class	-0.18
Working class	-0.48**
Drive to work	-0.55**

Note: Gentrification is defined as a neighborhood or census tract shifting from the bottom half of the distribution of home prices in the metropolitan area to the top half between 2000 and 2007. One asterisk indicates statistical significance at the 5 percent level, two indicate statistical significance at the 1 percent level.

Source: Analysis by Charlotta Mellander, based on data from Daniel Hartley, *Gentrification and Financial Health*, Federal Reserve Bank of Cleveland, 2013, as well as the US Census and the US Department of Labor, Bureau of Labor Statistics.

Appendix Table 3: Correlations for Economic Segregation

	Segregation-Inequality Index	Overall Economic Segregation Index	Income Segregation	Educational Segregation	Occupational Segregation Index
Segregation-Inequality Index	—	0.872**	0.641**	0.842**	0.854**
Overall Economic Segregation Index	0.872**	—	0.825**	0.935**	0.946**
Income segregation	0.641**	0.825**	—	0.677**	0.649**
Educational segregation	0.842**	0.935**	0.677**	—	0.852**
Occupational Segregation Index	0.854**	0.946**	0.649**	0.852**	—
Population	0.563**	0.643**	0.525**	0.621**	0.596**
Density	0.463**	0.560**	0.438**	0.557**	0.520**
Economic output per person	0.406**	0.405**	0.268**	0.405**	0.405**
Income	0.308**	0.291**	0.159**	0.279**	0.321**
Wages	0.426**	0.456**	0.249**	0.474**	0.477**
High-tech industry	0.587**	0.619**	0.479**	0.588**	0.599**
College grads	0.536**	0.465**	0.300**	0.431**	0.495**
Creative class	0.557**	0.532**	0.352**	0.503**	0.554**
Service class	-0.043	-0.124*	-0.109*	-0.162**	-0.079
Working class	-0.446**	-0.370**	-0.175**	-0.354**	-0.426**
Share who rent	0.420**	0.386**	0.157**	0.408**	0.431**
Housing costs	0.270**	0.312**	0.100	0.362**	0.342**
Take transit to work	0.369**	0.377**	0.232**	0.337**	0.417**
Drive alone to work	-0.243**	-0.230**	0.026	-0.265**	-0.317**
Liberal	0.305**	0.319**	0.240**	0.272**	0.335**
Conservative	-0.301**	-0.313**	-0.229**	-0.268**	-0.332**
Black	0.299**	0.292**	0.304**	0.234**	0.264**
White	-0.392**	-0.434**	-0.254**	-0.479**	-0.424**
Hispanic-Latino	0.237**	0.244**	0.018	0.380**	0.236**
Asian	0.272**	0.304**	0.094	0.317**	0.362**
Foreign born	0.379**	0.380**	0.073	0.479**	0.421**
Gay and lesbian	0.470**	0.422**	0.067	0.478**	0.514**

Note: One asterisk indicates statistical significance at the 5 percent level; two indicate statistical significance at the 1 percent level.

Source: See sources for measures and variables in Appendix text.

Appendix Table 4: Metro Rankings on the New Urban Crisis Index, Segregation-Inequality Index, and Overall Economic Segregation Index

METRO	NEW URBAN CRISIS INDEX		SEGREGATION-INEQUALITY INDEX		OVERALL ECONOMIC SEGREGATION INDEX	
	Rank	Score	Rank	Score	Rank	Score
Bridgeport-Stamford-Norwalk, CT	1	0.978	1	0.988	9	0.898
Los Angeles-Long Beach-Santa Ana, CA	2	0.972	3	0.967	10	0.893
New York-Northern New Jersey-Long Island, NY-NJ-PA	3	0.967	2	0.977	11	0.889
Gainesville, FL	4	0.952	5	0.959	14	0.870
College Station-Bryan, TX	5	0.944	4	0.964	36	0.788
San Francisco-Oakland-Fremont, CA	6	0.922	9	0.920	29	0.817
Santa Barbara-Santa Maria-Goleta, CA	7	0.914	15	0.892	45	0.774
Tallahassee, FL	8	0.912	11	0.904	1	0.947
Athens-Clarke County, GA	9	0.897	10	0.916	47	0.773
San Diego-Carlsbad-San Marcos, CA	10	0.884	31	0.848	24	0.831
Fresno, CA	11	0.879	22	0.866	19	0.854
Chicago-Naperville-Joliet, IL-IN-WI	12	0.878	17	0.889	15	0.868
Trenton-Ewing, NJ	13	0.875	8	0.922	2	0.933
Miami-Fort Lauderdale-Pompano Beach, FL	14	0.875	40	0.833	39	0.786
Boston-Cambridge-Quincy, MA-NH	15	0.874	21	0.875	34	0.799
Reno-Sparks, NV	16	0.872	26	0.860	17	0.856
Boulder, CO	17	0.857	14	0.896	89	0.689
Philadelphia-Camden-Wilmington, PA-NJ-DE-MD	18	0.852	12	0.903	13	0.873
Ann Arbor, MI	19	0.847	19	0.883	8	0.902
Austin-Round Rock, TX	20	0.845	18	0.885	3	0.925
Memphis, TN-MS-AR	21	0.842	29	0.853	16	0.867
Houston-Sugar Land-Baytown, TX	22	0.841	7	0.934	7	0.903
Dallas-Fort Worth-Arlington, TX	23	0.837	13	0.897	12	0.875
Columbus, GA-AL	24	0.836	25	0.861	32	0.807

Source: Martin Prosperity Index analysis, based on data from the US Census and the US Department of Labor, Bureau of Labor Statistics.

METRO	NEW URBAN CRISIS INDEX		SEGREGATION-INEQUALITY INDEX		OVERALL ECONOMIC SEGREGATION INDEX	
	Rank	Score	Rank	Score	Rank	Score
Durham, NC	25	0.833	6	0.935	23	0.835
Charlotte-Gastonia-Concord, NC-SC	26	0.831	15	0.892	33	0.805
Denver-Aurora, CO	27	0.829	32	0.844	21	0.841
Tucson, AZ	28	0.820	30	0.852	5	0.906
Atlanta-Sandy Springs-Marietta, GA	29	0.817	44	0.815	60	0.738
Charlottesville, VA	30	0.815	24	0.863	98	0.677
San Jose-Sunnyvale-Santa Clara, CA	31	0.811	48	0.804	49	0.766
Salinas, CA	32	0.811	61	0.762	38	0.787
Macon, GA	33	0.800	35	0.837	43	0.780
New Haven-Milford, CT	34	0.799	58	0.766	58	0.741
Brownsville-Harlingen, TX	35	0.788	42	0.828	128	0.610
New Orleans-Metairie-Kenner, LA	36	0.787	56	0.779	85	0.705
Tampa-St. Petersburg-Clearwater, FL	37	0.785	71	0.742	116	0.646
Greenville, NC	38	0.784	53	0.793	129	0.609
State College, PA	39	0.783	23	0.865	51	0.762
Santa Fe, NM	40	0.781	34	0.838	95	0.681
Birmingham-Hoover, AL	41	0.780	20	0.879	25	0.830
Cleveland-Elyria-Mentor, OH	42	0.778	41	0.829	22	0.837
El Paso, TX	43	0.774	45	0.811	56	0.742
Las Cruces, NM	44	0.772	39	0.833	99	0.675
Charleston-North Charleston-Summerville, SC	45	0.770	61	0.762	61	0.737
Baltimore-Towson, MD	46	0.769	54	0.791	27	0.823
Phoenix-Mesa-Scottsdale, AZ	47	0.769	76	0.733	20	0.842
Oxnard-Thousand Oaks-Ventura, CA	48	0.759	96	0.688	97	0.679

METRO	NEW URBAN CRISIS INDEX		SEGREGATION-INEQUALITY INDEX		OVERALL ECONOMIC SEGREGATION INDEX	
	Rank	Score	Rank	Score	Rank	Score
Corpus Christi, TX	49	0.758	48	0.804	103	0.672
Columbus, OH	50	0.757	42	0.828	4	0.912
McAllen-Edinburg-Mission, TX	51	0.756	50	0.803	122	0.624
Washington-Arlington-Alexandria, DC-VA-MD-WV	52	0.754	71	0.742	25	0.830
Lubbock, TX	53	0.753	33	0.840	87	0.702
San Antonio, TX	54	0.749	27	0.858	6	0.903
Providence-New Bedford-Fall River, RI-MA	55	0.747	85	0.715	126	0.611
Greensboro-High Point, NC	56	0.733	55	0.784	45	0.774
Santa Cruz-Watsonville, CA	57	0.729	118	0.641	213	0.441
Naples-Marco Island, FL	58	0.728	98	0.678	112	0.657
Bakersfield, CA	59	0.722	106	0.667	63	0.732
Jackson, MS	60	0.721	47	0.805	41	0.784
Lexington-Fayette, KY	61	0.720	36	0.836	52	0.762
Bloomington, IN	62	0.719	78	0.730	65	0.731
Seattle-Tacoma-Bellevue, WA	63	0.718	104	0.668	67	0.727
Albany, GA	64	0.718	77	0.732	91	0.687
Milwaukee-Waukesha-West Allis, WI	65	0.716	69	0.743	54	0.749
Albuquerque, NM	66	0.713	64	0.756	80	0.715
Napa, CA	66	0.713	114	0.644	212	0.442
Sacramento-Arden-Arcade-Roseville, CA	68	0.711	122	0.634	76	0.717
Ithaca, NY	69	0.710	87	0.712	68	0.723
Cape Coral-Fort Myers, FL	70	0.709	113	0.645	172	0.521
Nashville-Davidson-Murfreesboro-Franklin, TN	71	0.704	65	0.755	28	0.821
Auburn-Opelika, AL	72	0.704	73	0.740	161	0.540

METRO	NEW URBAN CRISIS INDEX		SEGREGATION-INEQUALITY INDEX		OVERALL ECONOMIC SEGREGATION INDEX	
	Rank	Score	Rank	Score	Rank	Score
Sebastian-Vero Beach, FL	73	0.700	104	0.668	136	0.596
Orlando-Kissimmee, FL	74	0.697	132	0.608	157	0.548
Winston-Salem, NC	75	0.696	51	0.803	90	0.689
Greenville-Mauldin-Easley, SC	76	0.694	46	0.809	75	0.718
Hartford-West Hartford-East Hartford, CT	76	0.694	86	0.713	100	0.674
Lawrence, KS	78	0.692	110	0.651	189	0.493
Raleigh-Cary, NC	79	0.689	58	0.766	37	0.787
Muncie, IN	80	0.688	61	0.762	35	0.795
Akron, OH	81	0.685	70	0.743	58	0.741
Waco, TX	82	0.684	82	0.723	115	0.647
Laredo, TX	83	0.683	125	0.626	53	0.752
Fort Collins-Loveland, CO	84	0.682	111	0.649	217	0.424
Detroit-Warren-Livonia, MI	85	0.681	109	0.656	18	0.854
Chico, CA	86	0.681	135	0.599	202	0.466
Iowa City, IA	87	0.679	57	0.777	83	0.711
Mobile, AL	88	0.679	91	0.699	132	0.606
Savannah, GA	89	0.678	124	0.630	117	0.644
Columbia, SC	90	0.676	67	0.750	62	0.733
Columbia, MO	91	0.673	88	0.703	167	0.528
Augusta-Richmond County, GA-SC	92	0.671	63	0.761	84	0.710
Colorado Springs, CO	93	0.670	115	0.644	66	0.729
Indianapolis-Carmel, IN	94	0.667	81	0.725	31	0.812
Jacksonville, FL	94	0.667	127	0.623	114	0.649
Cincinnati-Middletown, OH-KY-IN	96	0.659	84	0.717	101	0.673

METRO	NEW URBAN CRISIS INDEX		SEGREGATION-INEQUALITY INDEX		OVERALL ECONOMIC SEGREGATION INDEX	
	Rank	Score	Rank	Score	Rank	Score
Morgantown, WV	97	0.655	28	0.857	108	0.665
Richmond, VA	98	0.651	120	0.637	30	0.812
Tyler, TX	99	0.647	75	0.739	133	0.602
Minneapolis-St. Paul-Bloomington, MN-WI	100	0.647	121	0.635	136	0.596
Portland-Vancouver-Beaverton, OR-WA	101	0.646	144	0.578	143	0.581
Dayton, OH	102	0.646	93	0.693	86	0.702
Midland, TX	103	0.642	37	0.836	120	0.636
Knoxville, TN	104	0.641	66	0.753	105	0.669
Pittsburgh, PA	105	0.640	51	0.803	92	0.686
Oklahoma City, OK	106	0.638	67	0.750	55	0.743
Blacksburg-Christiansburg-Radford, VA	107	0.636	80	0.727	118	0.642
Riverside-San Bernardino-Ontario, CA	107	0.636	165	0.516	103	0.672
Champaign-Urbana, IL	109	0.634	108	0.661	48	0.769
Huntsville, AL	109	0.634	38	0.834	72	0.719
Kalamazoo-Portage, MI	111	0.633	112	0.647	165	0.531
Little Rock-North Little Rock-Conway, AR	112	0.630	73	0.740	70	0.723
Tuscaloosa, AL	113	0.624	128	0.622	64	0.731
Niles-Benton Harbor, MI	114	0.616	79	0.728	141	0.586
Palm Bay-Melbourne-Titusville, FL	115	0.614	156	0.546	235	0.384
Montgomery, AL	116	0.613	115	0.644	81	0.713
Toledo, OH	116	0.613	117	0.643	71	0.721
Atlantic City-Hammonton, NJ	118	0.612	181	0.487	218	0.423
Wilmington, NC	118	0.612	150	0.561	145	0.579
Santa Rosa-Petaluma, CA	120	0.610	181	0.487	264	0.320

METRO	NEW URBAN CRISIS INDEX		SEGREGATION-INEQUALITY INDEX		OVERALL ECONOMIC SEGREGATION INDEX	
	Rank	Score	Rank	Score	Rank	Score
Brunswick, GA	121	0.607	90	0.701	110	0.661
Jackson, TN	122	0.606	133	0.606	140	0.587
Modesto, CA	123	0.605	186	0.482	234	0.387
Rochester, NY	124	0.604	107	0.663	96	0.681
Virginia Beach-Norfolk-Newport News, VA-NC	125	0.602	165	0.516	121	0.634
Port St. Lucie, FL	126	0.601	187	0.480	248	0.347
Kansas City, MO-KS	127	0.601	103	0.669	40	0.785
St. Louis, MO-IL	127	0.601	101	0.671	76	0.717
Shreveport-Bossier City, LA	129	0.596	100	0.674	107	0.667
Merced, CA	130	0.594	185	0.484	243	0.362
Salt Lake City, UT	131	0.593	144	0.578	94	0.682
Eugene-Springfield, OR	132	0.592	175	0.497	187	0.495
Corvallis, OR	133	0.586	123	0.633	205	0.453
Ames, IA	134	0.585	92	0.694	146	0.577
Lafayette, IN	135	0.584	136	0.597	124	0.616
Gainesville, GA	136	0.582	155	0.547	184	0.497
Jonesboro, AR	137	0.581	99	0.677	160	0.545
Pittsfield, MA	138	0.575	143	0.578	292	0.273
Visalia-Porterville, CA	139	0.574	190	0.469	138	0.593
Flint, MI	140	0.573	152	0.555	149	0.570
Las Vegas-Paradise, NV	141	0.572	204	0.447	78	0.717
Honolulu, HI	142	0.572	196	0.459	125	0.612
Stockton, CA	143	0.570	208	0.433	155	0.557
Madison, WI	144	0.569	141	0.581	129	0.609

METRO	NEW URBAN CRISIS INDEX		SEGREGATION-INEQUALITY INDEX		OVERALL ECONOMIC SEGREGATION INDEX	
	Rank	Score	Rank	Score	Rank	Score
Decatur, IL	145	0.569	83	0.721	151	0.568
Worcester, MA	146	0.566	153	0.555	156	0.553
Amarillo, TX	147	0.565	89	0.701	42	0.783
Hattiesburg, MS	148	0.565	129	0.617	185	0.496
Abilene, TX	149	0.563	97	0.685	69	0.723
El Centro, CA	150	0.562	203	0.448	314	0.228
Madera, CA	151	0.560	212	0.429	179	0.503
Tulsa, OK	152	0.559	119	0.640	111	0.658
Lansing-East Lansing, MI	153	0.556	139	0.581	74	0.719
Burlington-South Burlington, VT	154	0.555	193	0.463	231	0.394
Baton Rouge, LA	155	0.551	101	0.671	81	0.713
Monroe, LA	156	0.550	95	0.689	134	0.600
Louisville-Jefferson County, KY-IN	157	0.548	130	0.613	50	0.762
Norwich-New London, CT	158	0.548	171	0.504	158	0.547
Bloomington-Normal, IL	159	0.547	94	0.692	88	0.699
Fayetteville, NC	160	0.543	199	0.455	232	0.391
Chattanooga, TN-GA	161	0.541	138	0.582	199	0.472
Springfield, MA	162	0.540	173	0.500	139	0.593
Valdosta, GA	163	0.536	167	0.514	168	0.528
Boise City-Nampa, ID	164	0.535	177	0.494	206	0.449
Flagstaff, AZ	165	0.535	189	0.474	162	0.536
Buffalo-Niagara Falls, NY	166	0.533	131	0.609	93	0.682
Pueblo, CO	167	0.531	178	0.494	123	0.622
Ocean City, NJ	168	0.530	227	0.391	237	0.380

METRO	NEW URBAN CRISIS INDEX		SEGREGATION-INEQUALITY INDEX		OVERALL ECONOMIC SEGREGATION INDEX	
	Rank	Score	Rank	Score	Rank	Score
Redding, CA	169	0.529	230	0.385	295	0.268
Carson City, NV	170	0.528	159	0.532	193	0.489
Poughkeepsie-Newburgh-Middletown, NY	171	0.528	209	0.430	207	0.448
Omaha-Council Bluffs, NE-IA	172	0.526	139	0.581	56	0.742
Bowling Green, KY	173	0.518	134	0.601	170	0.523
Fayetteville-Springdale-Rogers, AR-MO	174	0.515	146	0.570	213	0.441
Provo-Orem, UT	174	0.515	210	0.429	181	0.500
Myrtle Beach-North Myrtle Beach-Conway, SC	176	0.513	207	0.440	245	0.359
Salisbury, MD	177	0.510	221	0.401	277	0.298
Manchester-Nashua, NH	178	0.507	215	0.417	238	0.378
Yuba City, CA	179	0.506	235	0.374	280	0.296
Rome, GA	180	0.500	168	0.511	342	0.140
Lakeland-Winter Haven, FL	181	0.497	213	0.424	150	0.569
South Bend-Mishawaka, IN-MI	182	0.495	169	0.510	152	0.567
Barnstable Town, MA	183	0.492	245	0.358	332	0.164
Deltona-Daytona Beach-Ormond Beach, FL	183	0.492	235	0.374	246	0.359
Allentown-Bethlehem-Easton, PA-NJ	185	0.488	200	0.453	165	0.531
Florence, SC	186	0.485	142	0.579	236	0.382
Grand Rapids-Wyoming, MI	187	0.483	192	0.464	126	0.611
San Luis Obispo-Paso Robles, CA	188	0.481	262	0.318	260	0.324
Rochester, MN	189	0.478	154	0.553	177	0.506
Portland-South Portland-Biddeford, ME	190	0.477	222	0.401	277	0.298
Medford, OR	191	0.476	251	0.346	266	0.317
Lake Charles, LA	192	0.476	126	0.623	201	0.467

METRO	NEW URBAN CRISIS INDEX		SEGREGATION-INEQUALITY INDEX		OVERALL ECONOMIC SEGREGATION INDEX	
	Rank	Score	Rank	Score	Rank	Score
Rapid City, SD	192	0.476	184	0.485	223	0.416
Panama City-Lynn Haven, FL	194	0.470	233	0.378	182	0.499
Syracuse, NY	195	0.467	165	0.516	119	0.638
Kennewick-Pasco-Richland, WA	196	0.465	157	0.545	72	0.719
Albany-Schenectady-Troy, NY	197	0.464	176	0.497	142	0.584
Binghamton, NY	198	0.463	149	0.561	220	0.422
Gulfport-Biloxi, MS	199	0.462	210	0.429	296	0.268
Hot Springs, AR	200	0.456	195	0.460	343	0.136
Lafayette, LA	201	0.455	137	0.590	211	0.444
Spokane, WA	201	0.455	216	0.417	165	0.531
Winchester, VA-WV	203	0.453	228	0.389	297	0.267
Johnson City, TN	204	0.452	150	0.561	247	0.357
Rockford, IL	205	0.451	225	0.396	154	0.559
Roanoke, VA	206	0.448	179	0.493	135	0.597
Lincoln, NE	207	0.444	170	0.509	144	0.579
Missoula, MT	208	0.442	237	0.372	324	0.199
Springfield, IL	209	0.440	147	0.566	44	0.775
Columbus, IN	210	0.440	163	0.518	230	0.396
Wichita, KS	211	0.437	162	0.521	103	0.672
Beaumont-Port Arthur, TX	212	0.435	148	0.565	147	0.575
Prescott, AZ	213	0.433	266	0.314	305	0.254
Gadsden, AL	214	0.432	172	0.501	190	0.491
Saginaw-Saginaw Township North, MI	215	0.430	219	0.405	188	0.494
Spartanburg, SC	216	0.428	174	0.498	174	0.517

METRO	NEW URBAN CRISIS INDEX		SEGREGATION-INEQUALITY INDEX		OVERALL ECONOMIC SEGREGATION INDEX	
	Rank	Score	Rank	Score	Rank	Score
Des Moines-West Des Moines, IA	217	0.422	191	0.468	108	0.665
Rocky Mount, NC	218	0.422	244	0.359	244	0.361
Battle Creek, MI	219	0.421	230	0.385	257	0.329
Dothan, AL	220	0.416	161	0.528	267	0.315
Hanford-Corcoran, CA	221	0.416	270	0.296	106	0.668
Odessa, TX	222	0.414	158	0.545	203	0.465
Palm Coast, FL	223	0.414	297	0.239	304	0.259
Killeen-Temple-Fort Hood, TX	224	0.413	226	0.393	226	0.411
Canton-Massillon, OH	225	0.410	198	0.456	163	0.532
San Angelo, TX	226	0.409	183	0.487	153	0.566
Alexandria, LA	227	0.408	188	0.476	241	0.364
Punta Gorda, FL	228	0.406	278	0.286	340	0.143
Pensacola-Ferry Pass-Brent, FL	229	0.403	269	0.299	254	0.332
Vallejo-Fairfield, CA	230	0.403	311	0.217	268	0.314
Charleston, WV	231	0.400	160	0.530	131	0.608
Greeley, CO	232	0.393	283	0.275	113	0.655
Fort Wayne, IN	233	0.390	180	0.489	79	0.716
Kingston, NY	234	0.388	299	0.234	307	0.248
Burlington, NC	235	0.384	240	0.367	225	0.412
Harrisonburg, VA	236	0.382	246	0.355	297	0.267
Wichita Falls, TX	237	0.381	201	0.451	197	0.480
Erie, PA	238	0.379	216	0.417	222	0.419
Sioux Falls, SD	239	0.377	202	0.448	200	0.469
Huntington-Ashland, WV-KY-OH	240	0.374	194	0.462	309	0.243

252

METRO	NEW URBAN CRISIS INDEX		SEGREGATION-INEQUALITY INDEX		OVERALL ECONOMIC SEGREGATION INDEX	
	Rank	Score	Rank	Score	Rank	Score
Ocala, FL	241	0.373	290	0.254	318	0.214
Yakima, WA	242	0.370	267	0.307	170	0.523
Bellingham, WA	243	0.368	303	0.230	311	0.234
Coeur d'Alene, ID	244	0.366	291	0.252	354	0.097
Muskegon-Norton Shores, MI	245	0.365	282	0.276	233	0.388
Asheville, NC	246	0.363	248	0.353	274	0.302
Salem, OR	247	0.362	312	0.216	251	0.337
Springfield, MO	248	0.360	241	0.366	208	0.448
Davenport-Moline-Rock Island, IA-IL	249	0.359	206	0.440	239	0.377
Lynchburg, VA	249	0.359	218	0.415	192	0.489
Harrisburg-Carlisle, PA	251	0.358	224	0.398	169	0.524
Bend, OR	252	0.355	328	0.176	321	0.208
Fargo, ND-MN	253	0.352	219	0.405	319	0.213
Lima, OH	254	0.352	236	0.373	185	0.496
Anderson, SC	255	0.351	214	0.422	249	0.343
Sandusky, OH	256	0.349	251	0.346	317	0.218
Peoria, IL	257	0.346	205	0.443	178	0.504
Wheeling, WV-OH	257	0.346	196	0.459	271	0.311
Anchorage, AK	259	0.344	273	0.292	216	0.425
Scranton-Wilkes-Barre, PA	260	0.343	250	0.348	258	0.328
Youngstown-Warren-Boardman, OH-PA	261	0.339	242	0.364	180	0.501
Jacksonville, NC	262	0.338	321	0.164	262	0.322
Bremerton-Silverdale, WA	263	0.334	321	0.189	293	0.271
Holland-Grand Haven, MI	263	0.334	275	0.292	290	0.279

METRO	NEW URBAN CRISIS INDEX		SEGREGATION-INEQUALITY INDEX		OVERALL ECONOMIC SEGREGATION INDEX	
	Rank	Score	Rank	Score	Rank	Score
Olympia, WA	265	0.333	309	0.219	283	0.288
Elmira, NY	266	0.330	223	0.400	148	0.573
Lewiston-Auburn, ME	267	0.329	322	0.188	334	0.158
Reading, PA	268	0.329	272	0.294	215	0.438
Vineland-Millville-Bridgeton, NJ	269	0.328	333	0.161	308	0.243
Clarksville, TN-KY	270	0.327	284	0.269	176	0.506
Oshkosh-Neenah, WI	271	0.327	246	0.355	256	0.330
Evansville, IN-KY	272	0.322	239	0.370	183	0.498
Warner Robins, GA	272	0.322	231	0.382	284	0.287
Ogden-Clearfield, UT	274	0.322	273	0.292	219	0.423
Topeka, KS	275	0.321	233	0.378	210	0.444
Bangor, ME	276	0.318	281	0.281	287	0.285
Hinesville-Fort Stewart, GA	277	0.317	339	0.135	281	0.294
Dalton, GA	278	0.313	260	0.322	175	0.507
Duluth, MN-WI	279	0.309	253	0.342	259	0.325
Jackson, MI	280	0.307	293	0.246	204	0.454
Logan, UT-ID	281	0.303	284	0.269	227	0.405
Grand Forks, ND-MN	282	0.303	238	0.371	323	0.201
Sumter, SC	283	0.298	276	0.290	250	0.337
Cumberland, MD-WV	284	0.298	249	0.352	339	0.147
Terre Haute, IN	285	0.296	263	0.316	220	0.422
Pine Bluff, AR	286	0.292	271	0.296	272	0.309
Grand Junction, CO	287	0.290	318	0.204	306	0.251
Pascagoula, MS	288	0.288	254	0.341	228	0.401

254

METRO	NEW URBAN CRISIS INDEX		SEGREGATION-INEQUALITY INDEX		OVERALL ECONOMIC SEGREGATION INDEX	
	Rank	Score	Rank	Score	Rank	Score
Utica-Rome, NY	289	0.287	257	0.335	198	0.476
Cheyenne, WY	290	0.284	267	0.307	252	0.334
Racine, WI	291	0.283	307	0.219	302	0.263
Anniston-Oxford, AL	292	0.283	265	0.315	288	0.285
Yuma, AZ	293	0.283	317	0.205	196	0.482
Longview, WA	294	0.281	324	0.182	261	0.323
Victoria, TX	295	0.278	243	0.361	262	0.322
Springfield, OH	296	0.274	301	0.233	195	0.482
Eau Claire, WI	297	0.271	293	0.246	327	0.188
Kokomo, IN	298	0.267	264	0.316	242	0.363
Altoona, PA	299	0.266	258	0.332	289	0.280
Longview, TX	300	0.266	255	0.338	335	0.158
Kingsport-Bristol-Bristol, TN-VA	301	0.263	259	0.331	329	0.187
Texarkana, TX-Texarkana, AR	302	0.263	261	0.320	282	0.292
Idaho Falls, ID	303	0.257	289	0.256	331	0.169
Anderson, IN	304	0.256	305	0.228	194	0.486
Houma-Bayou Cane-Thibodaux, LA	305	0.255	256	0.338	265	0.319
Kankakee-Bradley, IL	306	0.252	329	0.166	240	0.374
Dover, DE	307	0.248	337	0.139	355	0.089
Lake Havasu City-Kingman, AZ	308	0.247	353	0.097	332	0.164
Joplin, MO	309	0.242	307	0.219	325	0.195
Danville, VA	310	0.239	327	0.177	313	0.232
Hickory-Lenoir-Morganton, NC	311	0.239	302	0.231	320	0.210
Florence-Muscle Shoals, AL	312	0.237	277	0.287	336	0.155

METRO	NEW URBAN CRISIS INDEX		SEGREGATION-INEQUALITY INDEX		OVERALL ECONOMIC SEGREGATION INDEX	
	Rank	Score	Rank	Score	Rank	Score
Sioux City, IA-NE-SD	312	0.237	280	0.282	158	0.547
Green Bay, WI	314	0.237	309	0.219	269	0.314
Fairbanks, AK	315	0.235	338	0.136	291	0.277
Cedar Rapids, IA	316	0.233	279	0.286	253	0.333
St. Cloud, MN	316	0.233	316	0.206	301	0.264
Mount Vernon-Anacortes, WA	318	0.227	357	0.061	337	0.153
Pocatello, ID	318	0.227	295	0.245	273	0.307
La Crosse, WI-MN	320	0.222	292	0.247	312	0.233
Bay City, MI	321	0.219	288	0.257	352	0.113
Lancaster, PA	321	0.219	330	0.166	270	0.314
Mansfield, OH	321	0.219	298	0.237	173	0.517
Goldsboro, NC	324	0.218	326	0.181	341	0.141
Janesville, WI	325	0.218	342	0.128	275	0.299
Fort Smith, AR-OK	326	0.214	286	0.261	299	0.266
Johnstown, PA	327	0.198	287	0.258	229	0.399
Billings, MT	328	0.195	324	0.182	286	0.285
Waterloo-Cedar Falls, IA	329	0.192	300	0.234	191	0.490
Hagerstown-Martinsburg, MD-WV	330	0.190	348	0.108	350	0.116
St. George, UT	331	0.189	359	0.032	357	0.074
Danville, IL	332	0.189	314	0.208	224	0.416
Dubuque, IA	333	0.187	306	0.221	208	0.448
Monroe, MI	333	0.187	349	0.103	358	0.049
Bismarck, ND	335	0.186	296	0.243	348	0.118
York-Hanover, PA	335	0.186	344	0.119	275	0.299

METRO	NEW URBAN CRISIS INDEX		SEGREGATION-INEQUALITY INDEX		OVERALL ECONOMIC SEGREGATION INDEX	
	Rank	Score	Rank	Score	Rank	Score
Sherman-Denison, TX	337	0.184	335	0.154	351	0.115
Lawton, OK	338	0.184	332	0.162	279	0.296
Great Falls, MT	339	0.182	323	0.185	255	0.331
Michigan City-La Porte, IN	340	0.182	341	0.129	322	0.203
Parkersburg-Marietta-Vienna, WV-OH	341	0.179	303	0.230	330	0.183
Glens Falls, NY	342	0.175	354	0.095	328	0.188
Wenatchee, WA	343	0.171	351	0.101	347	0.120
Williamsport, PA	343	0.171	345	0.117	346	0.132
Elkhart-Goshen, IN	345	0.170	355	0.089	343	0.136
Elizabethtown, KY	346	0.170	336	0.150	315	0.224
Decatur, AL	347	0.168	313	0.209	302	0.263
Farmington, NM	348	0.159	315	0.206	300	0.265
Morristown, TN	348	0.159	334	0.160	353	0.099
Owensboro, KY	350	0.155	319	0.196	294	0.269
Casper, WY	351	0.152	320	0.190	345	0.133
Appleton, WI	352	0.150	343	0.127	316	0.224
Sheboygan, WI	353	0.143	346	0.114	338	0.150
Lewiston, ID-WA	354	0.129	350	0.102	356	0.075
St. Joseph, MO-KS	355	0.118	340	0.131	310	0.240
Lebanon, PA	356	0.104	347	0.111	285	0.286
Wausau, WI	357	0.101	351	0.101	349	0.117
Fond du Lac, WI	358	0.099	358	0.050	359	0.029
Jefferson City, MO	359	0.062	356	0.082	326	0.189

ACKNOWLEDGMENTS

The idea for this book came out of a conversation I had about another book I thought I wanted to write. It was the summer of 2013, and I was in New York City to discuss the ideas for that book with prospective editors and publishers. On a balmy evening, I sat down in the lounge of SoHo's Crosby Hotel to chat with the team from Basic Books. As I labored to explain the re-urbanizing trend I was seeing, Lara Heimert, Basic's publisher, interrupted me: "What you're talking about is a New Urban Crisis. Write *that* book." She was right, of course. Almost before I knew it, I was busily working away.

But first, I needed to retool myself. My earliest research was in housing and urban affairs, but I had spent the bulk of my career focusing on the factors underpinning urban and regional innovation and economic growth. For this book, I would need to take a deep dive into the field of urban sociology—in particular, its research on urban poverty, concentrated disadvantage, and the persistent effects of neighborhoods. Working with my team at the Martin Prosperity Institute (MPI) at the University of Toronto's Rotman School of Management, I embarked on a series of research projects on the geographies of inequality and economic segregation, the myths and realities of gentrification, the geography of billionaires and the incursion of the super-rich in our cities, the extent and challenges of startup urbanism, the deep new divides crisscrossing our cities and suburbs, and the enormous challenges of global urbanization. As I plumbed the depths of the New Urban Crisis and mapped its fault lines across cities, suburbs, and entire metro areas, I realized that I was seeing a pattern that neither urban economics, with its traditional preoccupation with concentrated advantage, nor urban sociology, with its preoccupation with concentrated disadvantage, had seen in its entirety. By wedding their complementary insights, I could begin to forge a synthesis and perhaps a new way of understanding it.

ACKNOWLEDGMENTS

A massive project like this one is a group effort, and I incurred a huge heap of debts along the way. Heimert is everything an author would want in a publisher; she helped identify and hone the big idea and both pushed me and worked tirelessly beside me to ensure that my writing conveyed my ideas as clearly and straightforwardly as possible. My agent, Jim Levine, believed in this project from the start, stuck with it throughout the many stages of its evolution, and ensured that it found a perfect home.

Arthur Goldwag is a font of ideas as well as one of the very best writers and editors around. He is a terrific sounding board for my ideas who helps me set them down in writing in a clearer and sharper way. Charlotta Mellander is a statistical wiz who shaped the key indicators and statistical analyses used in the book. Brian Distelberg of Basic Books made sure the final edit was as tight and as focused as could be. Kathy Streckfus provided a detailed copyedit, and Melissa Veronesi shepherded the book through production in a timely and efficient manner.

I am especially grateful to my research team at the MPI, including several who have moved on to bigger and better things, for their work on various research projects that shaped and informed this book. Karen King served as overall project manager, supervising and organizing everything from the data and analysis to the editing and the references and the construction of maps, charts, and tables. Isabel Ritchie and Taylor Blake made the maps and aided with data analysis. Michelle Hopgood put together the graphics. Kim Silk and Ian Gormely helped pull together the source material and references. Patrick Adler, Taylor Brydges, and Zara Matheson collaborated on the original maps and analysis for the chapter on the Patchwork Metropolis.

The MPI is a fantastic place to work. Roger Martin is the reason I am at the Rotman School to begin with. Jamison Steeve, MPI's executive director, stewards the institute. Vass Bednar played a key role in steering the MPI Cities Initiative, keeping our projects on track and our budgets in order, and building our culture. Valeria Sladojevic-Sola and Quinn Davidson keep the institute running on a day-to-day basis. The late Joe Rotman and the Rotman family provided the funding that supports our work at the MPI.

Steven Pedigo, my colleague at the NYU Urban Lab and director of research for the Creative Class Group (CCG), keeps me steeped in the professional practice of urban economic development, helping to deepen my understanding of the practical implications of the issues discussed in this book for real-world communities. Reham Alexander of the CCG supports my various engagements with effortless efficiency, keeping me on track and on time no matter how far afield I roam.

ACKNOWLEDGMENTS

My *Atlantic* editorial fellows over the past couple of years—Aria Bendix, Stephanie Garlock, Sara Johnson, Aarian Marshall, and Andrew Small—have assisted me in researching and developing my posts at *CityLab*, many of which have been the starting points for the lines of inquiry I've expanded and fleshed out in these pages.

My colleagues Mark Rosenberg and Brian Shriner at Florida International University provided a great space at the Miami Beach Urban Studio for me to think and write during our breaks from the cold Canadian winter.

I am grateful to the many people who provided helpful comments and ideas on various chapters and drafts of this book—in particular, Patrick Adler, Luis Bettencourt, Boyd Cohen, Kim-Mai Cutler, Jan Doering, Melanie Fasche, Jose Lobo, Robert Manduca, Gabe Metcalfe, Seth Pinksy, Aaron Renn, Jonathan Rothwell, Rob Sampson, Pat Sharkey, Dan Silver, Greg Spencer, and Lyman Stone.

I am fortunate to have a large extended family that is the source of great comfort and joy. My deepest thanks are reserved for my wife, Rana. She is a true force of nature who helps me focus and sharpen my ideas, tells me when they sound right *or* wrong, and sweats the details of our business and life so that I can focus on projects like this one. The love of my life, she fills each and every day with her boundless energy and passion for living. In the process of writing the original edition of this book, we had our first daughter, Mila Simone. Then during the preparation of the paperback edition, we had our second, Valentina Rose. I dedicate this book to both of them.

NOTES

PREFACE

1. *Report of the National Advisory Commission on Civil Disorders* (Kerner Commission Report) (Washington, DC: US Government Printing Office, 1968); Max Herman, *Summer of Rage: An Oral History of the 1967 Newark and Detroit Riots* (Bern: Peter Lang, 2013); Kevin Mumford, *Newark: A History of Race, Rights, and Riots in America* (New York: New York University Press, 2008); Sidney Fine, *Violence in the Model City: The Cavanagh Administration, Race Relations, and the Detroit Riot of 1967* (Ann Arbor: University of Michigan Press, 1989); Thomas J. Sugrue, *The Origins of the Urban Crisis: Race and Inequality in Postwar Detroit* (Princeton, NJ: Princeton University Press, 1996).

2. Richard Florida, *The Rise of the Creative Class: And How It's Transforming Work, Leisure, Community, and Everyday Life* (New York: Basic Books, 2002); Florida, *The Rise of the Creative Class Revisited* (New York: Basic Books, 2012).

3. Thomas Piketty, *Capital in the Twenty-First Century* (Cambridge, MA: Belknap Press of Harvard University Press, 2013); Richard Florida, "The New American Dream," *Washington Monthly*, March 2003; Richard Florida, *The Flight of the Creative Class* (New York: HarperCollins, 2005).

4. Richard Florida, "More Losers Than Winners in America's New Economic Geography," *CityLab*, January 30, 2013, www.citylab.com/work/2013/01/more-losers-winners-americas-new-economic-geography/4465.

5. Joel Kotkin, "Richard Florida Concedes the Limits of the Creative Class," *Daily Beast*, March 20, 2013, www.thedailybeast.com/articles/2013/03/20/richard-florida-concedes-the-limits-of-the-creative-class.html; Richard Florida, "Did I Abandon My Creative Class Theory? Not So Fast, Joel Kotkin," *Daily Beast*, March 21, 2013, www.thedailybeast.com/articles

/2013/03/21/did-i-abandon-my-creative-class-theory-not-so-fast-joel-kotkin
.html.

6. Richard Florida, "How Rob Ford's Pride Snub Hurts the City of Toronto," *Toronto Star*, April 23, 2012, www.thestar.com/opinion/editorial
opinion/2012/04/23/how_rob_fords_pride_snub_hurts_the_city_of
_toronto.html; Richard Florida, "Toronto Needs a Muscular Mayor," *Globe
and Mail*, November 30, 2012, www.theglobeandmail.com/globe-debate
/richard-florida-toronto-needs-a-muscular-mayor/article5822048; Richard
Florida, "What Toronto Needs Now: Richard Florida Offers a Manifesto
for a New Model of Leadership," *Toronto Life*, October 22, 2012, www
.torontolife.com/informer/features/2012/10/22/what-toronto-needs-now.
See also Zack Taylor, "Who Votes for a Mayor Like Rob Ford?," *The Conversation*, November 13, 2013, http://theconversation.com/who-votes-for
-a-mayor-like-rob-ford-20193; Zack Taylor, "Who Elected Rob Ford, and
Why? An Ecological Analysis of the 2010 Toronto Election," Paper presented at the Canadian Political Science Association Conference, Waterloo,
Ontario, May 2011, www.cpsa-acsp.ca/papers-2011/Taylor.pdf.

7. The person who first identified this development is my University of
Toronto colleague J. David Hulchanski, in "The Three Cities Within Toronto: Income Polarization Among Toronto's Neighborhoods, 1970–2005,"
Cities Centre, University of Toronto, 2010, www.urbancentre.utoronto.ca
/pdfs/curp/tnrn/Three-Cities-Within-Toronto-2010-Final.pdf. See also Richard Florida, "No Longer One Toronto," *Globe and Mail*, October 22, 2010,
www.theglobeandmail.com/opinion/no-longer-one-toronto/article4329894.

CHAPTER 1: THE URBAN CONTRADICTION

1. The urban optimists include Harvard University's Edward Glaeser,
Bruce Katz of the Brookings Institution, and the political theorist Benjamin
Barber. See Edward Glaeser, *The Triumph of the City: How Our Greatest Invention Makes Us Richer, Smarter, Greener, Healthier, and Happier*
(New York: Penguin, 2011); Bruce Katz and Jennifer Bradley, *The Metropolitan Revolution: How Cities and Metros Are Fixing Our Broken Politics
and Fragile Economy* (Washington, DC: Brookings Institution Press, 2013);
Benjamin Barber, *If Mayors Ruled the World: Dysfunctional Nations, Rising Cities* (New Haven, CT: Yale University Press, 2013).

2. The pessimists include the Marxist geographer David Harvey and
urban theorist Mike Davis, among others. Harvey wrote: "None of this new
development could have occurred without massive population displacements

and dispossessions, wave after wave of creative destruction that has taken not only a physical toll but destroyed social solidarities, exaggerated social inequalities, swept aside any pretenses of democratic urban governance, and has increasingly looked to militarized police surveillance and terror as its primary mode of social regulation." See David Harvey, "The Crisis of Planetary Urbanization," Post: Notes on Modern and Contemporary Art Around the Globe, Museum of Modern Art, November 18, 2014, http://post.at.moma.org/content_items/520-the-crisis-of-planetary-urbanization; Mike Davis, *Planet of Slums* (New York: Verso, 2006).

3. I was especially influenced by the work of Robert Sampson and Patrick Sharkey. See Robert J. Sampson, *Great American City: Chicago and the Enduring Neighborhood Effect* (Chicago: University of Chicago Press, 2012); Patrick Sharkey, *Stuck in Place: Urban Neighborhoods and the End of Progress Toward Racial Equality* (Chicago: University of Chicago Press, 2013). Some of the key research studies by my team that inform this book include: Richard Florida and Charlotta Mellander, "The Geography of Inequality: Difference and Determinants of Wage and Income Inequality across US Metros," *Regional Studies* 50, no. 1 (2014): 1–14; Richard Florida, Zara Matheson, Patrick Adler, and Taylor Brydges, *The Divided City and the Shape of the New Metropolis* (Toronto: Martin Prosperity Institute, Rotman School of Management, University of Toronto, 2015), http://martinprosperity.org/media/Divided-City.pdf; Richard Florida and Charlotta Mellander, *Segregated City: The Geography of Economic Segregation in America's Metros* (Toronto: Martin Prosperity Institute, Rotman School of Management, University of Toronto, 2016), http://martinprosperity.org/media/Segregated%20City.pdf.

4. In the 1970s, one of my Rutgers professors likened America's urban centers to veritable "sandboxes," where the poor minorities who were left in them were pacified and distracted by programs that were underwritten by federal transfer payments. See George Sternlieb, "The City as Sandbox," *National Affairs*, no. 25 (Fall 1971): 14–21, www.nationalaffairs.com/public_interest/detail/the-city-as-sandbox.

5. Richard Florida and Karen King, *Rise of the Global Startup City: The Geography of Venture Capital Investment in Cities and Metro Areas Across the Globe* (Toronto: Martin Prosperity Institute, Rotman School of Management, University of Toronto, 2016), http://martinprosperity.org/media/Rise-of-the-Global-Startup-City.pdf.

6. The phrase "plutocratization" is from Simon Kuper, "Priced Out of Paris," *Financial Times*, June 14, 2013, www.ft.com/intl/cms/s/2/a096d1do-d2ec-11e2-aac2-00144feab7de.html.

7. For the shrinking of the middle class in metropolitan areas, see Pew Research Center, *America's Shrinking Middle Class: A Close Look at Changes Within Metropolitan Areas*, May 11, 2016, www.pewsocialtrends.org /2016/05/11/americas-shrinking-middle-class-a-close-look-at-changes-within -metropolitan-areas. For the 1970–2012 figures on the share of families living in middle-class neighborhoods, see Kendra Bischoff and Sean Reardon, "The Continuing Increase in Income Segregation, 2007–2012," Stanford University, Center for Education and Policy Analysis, March 2016, https://cepa.stanford.edu/sites/default/files/the%20continuing%20increase%20 in%20income%20segregation%20march2016.pdf.

8. Elizabeth Kneebone, "The Growth and Spread of Concentrated Poverty, 2000 to 2008–2012," Brookings Institution, July 31, 2014, www .brookings.edu/research/interactives/2014/concentrated-poverty.

9. The concept of urbanization without growth is from Remi Jedwab and Dietrich Vollrath, "Urbanization Without Growth in Historical Perspective," *Explorations in Economic History* 57 (July 2015): 1–94. The data on global slums is from UN-Habitat. See UN-Habitat, *State of the World's Cities 2010/2011: Bridging the Urban Divide* (New York: Routledge, 2010), https://sustainabledevelopment.un.org/content/documents /11143016_alt.pdf, 7. Also see UN-Habitat, *Urbanization and Development: Emerging Futures*, World Cities Report 2016, http://wcr.unhabitat .org/wp-content/uploads/sites/16/2016/05/WCR-%20Full-Report-2016.pdf.

10. The mega-region figures are from Richard Florida, Charlotta Mellander, and Tim Gulden, "Global Metropolis: Assessing Economic Activity in Urban Centers Based on Nighttime Satellite Images," *Professional Geographer*, April 2012, 178–187; Richard Florida, Tim Gulden, and Charlotta Mellander, "The Rise of the Mega-Region," *Cambridge Journal of Regions, Economy and Society* 1, no. 3 (2008): 459–476. The venture capital figures are from Richard Florida and Karen King, *Venture Capital Goes Urban: Tracking Venture Capital and Startup Activity Across US Zip Codes* (Toronto: Martin Prosperity Institute, Rotman School of Management, University of Toronto, 2016), http://martinprosperity.org/media /Startup-US-2016_Venture-Capital-Goes-Urban.pdf; Richard Florida and Karen King, *The Rise of the Urban Startup Neighborhood: Mapping Micro-Clusters of Venture Capital–Based Startups* (Toronto: Martin Prosperity Institute, Rotman School of Management, University of Toronto, 2016), http://martinprosperity.org/media/Startup-US-2016_Rise-of-the-Urban -Startup-Neighborhood.pdf.

11. The concept of the urban land nexus was first advanced by the geographer Allen J. Scott in *The Urban Land Nexus and the State* (London: Pion Press, 1980). See also Allen J. Scott and Michael Storper, "The Nature of Cities: The Scope and Limits of Urban Theory," *International Journal of Urban and Regional Research* 39, no. 1 (2015): 1–15.

CHAPTER 2: WINNER-TAKE-ALL URBANISM

1. Geoff Manaugh and Kelsey Campbell-Dollaghan, "Sneak Peek of Sim-City: Cities of Tomorrow," *Gizmodo*, October 11, 2013, http://gizmodo.com /sneak-peek-of-simcity-cities-of-the-future-1443653857.

2. As far as I can tell, the phrase superstar cities was introduced in a 2013 study by economists Joseph Gyourko, Christopher Mayer, and Todd Sinai to identify US cities where housing prices consistently outpaced prices in other cities and appreciated at a rapid clip. See their article "Superstar Cities," *American Economic Journal: Economic Policy* 5, no. 4 (2013): 167–199.

3. Robert Frank and Philip J. Cook, *The Winner-Take-All Society: Why the Few at the Top Get So Much More Than the Rest of Us* (New York: Penguin, 1996); Sherwin Rosen, "The Economics of Superstars," *American Economic Review* 71, no. 5 (1981): 845–858.

4. The ratio rose to 30 to 1 in 1978, and 123 to 1 in 1995. By 2000, around the time Frank and Cook were developing their theory, it was 383 to 1, and it has hovered around 300 to 1 since the economic crisis of 2008. See Lawrence Mishel and Jessica Schieder, "Stock Market Headwinds Meant Less Generous Year for Some CEOs," Economic Policy Institute, July 12, 2016, www.epi.org/files/pdf/109799.pdf; Ric Marshall and Linda-Eling Lee, *Are CEOs Paid for Performance? Evaluating the Effectiveness of Equity Incentives*, MSCI Research Insight, July 2016, www.msci.com /documents/10199/91a7f92b-d4ba-4d29-ae5f-8022f9bb944d; Theo Francis, "Best-Paid CEOs Run Some of Worst-Performing Companies," *Wall Street Journal*, July 25, 2016, www.wsj.com/articles/best-paid-ceos-run-some-of -worst-performing-companies-1469419262. The study, not surprisingly, calls for dramatically paring back equity-based compensation.

5. My colleague Derek Thompson at *The Atlantic* refers to it as the rich-get-richer principle. See Derek Thompson, "The Richest Cities for Young People: 1980 vs. Today," *The Atlantic*, February 15, 2015, www.theatlantic .com/business/archive/2015/02/for-great-american-cities-the-rich-dont -always-get-richer/385513.

6. The Superstar City Index uses five measures: The first is Economic Power, based on economic output and economic output per capita from the Brookings Institution's *Global Metro Monitor*. See Joseph Parilla, Jesus Leal Trujillo, and Alan Berube, *Global Metro Monitor 2014: An Uncertain Recovery*, Brookings Institution, 2014, www.brookings.edu/~/media/Research /Files/Reports/2015/01/22-global-metro-monitor/bmpp_GMM_final.pdf ?la=en. The second is Financial Power, based on the Global Financial Centres Index, which measures a range of factors related to a city's banking, finance, and investment industries. See Mark Yeandle, Nick Danev, and Michael Mainelli, *The Global Financial Centres Index*, Z/Yen Group, 2014, www.zyen.com/research/gfci.html. Next is Global Competitiveness, which is based on *The Economist*'s Global City Competiveness Index, which is the third measure, and A. T. Kearney's Global Cities Index, the fourth measure. Both of these track elements of business activity, talent, and competitiveness among global cities. See Citigroup, *Hot Spots 2025: Benchmarking the Future Competitiveness of Cities*, Economist Intelligence Unit, 2013, www .citigroup.com/citi/citiforcities/pdfs/hotspots2025.pdf; Mike Hales, Erik R. Peterson, Andres Mendoza, and Johan Gott, *Global Cities, Present and Future: 2014 Global Cities Index and Emerging Cities Outlook*, AT Kearney, 2014, www.atkearney.com/research-studies/global-cities-index/full-report. The fifth measure is Quality of Life, based on the UN City Prosperity Index, which measures prosperity along five dimensions: productivity, infrastructure, quality of life, equity and social inclusion, and environmental sustainability. See UN-Habitat, *State of the World's Cities 2012/2013: Prosperity of Cities* (New York: Routledge, 2013), https://sustainabledevelopment .un.org/content/documents/745habitat.pdf.

7. Richard Florida, "The World Is Spiky," *Atlantic Monthly* (October 2005), 48–51, www.theatlantic.com/past/docs/images/issues/200510/world -is-spiky.pdf.

8. John Schoales, "Alpha Clusters: Creative Innovation in Local Economies," *Economic Development Quarterly* 20, no. 2 (2006): 162–177.

9. See, for example, Luís M. A. Bettencourt, José Lobo, Deborah Strumsky, and Geoffrey B. West, "Urban Scaling and Its Deviations: Revealing the Structure of Wealth, Innovation, and Crime Across Cities," *PLOS ONE* (November 10, 2010).

10. Richard Florida, Hugh Kelly, Steven Pedigo, and Rosemary Scanlon, *New York City: The Great Reset*, NYU School of Professional Studies, July 2015, www.pageturnpro.com/New-York-University/67081-The-Great-Reset /default.html#page/1.

11. Richard Florida, "Why Some Cities Lose When Others Win," *CityLab*, March 30, 2012, www.citylab.com/work/2012/03/why-some-cities -lose-when-others-win/1611; Aaron M. Renn, "The Great Reordering of the Urban Hierarchy," *New Geography*, March 26, 2012, www.newgeography .com/content/002745-the-great-reordering-urban-hierarchy.

12. These data are from Zillow's Research Data site, www.zillow.com/ research/data. It is important to point out that Zillow's data exclude the following nondisclosure states: Alaska, Idaho, Indiana, Kansas, Louisiana, Maine, Mississippi, Missouri, Montana, New Mexico, North Dakota, Texas, Utah, and Wyoming. Still, Zillow provides a useful perspective into the enormous gaps in housing prices between superstar cities and superstar neighborhoods and much of the rest of the country.

13. On clustering, see Alfred Marshall, *Principles of Economics* (London: Macmillan, 1890); Jane Jacobs, *The Economy of Cities* (New York: Random House,1969); Paul Krugman, "Increasing Returns and Economic Geography," *Journal of Political Economy* 99, no. 3 (June 1991): 483–499; Robert E. Lucas, "On the Mechanics of Economic Development," *Journal of Monetary Economics* 22, no. 1 (1988): 3–42. On diversity and immigration, see AnnaLee Saxenian, *The New Argonauts: Regional Advantage in a Global Economy* (Cambridge, MA: Harvard University Press, 2007); Vivek Wadhwa, AnnaLee Saxenian, and F. Daniel Siciliano, *America's New Immigrant Entrepreneurs: Then and Now* (Kansas City, MO: Kauffman Foundation, 2012), www.kauffman.org/~/media/kauffman_org /research%20reports%20and%20covers/2012/10/then_and_now_americas _new_immigrant_entrepreneurs.pdf.

14. William Alonso, "A Theory of the Urban Land Market," *Regional Science* 6, no. 1 (1960): 149–157; William Alonso, *Location and Land Use* (Cambridge, MA: Harvard University Press, 1964).

15. Willie Larson, *New Estimates of Value of Land of the United States*, Bureau of Economic Analysis, 2015, www.bea.gov/papers/pdf/new-estimates -of-value-of-land-of-the-united-states-larson.pdf; Richard Florida, "The Real Role of Land Values in the United States," *CityLab*, April 10, 2015, www .citylab.com/housing/2015/04/the-real-role-of-land-values-in-the-united -states/389862.

16. These data are from Joe Cortright, "The Market Cap of Cities," *City Observatory*, January 1, 2016, http://cityobservatory.org/the-market-cap -of-cities. Cortright combined Zillow estimates for owner-occupied housing of $28.4 trillion with his own estimates of the value of rental housing of $5.8 trillion. Cortright explained via e-mail that he used Zillow's base estimates

of annual gross rent for the United States and metro areas to calculate his estimate of rental value. To come up with the total value of US rental housing, for example, he used Zillow's estimate of $535 billion in gross rent to calculate annual net income from rental housing of $350 billion based on net operating income of 65 percent. He then capitalized that at 6 percent to come up with the $5.8 trillion figure. The base data for both owner and rental housing are from Svenja Gudell, "How Much Would It Cost to Buy Every Home in America?" Zillow Blog, December 30, 2015, www.zillow .com/research/total-housing-value-2015-11535.

17. Gyourko, Mayer, and Sinai, "Superstar Cities."

18. These data are from Anna Scherbina and Jason Barr, "Manhattan Real Estate: What's Next," *Real Clear Markets*, February 8, 2016, www .realclearmarkets.com/articles/2016/02/08/manhattan_real_estate_whats _next_101995.html.

19. The term NIMBY grew in use in the United States in the 1980s, but some date its origin as far back as the 1950s. See Michael Dear, "Understanding and Overcoming the NIMBY Syndrome," *Journal of the American Planning Association* 58, no. 3 (1992): 288–300. There is a rapidly expanding literature on the effects of NIMBYism and land use restrictions on housing costs and urban development. See, Edward Glaeser, *The Triumph of the City* (New York: Penguin, 2011); Ryan Avent, *The Gated City* (Seattle: Amazon Digital Services, 2014); Ryan Avent, "One Path to Better Jobs: More Density in Cities," *New York Times*, September 3, 2011, www.nytimes.com/2011/09/04 /opinion/sunday/one-path-to-better-jobs-more-density-in-cities.html; Matthew Yglesias, *The Rent Is Too Damn High* (New York: Simon and Schuster, 2012); Matthew Yglesias, "NIMBYs Are Killing the National Economy," *Vox*, April 25, 2014, www.vox.com/2014/4/25/5650816 /NIMBYs-are-killing-the-national-economy. On the increase in court cases about land use issues, see Peter Ganong and Daniel Shoag, "Why Has Regional Income Convergence in the U.S. Declined?," Harvard University, January 2015, http://papers.ssrn.com/sol3/papers.cfm?abstract_id=2081216.

20. Richard Florida, "Bring on the Jets at Island Airport," *Toronto Star*, December 17, 2013, www.thestar.com/opinion/commentary/2013/12/17 /bring_on_the_jets_at_the_island_airport.html; Richard Florida, Charlotta Mellander, and Thomas Holgersson, "Up in the Air: The Role of Airports for Regional Economic Development," *Annals of Regional Science* 54, no. 1 (2015): 197–214; Jordan Press, "Trudeau Government Says No to Expansion of Toronto Island Airport," *Toronto Star*, November 21, 2015, www.the

star.com/news/canada/2015/11/27/trudeau-government-says-no-to-expansion
-of-toronto-island-airport.html.

21. Hans Brems, "Cantillon Versus Marx: The Land Theory and the Labor Theory of Value," *History of Political Economy* 10, no. 4 (1978): 669–678; Anthony Brewer, "Cantillon and the Land Theory of Value," *History of Political Economy* 20, no. 1 (1988): 1–14; David Ricardo, "On Rent," in *On the Principles of Political Economy and Taxation* (London: John Murray, 1821), chap. 2, available at www.econlib.org/library/Ricardo/ricP .html; Adam Smith, *The Wealth of Nations*, Bantam Classics Reprint (New York: Bantam, 2003 [1776]).

22. Ryan Avent, "The Parasitic City," *The Economist*, June 3, 2013, www .economist.com/blogs/freeexchange/2013/06/london-house-prices; Noah Smith, "Piketty's Three Big Mistakes," *Bloomberg View*, March 27, 2015, www.bloombergview.com/articles/2015-03-27/piketty-s-three-big-mistakes -in-inequality-analysis. Emphasis is from the original.

23. On the original Luddites, see Kirkpatrick Sale, *Rebels Against the Future: The Luddites and Their War on the Industrial Revolution: Lessons for the Computer* (Boston: Addison-Wesley, 1995).

24. Chang-Tai Hsieh and Enrico Moretti, "Why Do Cities Matter? Local Growth and Aggregate Growth," NBER Working Paper no. 21154, National Bureau of Economic Research, May 2015. Economists Jason Furman, a former chairman of the President's Council of Economic Advisers, and Peter Orszag, a former director of the Office of Management and Budget, noted that "zoning regulations are best interpreted as real estate market supply constraints. Taking various forms—limiting height restrictions, highly restrictive minimum lot sizes, complicated permitting processes, or prohibitions on multifamily structures, to name just a few—such regulations effectively limit the number of housing units or non-residential buildings that can be built in a given area." See their article "Firm-Level Perspective on the Role of Rents in the Rise in Inequality," Presentation at "A Just Society" Centennial Event in Honor of Joseph Stiglitz, Columbia University, October 16, 2015, 7–8, www.whitehouse.gov/sites/default/files /page/files/20151016_firm_level_perspective_on_role_of_rents_in_inequal-ity.pdf. See also "Inclusive Growth in the United States," in *2016 Economic Report of the President* (Washington, DC: President's Council of Economic Advisers, 2016), chap. 1, p. 44. On top of this, such restrictions contribute significantly to the geographic segregation and isolation of the rich and poor. Also see Michael C. Lens and Paavo Monkkonen, "Do Strict Land

Use Regulations Make Metropolitan Areas More Segregated by Income?" *Journal of the American Planning Association* 82, no. 1 (2016): 6–121. Such land use regulations are so restrictive that they have been dubbed "the new exclusionary zoning." See John Mangin, "The New Exclusionary Zoning," *Stanford Law and Policy Review* 29, no. 1 (January 2014): 91–120; William Fischel, *Zoning Rules! The Economics of Land Use Regulation*, Lincoln Institute of Land Policy, 2015.

25. The data and graph are from a study by Issi Romem, chief economist with the real estate site BuildZoom. See Issi Romem, "Has the Expansion of American Cities Slowed Down?" BuildZoom, May 15, 2016, www .buildzoom.com/blog/cities-expansion-slowing. This discussion is also based on Richard Florida, "Blame Geography for High Housing Prices?" *CityLab*, April 18, 2016, www.citylab.com/housing/2016/04/blame-geography-for -high-housing-prices/478680. Austin is a bit deceiving: Despite its relatively modest housing price growth, the metro area has had a serious problem with housing affordability. Its housing prices may be lower than San Francisco's, Boston's, or DC's, but its median income is also lower, and roughly half its renters face substantial cost burdens.

26. Albert Saiz, "The Geographic Determinants of Housing Supply," *Quarterly Journal of Economics* 125, no. 3 (2010): 1253–1296; Yonah Freemark, "Reorienting Our Discussion of Urban Growth," The Transport Politic, July 6, 2016, www.thetransportpolitic.com/2016/07/06/reorienting-our-discussion -of-city-growth. Freemark's analysis charted population change in America's one hundred largest cities, comparing the change in overall population to the change in the built-up areas of those cities (areas with a population density of 4,000 people per square mile or more), with central areas in and around the urban core defined as those within 1.5 to 3 miles of city hall.

27. See Enrico Moretti, *The New Geography of Jobs* (Boston: Houghton Mifflin Harcourt, 2012).

28. Richard Florida, "Cost of Living Is Really All About Housing," *CityLab*, July 21, 2014, www.citylab.com/housing/2014/07/cost-of-living-is-really -all-about-housing/373128; Richard Florida, "The U.S. Cities with the Most Leftover to Spend . . . After Paying for Housing," *CityLab*, December 23, 2011, www.citylab.com/housing/2011/12/us-cities-with-most-spend -after-paying-housing/778.

29. Average wages are positively correlated with metropolitan populations (0.58), as are wages for the three classes of workers: knowledge, professional, and creative workers (0.69); service workers (0.46); and blue-collar workers (0.28).

30. The correlation between housing cost and creative-class wages left over after paying for housing is positive and significant (0.58). The correlations between housing costs and wages left over after paying for housing are negative and significant for the service class (−0.36) and the working class (−0.20).

31. Thomas Piketty, *Capital in the Twenty-First Century* (Cambridge, MA: Belknap Press of Harvard University Press, 2013); Matthew Rognlie, "Deciphering the Fall and Rise in the Net Capital Share," *Brookings Papers on Economic Activity*, Brookings Institution, March 2015, www.brookings .edu/~/media/projects/bpea/spring-2015/2015a_rognlie.pdf. While some have jumped on Rognlie's work as somehow criticizing or upending Piketty's arguments and conclusions, I prefer to see it as clarifying and focusing attention on the role that housing plays in mounting inequality. Felix Salmon referred to the "physical manifestation of r > g" in his "Lessons from a $110 Million Penthouse," *Medium*, June 8, 2014, https://medium.com /@felixsalmon/lessons-from-a-110-million-penthouse-ca23db711df2.

CHAPTER 3: CITY OF ELITES

1. David Byrne, "If the 1% Stifles New York's Creative Talent, I'm Out of Here," *The Guardian*, October 7, 2013, www.theguardian.com/commentis free/2013/oct/07/new-york-1percent-stifles-creative-talent.

2. This quotation is from a 2010 conversation between Smith and writer Jonathan Lethem at Cooper Union. See Jeremiah Moss, "Find a New City," Jeremiah's Vanishing New York, May 3, 2010, http://vanishingnewyork .blogspot.ca/2010/05/find-new-city.html.

3. Moby, "I Left New York for LA Because Creativity Requires the Freedom to Fail," *The Guardian*, February 3, 2014, www.theguardian.com /commentisfree/2014/feb/03/leave-new-york-for-los-angeles.

4. See Scott Timberg, *Culture Crash: The Killing of the Creative Class* (New Haven, CT: Yale University Press, 2015); Sarah Kendzior, "Expensive Cities Are Killing Creativity," *Al Jazeera*, December 17, 2013, www.aljazeera .com/indepth/opinion/2013/12/expensive-cities-are-killing-creativity-20131 21065856922461.html.

5. Marcus Fairs, "London Could Follow New York and Lose Its Creative Class Warns Rohan Silva," *Dezeen*, July 10, 2015, www.dezeen .com/2015/07/10/creative-people-designers-new-york-move-los-angeles -cautionary-tale-london-warns-rohan-silva; Alex Proud, "'Cool' London Is Dead, and the Rich Kids Are to Blame," *The Telegraph*, April 7, 2014, www

.telegraph.co.uk/men/thinking-man/10744997/Cool-London-is-dead-and
-the-rich-kids-are-to-blame.html.

6. Statistically speaking, for all three of these groups—business professionals, techies, and creatives—the correlations between housing costs and
the amount of money they have left over after paying for housing are positive and significant, while the correlation for the service class is negative.
The correlations between housing costs and the amount of wages left over
after paying for housing are as follows: business professionals (0.60); techies
and scientists (0.44); and artists, musicians, and cultural creatives (0.42).
The BLS data for artists and cultural creatives pertain only to those who report creative work as their primary occupation, and thus exclude struggling
or younger artists whose primary occupation may be something else. Although we tend to think of the aspiring artist working in a non-creative job
as unique, young people in many occupations may have different jobs as they
transition from college or graduate school to their preferred career.

7. On London, see Jonathan Prynn, Mira Bar-Hillel, and Lindsay Watling,
"London's £3bn Ghost Mansions: 'Foreign Investors Are Using Capital's
Finest Homes as Real-Life Monopoly Pieces,'" *Evening Standard*, February
14, 2014, www.standard.co.uk/news/london/londons-3bn-ghost-mansions
-foreign-investors-are-using-capitals-finest-homes-as-reallife-monopoly
-pieces-9128782.html. On New York, see Sam Roberts, "Homes Dark and
Lifeless, Kept by Out-of-Towners," *New York Times*, July 6, 2011, www
.nytimes.com/2011/07/07/nyregion/more-apartments-are-empty-yet-rented-
or-owned-census-finds.html; Julie Satow, "Pieds-À-Terre Owners Dominate
Some New York Buildings," *New York Times*, October 24, 2014, www.ny
times.com/2014/10/26/realestate/pieds-terre-owners-dominate-some-new
-york-buildings.html.

8. On foreign buyers in London, see Patrick Worrall, "FactCheck: Are
the Super-Rich Killing 'Cool London'?," BBC Channel 4 Fact Check Blog,
April 14, 2014, http://blogs.channel4.com/factcheck/factcheck-superrich
-driving-property-prices/18073. On the displacement of established London elites by the global super-rich, see Luna Glucksburg, "Is This Displacement? Pushing the Boundaries of Super-Gentrification in London's Alpha
Territory," Paper presented to the Royal Geographical Society (with IBG)
Annual International Conference in London, August 31, 2016. The term
"oligarchification" is from Feargus O'Sullivan, "No One Feels Sorry for
the Latest Victims of London's 'Gentrification,'" *CityLab*, September 2,
2016, www.citylab.com/housing/2016/09/the-latest-victims-of-london
-gentrification-are-the-rich/498536.

9. Louise Story and Stephanie Saul, "Stream of Foreign Wealth Flows to Elite New York Real Estate," *New York Times,* February 7, 2015, www .nytimes.com/2015/02/08/nyregion/stream-of-foreign-wealth-flows-to-time -warner-condos.html; "Story and Saul: The Hidden Money Buying Condos at the Time Warner Center," *New York Times,* February 7, 2015, www.nytimes.com/2015/02/08/nyregion/the-hidden-money-buying -up-new-york-real-estate.html; Octavio Nuiry, "Are Foreigners Stashing Billions in U.S. Real Estate?" *Housing News Report,* September 2015, https:// issuu.com/ftmagazine/docs/housingnewsreport_sept; Saskia Sassen, "Who Owns Our Cities—and Why This Urban Takeover Should Concern Us All," *The Guardian,* November 24, 2015, www.theguardian.com/cities/2015/nov/24 /who-owns-our-cities-and-why-this-urban-takeover-should-concern-us-all.

10. Thorstein Veblen, *The Theory of the Leisure Class: An Economic Study of Institutions* (Mineola, NY: Dover Publications, 1994 [1899]).

11. Richard Florida, Charlotta Mellander, and Isabel Ritchie, *The Geography of the Global Super-Rich* (Toronto: Martin Prosperity Institute, Rotman School of Management, University of Toronto, 2016), http://martin prosperity.org/media/The-Geography-of-the-Global-Super-Rich.pdf. Our figures are based on *Forbes* data that cover 1,826 billionaires worldwide. These billionaires account for roughly 0.00003 percent of the world's population but hold total wealth of $7 trillion, roughly equivalent to 10 percent of global economic output. We identified billionaires by primary residence and aggregated them by global metropolitan areas. The number and net worth of billionaires are positively correlated with population size (0.41, 0.33), economic output (0.68, 0.61), the Global City Competitiveness Index (0.47, 0.49), and the Global Financial Centre's Index (0.49, 0.52). Even though the biggest superstar cities have the most billionaires, some billionaires still reside in the smaller cities where they generated their wealth— such as the Walton family of Walmart fame in Bentonville, Arkansas, and Warren Buffet in Omaha, Nebraska.

12. Knight Frank, *The Wealth Report—2015,* www.knightfrank.com /research/the-wealth-report-2015-2716.aspx.

13. Richard Florida and Martin Kenney, "Venture Capital, High Technology, and Regional Development," *Regional Studies* 22, no. 1 (1988): 33–48; Richard Florida and Martin Kenney, "Venture Capital–Financed Innovation in the U.S.," *Research Policy* 17 (1988): 119–137; Richard Florida and Donald Smith, "Venture Capital Formation, Investment, and Regional Industrialization," *Annals of the Association of American Geographers* 83, no. 3 (September 1993): 434–451.

14. Richard Florida, "The Joys of Urban Tech," *Wall Street Journal*, August 31, 2012, www.wsj.com/articles/SB10000872396390444914904577619441778073340; Richard Florida, "The Urban Tech Revolution," *Urban Land*, October 7, 2013, http://urbanland.uli.org/economy-markets-trends/the-urban-tech-revolution; Richard Florida and Charlotta Mellander, *Rise of the Startup City: The Changing Geography of the Venture Capital Financed Innovation* (Toronto: Martin Prosperity Institute, Rotman School of Management, University of Toronto, 2014), http://martinprosperity.org/media/StartupCity-CMR-FINAL-formatted.pdf.

15. Richard Florida and Karen King, *Venture Capital Goes Urban: Tracking Venture Capital and Startup Activity Across US Zip Codes* (Toronto: Martin Prosperity Institute, Rotman School of Management, University of Toronto, 2016), http://martinprosperity.org/content/venture-capital-goes-urban; Richard Florida and Karen King, *Rise of the Urban Startup Neighborhood: Mapping Micro-Clusters of Venture Capital–Based Startups* (Toronto: Martin Prosperity Institute, Rotman School of Management, University of Toronto, 2016), http://martinprosperity.org/content/rise-of-the-urban-startup-neighborhood. The correlations are 0.55 for density, 0.50 for college grads, and 0.50 for the creative class. The only correlations that were higher were for the concentration of tech industry, which creates the demand for venture capital in the first place, and wages. Appendix Table 1 provides the full results.

16. Max Nathan, Emma Vandore, and Rob Whitehead, *A Tale of Tech City: The Future of Inner East London's Digital Economy* (London: Centre for London, 2012).

17. Richard Florida and Karen King, *Rise of the Global Startup City: The Geography of Venture Capital Investment in Cities and Metro Areas Across the Globe* (Toronto: Martin Prosperity Institute, Rotman School of Management, University of Toronto, 2016), http://martinprosperity.org/content/rise-of-the-global-startup-city.

18. Alessandro Piol and Maria Teresa Cometto, *Tech and the City: The Making of New York's Startup Community* (San Francisco: Mirandola Press, 2013).

19. "Stern's Urbanization Project Hosts a Conversation with Richard Florida and Fred Wilson," NYU Stern School of Business, October 9, 2013, www.stern.nyu.edu/experience-stern/news-events/conversation-florida-wilson.

20. Paul Graham, "How to Be Silicon Valley," PaulGraham.com, May 2006, www.paulgraham.com/siliconvalley.html.

21. Rory Carroll, "Oakland: The City That Told Google to Get Lost," *The Guardian*, February 11, 2014, www.theguardian.com/technology/2014/feb/10/city-google-go-away-oakland-california; Ellen Huet, "Protesters Block, Vomit on Yahoo Bus in Oakland," SFGate, April 2, 2014, http://blog.sfgate.com/techchron/2014/04/02/protesters-block-vomit-on-yahoo-bus-in-oakland; Rebecca Solnit, "Diary: Google Invades," *London Review of Books*, February 7, 2013, 34–35, www.lrb.co.uk/v35/n03/rebecca-solnit/diary. On the local backlash to artists and art galleries in downtown Los Angeles, see Jennifer Medina, "Gentrification Protesters in Los Angeles Target Art Galleries," *New York Times*, November 5, 2016, www.nytimes.com/2016/11/05/us/los-angeles-gentrification-art-galleries.html.

22. Dan Morain, "Gentrification's Price: S.F. Moves: Yuppies In, the Poor Out," *Los Angeles Times*, April 3, 1985, http://articles.latimes.com/1985-04-03/news/mn-28445_1_san-francisco-s-skyline.

23. Paul Graham, "Economic Inequality," PaulGraham.com, January 2016, http://paulgraham.com/ineq.html.

24. Charlotta Mellander and I examined the connection between key facets of urban tech (the number of startups, the level of venture capital investment, the concentration of high-tech companies, and the like) and both housing affordability and inequality. Median monthly housing costs were closely correlated with high levels of innovation (0.49), high concentrations of high-tech industry (0.58) and venture capital startups (0.60), and investment (0.56). Wage inequality was positively correlated with innovation (0.44), the concentration of venture capital startups (0.60), and the amount of venture capital investment (0.55). See Appendix Table 1.

25. Philippe Aghion, Ufuk Akcigit, Antonin Bergeaud, Richard Blundell, and David Hémous, "Innovation and Top Income Inequality," NBER Working Paper no. 21247, National Bureau of Economic Research, June 2015, www.nber.org/papers/w21247.

26. Aki Ito, "San Franciscans View Tech Boom as Benefit at Cost of Diversity," *Bloomberg*, April 4, 2014, www.bloomberg.com/news/2014-04-04/san-franciscans-view-tech-boom-as-benefit-at-cost-of-diversity.html.

27. Richard Florida, Hugh Kelly, Rosemary Scanlon, and Steven Pedigo, *New York City: The Great Reset*, NYU School of Professional Studies, July 2015, www.pageturnpro.com/New-York-University/67081-The-Great-Reset/index.html; Richard Florida, "Resetting and Reimagining New York City's Economy," *CityLab*, July 29, 2015, www.citylab.com/politics/2015/07/resetting-and-reimagining-new-york-citys-economy/399815; Adam

Forman, *Creative New York*, Center for an Urban Future, June 2015, https://nycfuture.org/research/publications/creative-new-york-2015.

28. Juan Mateos-Garcia and Hasan Bakhshi, *The Geography of Creativity in the UK*, Nesta, July 2016, www.nesta.org.uk/sites/default/files/the _geography_of_creativity_in_the_uk.pdf. Greater London here is defined as its "Travel to Work Area," or TTWA.

29. Richard Florida, Charlotta Mellander, and Kevin Stolarick, "Geographies of Scope: An Empirical Analysis of Entertainment, 1970–2000," *Journal of Economic Geography* 12, no. 1 (2012): 183–204.

30. These figures are based on a measure called a location quotient, or LQ, which compares the share of economic activity in a metro to its expected national share. The actual LQs are as follows: for creative fields overall, Los Angeles 2.7, New York 2.2; for fine artists, LA 3.8, NY 1.5; for musicians and singers, NY 2.7, LA 2.2; for actors, LA 9.9, NY 2.6; for producers and directors, LA 6.7, NY 4.6; for writers and authors, 3.3 for both; for fashion designers, NY 9.9, LA 7.7. These data are for 2014.

31. Moby, "I Left New York for LA"; Charlynn Burd, "Metropolitan Migration Flows of the Creative Class by Occupation Using 3-Year 2006–2008 and 2009–2011 American Community Survey Data," Journey to Work and Migration Statistics Branch, Social, Economic, and Housing Statistics Division (SEHSD), US Census Bureau, Working Paper no. 2013-11, Presented at the 2013 Annual Meeting of the Association of American Geographers, Los Angeles, April 9–13, 2013.

32. Carl Grodach, Elizabeth Currid-Halkett, Nicole Foster, and James Murdoch, "The Location Patterns of Artistic Clusters: A Metro- and Neighborhood-Level Analysis," *Urban Studies* 51, no. 13 (2014): 2822–2843.

33. This analysis is based on data from Myspace originally organized by University of Toronto sociologist Dan Silver and the University of Chicago's Cultural Policy Center, which I downloaded in early 2007 at the peak of the site's popularity (it had more visitors than Google at the time). The data cover more than 3 million artists. Because of its online reach at the time, MySpace was well suited to documenting the role of place in pop music's commercial ecosystem in a digital environment. My Martin Prosperity Institute research team cleaned and organized these data by genre and location, generating usable data on more than 2 million acts in ten genres: rock, urban, pop, electronic, folk, country, Christian, Latin-Afro-Caribbean, experimental, and jazz. To identify the places that have the biggest influence on popular music, we created a Music Popularity Index, a composite measure of the fans, views, and plays accumulated. See Richard

Florida, "The Geography of America's Pop Music Entertainment Complex," *CityLab*, May 28, 2013, www.citylab.com/design/2013/05/geography -americas-pop-musicentertainment-complex/5219.

34. Richard Florida, "The Geography of Pop Music Superstars," *CityLab*, August 27, 2015, www.citylab.com/tech/2015/08/the-geography-of -pop-music-superstars/402445.

35. Shade Shutters, Rachata Muneepeerakul, and José Lobo, "Constrained Pathways to a Creative Urban Economy," Martin Prosperity Institute, Rotman School of Management, University of Toronto, April 2015, http:// martinprosperity.org/media/WP2015_Constrained-pathways-to-a-creative -urban-economy_Shutters-Muneepeerakul-Lobo.pdf. The study notes that it is extremely difficult for cities to break into this elite club. For one thing, they need to excel across the board; their industry mix and talent pool must be deep in all the skills, creative and otherwise, required for economic growth. And they have to be able to overcome the tremendous forces that act against the development of the creative economy, such as expensive housing prices and high living costs, and continuously attract a net influx of top talent. This is something only a very limited number of metros are able to do.

36. Jessica Floum, "Bay Area Economy Outpaces the US, China," *San Francisco Chronicle*, September 26, 2016, www.sfchronicle.com/business /article/Bay-Area-economy-outpaces-U-S-China-9289809.php.

CHAPTER 4: GENTRIFICATION AND ITS DISCONTENTS

1. Joe Coscarelli, "Spike Lee's Amazing Rant Against Gentrification: 'We Been Here!,'" *New York Magazine*, February 25, 2014, http://nymag .com/daily/intelligencer/2014/02/spike-lee-amazing-rant-against -gentrification.html. Lee's rant set off a firestorm of reaction. See John McWhorter, "Spike Lee's Racism Isn't Cute: 'M—— F—— Hipster' Is the New 'Honkey,'" *TIME*, February 28, 2014, http://time.com /10666/spike-lees-racism-isnt-cute-m-f-hipster-is-the-new-honkey; Gene Demby, "The One Problem with Spike Lee's Gentrification Argument," *Salon*, February 27, 2014, www.salon.com/2014/02/27/the_one_problem _with_spike_lees_gentrification_argument_partner.

2. Neil Smith, *New Urban Frontier: Gentrification and the Revanchist City* (London: Routledge, 1996); Neil Smith, "Toward a Theory of Gentrification: A Back to the City Movement by Capital, not People," *Journal of the American Planning Association* 45, no. 4 (1979); Neil Smith, "Gentrification and Uneven Development," *Economic Geography* 58, no. 2 (April

1982): 139–155; Neil Smith, "Of Yuppies and Housing: Gentrification, Social Restructuring, and the Urban Dream," *Environment and Planning D: Society and Space* 5, no. 2 (January 1987): 151–172.

3. Susie Cagle, "Fallacy of the Creative Class: Why Richard Florida's 'Urban Renaissance' Won't Save U.S. Cities," *Grist*, February 11, 2013, http://grist.org/cities/fallacy-of-the-creative-class.

4. Daniel Hertz, "There's Basically No Way Not to Be a Gentrifier," *CityLab*, April 23, 2014, www.citylab.com/housing/2014/04/theres-basically -no-way-not-be-gentrifier/8877.

5. Lance Freeman, "Five Myths About Gentrification," *Washington Post*, June 3, 2016, www.washingtonpost.com/opinions/five-myths-about -gentrification/2016/06/03/b6c80e56-1ba5-11e6-8c7b-6931e66333e7_story .html; Douglas Massey, "Comment on Jacob Vigdor, 'Does Gentrification Harm the Poor?'" *Brookings-Wharton Papers on Urban Affairs*, 2002, 174–176.

6. Ruth Glass, *London: Aspects of Change* (London: MacGibbon and Kee, 1964).

7. Tino Balio, *United Artists: The Company That Changed the Film Industry* (Madison: University of Wisconsin Press, 1987).

8. Dennis Gale, "Middle Class Resettlement in Older Urban Neighborhoods: The Evidence and the Implications," *Journal of the American Planning Association* 45, no. 3 (1979): 293–304.

9. Rosen, quoted in Wayne King, "Changing San Francisco Is Foreseen as a Haven for the Wealthy and Childless," *New York Times*, June 9, 1981, www.nytimes.com/1981/06/09/us/changing-san-francisco-is-foreseen-as-a -haven-for-wealthy-and-childless.html.

10. William Easterly, Laura Freschi, and Steven Pennings, "A Long History of a Short Block: Four Centuries of Development Surprises on a Single Stretch of New York City Street," NYU Development Research Institute, DRI Working Paper no. 96, 2014, http://static1.squarespace.com/static/5451873de4b 008f3c5898336/t/54cfbedee4b092432af5f5f8/1422900969104/DRIw1 .pdf. The project website is www.greenestreet.nyc. See also Laura Bliss, "The Economic Lessons in a Single New York City Block," *CityLab*, August 3, 2015, www.citylab.com/design/2015/08/the-economics-lessons-in-a -single-new-york-city-block/400154.

11. Yonah Freemark, "Reorienting Our Discussion of Urban Growth," The Transport Politic, July 6, 2016, www.thetransportpolitic.com/2016 /07/06/reorienting-our-discussion-of-city-growth. Of these one hundred largest cities, fifty-three saw population growth in the urban center (the area within 1.5 miles of city hall) between 2000 and 2014, and fifty-one

did between 1990 and 2000. This compares to thirty-five between 1980 and 1990, six between 1970 and 1980, and five between 1960 and 1970.

12. Jed Kolko, "Urban Revival? Not for Most Americans," JedKolko .com, March 30, 2016, http://jedkolko.com/2016/03/30/urban-revival-not-for -most-americans.

13. Markus Moos, "From Gentrification to Youthification: The Increasing Importance of Young Age in Delineating High-Density Living," *Urban Studies* 53, no. 14 (November 2016): 2903–2920, http://usj.sagepub.com/content /53/14/2903.long.

14. Terra McKinnish, Randall Walsh, and T. Kirk White, "Who Gentrifies Low-Income Neighborhoods?," *Journal of Urban Economics* 67, no. 2 (2010): 180–193. The study also notes that gentrification had substantial negative effects on less-educated blacks. Black households whose heads did not complete high school were the most likely to be pushed out of gentrifying neighborhoods, while those that remained saw much more modest growth in their incomes.

15. Nathaniel Baum-Snow and Daniel Hartley, "Accounting for Central Neighborhood Change, 1980–2010," Federal Reserve Bank of Chicago, September 2016, www.chicagofed.org/publications/working-papers/2016 /wp2016-09.

16. Miriam Zuk, Ariel Bierbaum, Karen Chapple, Karolina Gorska, Anastasia Loukaitou-Sideris, Paul Ong, and Trevor Thomas, *Gentrification, Displacement, and the Role of Public Investment: A Literature Review*, Federal Reserve Bank of San Francisco, 2015, www.frbsf.org/community -development/publications/working-papers/2015/august/gentrification -displacement-role-of-public-investment/.

17. Sam Bass Warner Jr., *Streetcar Suburbs: The Process of Growth in Boston, 1870–1900* (Cambridge, MA: Harvard University Press, 1978).

18. Lena Edlund, Cecilia Machado, and Michaela Sviatchi, "Bright Minds, Big Rent: Gentrification and the Rising Returns to Skill," NBER Working Paper no. 21729, National Bureau of Economic Research, November 2015, www.nber.org/papers/w21729. Also see Victor Couture and Jessie Handbury, "Urban Revival in America, 2000 to 2010," Presented at the American Economic Association Annual Meeting, 2015, http://faculty.haas .berkeley.edu/couture/download/Couture_Handbury_Revival.pdf.

19. Daniel Hartley, *Gentrification and Financial Health*, Federal Reserve Bank of Cleveland, 2013, www.clevelandfed.org/newsroom-and -events/publications/economic-trends/2013-economic-trends/et-20131106 -gentrification-and-financial-health.aspx.

20. Gentrification is positively correlated with population size (0.59) and density (0.44); per capita income (0.61) and wages (0.62); the share of science and technology workers in a metro (0.32); the concentration of high-tech industry (0.58); the share of the workforce that consists of members of the creative class (0.55); and the share of adults who are college graduates (0.51). It is negatively correlated with the share of blue-collar workers in an area (-0.48). It is positively correlated with the share of commuters who use transit (0.61) and negatively correlated with the share who drive to work alone (-0.55). See Appendix Table 2.

21. James Tankersley, "Why the PR Industry Is Sucking Up Pulitzer Winners," *Washington Post*, *Wonkblog*, April 24, 2015, www.washington post.com/blogs/wonkblog/wp/2015/04/23/why-the-pr-industry-is-sucking -up-pulitzer-winners.

22. Michael Barton, "An Exploration of the Importance of the Strategy Used to Identify Gentrification," *Urban Studies*, December 3, 2014; Richard Florida, "No One's Very Good at Correctly Identifying Gentrification," *CityLab*, December 15, 2014, www.citylab.com/housing/2014/12/no-ones -very-good-at-correctly-identifying-gentrification/383724.

23. NYU Furman Center for Real Estate and Urban Policy, *State of New York City's Housing and Neighborhoods in 2015*, May 2016, http://furman center.org/files/sotc/NYUFurmanCenter_SOCin2015_9JUNE2016.pdf.

24. These data were provided by PropertyShark.com.

25. Lance Freeman, "Displacement or Succession?," *Urban Affairs Review* 40, no. 4 (2005): 463–491; Lance Freeman and Frank Braconi, "Gentrification and Displacement: New York City in the 1990s," *Journal of the American Planning Association* 70, no. 1 (2004): 39–52; Lance Freeman, "Neighborhood Diversity, Metropolitan Segregation, and Gentrification: What Are the Links in the US?," *Urban Studies* 46, no. 10 (2009): 2079–2101. On the effects of gentrification on homeowners and renters, see Isaac William Martin and Kevin Beck, "Gentrification, Property Tax Limitation, and Displacement," *Urban Affairs Review*, September 2, 2016, http://uar.sagepub.com/content/early/2016/08/31/10780874166669 59.abstract. Also see Kathe Newman, "The Right to Stay Put, Revisited: Gentrification and Resistance to Displacement in New York City," *Urban Studies* 43, no. 1 (2006): 23–57; Ingrid Gould Ellen and Katherine M. O'Regan, "How Low Income Neighborhoods Change: Entry, Exit, and Enhancement," *Regional Science and Urban Economics* 41, no. 2 (2011): 89–97.

26. Lei Ding, Jackelyn Hwang, and Eileen Divringi, "Gentrification and Residential Mobility in Philadelphia," Federal Reserve Bank of Philadelphia, October 2015.

27. Furman Center, *State of New York City's Housing and Neighborhoods in 2015*, http://furmancenter.org/research/sonychan.

28. Miriam Zuk, *Regional Early Warning System for Displacement*, Centre for Community Innovation, 2015, www.urbandisplacement.org /sites/default/files/images/rews_final_report_07_23_15.pdf.

29. Coscarelli, "Spike Lee's Amazing Rant Against Gentrification."

30. Jackelyn Hwang, "The Social Construction of a Gentrifying Neighborhood Reifying and Redefining Identity and Boundaries in Inequality," *Urban Affairs Review* 52, no. 1 (January 2016): 98–128.

31. Sharon Zukin, Scarlett Lindeman, and Laurie Hurson, "The Omnivore's Neighborhood? Online Restaurant Reviews, Race, and Gentrification," *Journal of Consumer Culture* (October 2015).

32. Jackelyn Hwang and Robert J. Sampson, "Divergent Pathways of Gentrification: Racial Inequality and the Social Order of Renewal in Chicago Neighborhoods," *American Sociological Review* 79, no. 4 (August 2014): 726–751.

33. Joseph Cortright and Dillon Mahmoudi, *Neighborhood Change, 1970 to 2010: Transition and Growth in Urban High Poverty Neighborhoods*, Impresa Economics, May 2014, http://dillonm.io/articles/Cortright _Mahmoudi_2014_Neighborhood-Change.pdf.

CHAPTER 5: THE INEQUALITY OF CITIES

1. Sam Roberts, "Mayor Making It No Secret: He'll Endorse Quinn in 2013," *New York Times*, August 28, 2011, www.nytimes.com/2011/08/29 /nyregion/in-private-bloomberg-backs-christine-quinn-as-successor.html.

2. Richard Florida, Hugh Kelly, Steven Pedigo, and Rosemary Scanlon, "New York City: The Great Reset," NYU School of Professional Studies, August 2015, www.pageturnpro.com/New-York-University/67081-The -Great-Reset/index.html.

3. Michael Bloomberg, "Cities Must Be Cool, Creative, and in Control," *Financial Times*, March 27, 2012, www.ft.com/cms/s/0/c09235b6-72ac-11e1 -ae73-00144feab49a.html#axzz3nuBbmXVR.

4. Michael Barbaro and Megan Thee-Brenan, "Poll Shows New Yorkers Are Deeply Conflicted over Bloomberg's Legacy," *New York Times*,

August 16, 2013, www.nytimes.com/2013/08/18/nyregion/what-new-yorkers
-think-of-mayor-bloomberg.html; Sam Roberts, "Gap Between Manhattan's Rich and Poor Is Greatest in US, Census Finds," *New York
Times*, September 17, 2014, www.nytimes.com/2014/09/18/nyregion/gap
-between-manhattans-rich-and-poor-is-greatest-in-us-census-finds.html;
"Cities and Their Millionaires," *The Economist*, May 9, 2013, www
.economist.com/blogs/graphicdetail/2013/05/daily-chart-7; Aoife Moriarty,
"Revealed: Global Cities with the Highest Percentage of Millionaires,"
Spears, July 22, 2014, www.spearswms.com/revealed-global-cities-with
-the-highest-percentage-of-millionaires.

5. "Laying the Foundation for Greatness: Bill de Blasio" (video), The
New School for Social Research, Milano School for International Affairs,
Management, and Urban Policy, May 30, 2013, http://new.livestream.com
/TheNewSchool/Bill-de-Blasio; Bill de Blasio, "A Foundation for Great-
ness," New York Public Advocate Archives, May 30, 2013, http://archive
.advocate.nyc.gov/jobs/speech.

6. Voting data are from exit polls as per the *New York Times*, www.ny
times.com/projects/elections/2013/general/nyc-mayor/exit-polls.html.

7. Thomas Piketty and Emmanuel Saez, "Income Inequality in the United
States, 1913–1998," *Quarterly Journal of Economics* 118, no. 1 (2003).

8. The gap between the top 1 percent and the rest is even larger in small,
ultra-rich enclaves where top celebrities and entertainers live alongside low-
paid service workers and the poor—places such as Jackson Hole, Wyoming,
where the 1 percent takes home 200 times as much as everyone else; or some
of the cities in Florida, including Naples (73 times as much), Vero Beach
(63 times), Key West (59 times), Miami (45 times); Bridgeport-Stamford in
Connecticut, which encompasses uber-wealthy Greenwich and Westport
on Fairfield County's Gold Coast (74 times as much); and Las Vegas (41
times). Data on metro areas, as well as the more recent data on national
trends, are from Estelle Sommeiller, Mark Price, and Ellis Wazeter, *Income
Inequality in the U.S. by State, Metropolitan Area, and County* (Washington, DC: Economic Policy Institute, 2016), www.epi.org/publication
/income-inequality-in-the-us/#epi-toc-8.

9. The Gini coefficient for nations is from the Central Intelligence Agency,
The World Factbook (Washington, DC: US Government Publishing Office,
2015), www.cia.gov/library/publications/the-world-factbook; for metros it is
from the US Census Bureau, "American Community Survey," www.census
.gov/programs-surveys/acs.

10. On the worsening trend in inequality across metros, see Richard Florida, "Where the Great Recession Made Inequality Worse," *CityLab*, August 4, 2014, www.citylab.com/politics/2014/08/where-the-great-recession-made-inequality-worse/375480/T; US Conference of Mayors, *U.S. Metro Economies: Income and Wage Gaps Across the U.S.*, Prepared by IHS Global Insight, 2014, http://usmayors.org/metroeconomies/2014/08/report.pdf. On comparing city to metro inequality, see Daniel Hertz, "Why Are Metropolitan Areas More Equal Than Their Central Cities?," *City Observatory*, September 22, 2015, http://cityobservatory.org/why-are-metropolitan-areas-more-equal-than-their-central-cities; Joe Cortright, "The Difficulty of Applying Inequality Measurements to Cities," *City Observatory*, July 30, 2015, http://cityobservatory.org/the-difficulty-of-applying-inequality-measurements-to-cities.

11. Alan Berube and Natalie Holmes, "City and Metropolitan Inequality on the Rise, Driven by Declining Incomes," Brookings Institution Metropolitan Policy Program, January 14, 2016, www.brookings.edu/research/papers/2016/01/14-income-inequality-cities-update-berube-holmes.

12. J. Chris Cunningham, "Measuring Wage Inequality Within and Across US Metropolitan Areas, 2003–2013," *Monthly Labor Review*, September 2015, www.bls.gov/opub/mlr/2015/article/measuring-wage-inequality-within-and-across-metropolitan-areas-2003-13.htm; Richard Florida, "Wage Inequality and America's Most Successful Cities," *CityLab*, October 7, 2015, www.citylab.com/work/2015/10/how-wage-inequality-is-playing-out-americas-most-successful-cities/409231.

13. Richard Florida and Charlotta Mellander, "The Geography of Inequality: Difference and Determinants of Wage and Income Inequality across US Metros," *Regional Studies*, 2014, 1–14; Richard Florida, "The Inequality of American Cities," *CityLab*, March 5, 2012, www.citylab.com/work/2012/03/inequality-american-cities/861; Richard Florida, "The Inequality Puzzle in U.S. Cities," *CityLab*, March 7, 2012, www.citylab.com/work/2012/03/inequality-puzzle-us-cities/858.

14. David H. Autor, Lawrence F. Katz, and Melissa S. Kearney, *The Polarization of the U.S. Labor Market* (Cambridge, MA: National Bureau of Economic Research, 2006), http://economics.mit.edu/files/584; David Autor and David Dorn, "The Growth of Low-Skill Service Jobs and the Polarization of the US Labor Market," *American Economic Review* 103, no. 5 (2013): 1553–1597; David H. Autor, Lawrence F. Katz, and Alan B. Krueger, "Computing Inequality: Have Computers Changed the Labor Market?,"

Quarterly Journal of Economics 113, no. 4 (1998): 1169–1213; David H. Autor, Frank Levy, and Richard J. Murnane, "The Skill Content of Recent Technological Change: An Empirical Exploration," *Quarterly Journal of Economics* 118, no. 4 (2003): 1279–1333.

15. Wage inequality is positively and significantly correlated with high-tech industry concentration (0.74); the share of the workforce employed in knowledge, professional, and creative occupations (0.68); and the share of adults who are college graduates (0.61).

16. William Julius Wilson, *The Truly Disadvantaged: The Inner City, the Underclass, and Public Policy* (Chicago: University of Chicago Press, 1987); William Julius Wilson, *When Work Disappears: The World of the New Urban Poor* (New York: Knopf, 1996).

17. The correlation between income inequality and poverty is 0.50, and the correlation between income inequality and race is 0.30.

18. See Barry Bluestone and Bennett Harrison, *The Great U-Turn: Corporate Restructuring and the Polarizing of America* (New York: Basic Books, 1988). Also see Dierk Herzer, "Unions and Income Inequality: A Panel Cointegration and Causality Analysis for the United States," *Economic Development Quarterly* (March 3, 2016).

19. Richard Florida, "Inequality and the Growth of Cities," *CityLab*, January 20, 2015, www.citylab.com/work/2015/01/inequality-and-the-growth-of-cities/384571; Richard Florida, "The Connection Between Successful Cities and Inequality," *CityLab*, January 6, 2015, www.citylab.com/politics/2015/01/the-connection-between-successful-cities-and-inequality/384243.

20. Ben Casselman makes the point that the low incomes of students contribute to inequality in college towns in his article "Inequality in College Towns," *FiveThirtyEight*, April 28, 2014, http://fivethirtyeight.com/features/inequality-in-college-towns.

21. Wage inequality is positively and significantly associated with both the size (0.48) and the density (0.38) of metros.

22. Nathaniel Baum-Snow and Ronni Pavan, "Understanding the City Size Wage Gap," *Review of Economic Studies* 79, no. 1 (2012): 88–127; Nathaniel Baum-Snow, Matthew Freedman, and Ronni Pavan, "Why Has Urban Inequality Increased?," Working Paper, Brown University, June 2014, http://restud.oxfordjournals.org/content/79/1/88.full.pdf+html.

23. Michael Zuckerman, "The Polarized Partisan Geography of Inequality," *The Atlantic*, April 7, 2014, www.theatlantic.com/politics/archive/2014/04/the-polarized-partisan-geography-of-inequality/360130; Joshua

Green and Eric Chemi, "Income Inequality Is Higher in Democratic Districts Than Republican Ones," *Bloomberg Businessweek*, May 12, 2014, www.bloomberg.com/news/articles/2014-05-12/income-inequality-is-higher-in-democratic-districts-than-republican-ones.

24. The correlation between wage inequality and liberalism measured as the share of Clinton votes is 0.42 and the correlation between wage inequality and conservatism measured as the share of Trump votes is −0.42. See Richard Florida, "Why Democrats Are Focused on Inequality: Liberal Metros Face the Worst of It," *CityLab*, June 4, 2014, www.citylab.com/politics/2014/06/why-democrats-are-focused-on-inequality-liberal-metros-face-the-worst-of-it/371827.

25. Edward Glaeser, Mathew Resseger, and Kristina Tobio, "Urban Inequality," *Journal of Regional Science* 49, no. 4 (October 2009): 617–646.

26. Chris Benner and Manuel Pastor, "Brother, Can You Spare Some Time? Sustaining Prosperity and Social Inclusion in America's Metropolitan Regions," *Urban Studies* 52, no. 7 (2015): 1339–1356; also, Tanvi Misra, "Another Reason to Promote Social Equity in U.S. Metros: Job Growth," *CityLab*, March 31, 2015, www.citylab.com/housing/2015/03/another-reason-to-promote-social-equity-in-us-metros-job-growth/389033.

27. *The 2016 Distressed Communities Index* (Washington, DC: Economic Innovation Group, 2016), http://eig.org/wp-content/uploads/2016/02/2016-Distressed-Communities-Index-Report.pdf.

28. Richard Shearer, John Ng, Alan Berube, and Alec Friedhoff, "Growth, Prosperity, and Inclusion in the 100 Largest U.S. Metro Areas," *Brookings Metro Monitor 2016*, Brookings Institution Metropolitan Policy Program, January 2016, www.brookings.edu/research/reports2/2016/01/metro-monitor#V0G10420.

29. Richard Florida, Charlotta Mellander, and Karen King, *The Global Creativity Index 2015* (Toronto: Martin Prosperity Institute, Rotman School of Management, University of Toronto, 2015), http://martinprosperity.org/content/the-global-creativity-index-2015/; Richard Florida, "Greater Competitiveness Does Not Have to Mean Greater Inequality," *CityLab*, October 11, 2011, www.citylab.com/work/2011/10/greater-competitiveness-does-not-greater-inequality/230.

30. Jonathan Ostry, Andrew Berg, and Charalambos Tsangarides, *Redistribution, Inequality, and Growth* (Washington, DC: International Monetary Fund, 2014), www.imf.org/external/pubs/ft/sdn/2014/sdn1402.pdf.

CHAPTER 6: THE BIGGER SORT

1. Statistics for Baltimore are from the following sources. Creative economy: Shade Shutters, Rachata Muneepeerakul, and José Lobo, "Constrained Pathways to a Creative Urban Economy," Martin Prosperity Institute, Rotman School of Management, University of Toronto, April 2015, http://martinprosperity.org/media/WP2015_Constrained-pathways-to-a -creative-urban-economy_Shutters-Muneepeerakul-Lobo.pdf. Black income: Joel Kotkin, "The Cities Where African Americans Are Doing the Best Economically," *Forbes*, January 15, 2015, www.forbes.com/pictures /femi45jlhh/no-4-baltimore-md. Concentrated poverty and affluence: Edward G. Goetz, Tony Damiano, and Jason Hicks, "American Urban Inequality: Racially Concentrated Affluence," Lincoln Land Institute, 2015. Limited economic mobility: Raj Chetty and Nathaniel Hendren, "The Impacts of Neighborhoods on Intergenerational Mobility: Childhood Exposure Effects and County-Level Estimates," NBER Working Paper, National Bureau of Economic Research, May 2015. Crime and violence: Richard Florida and John Roman, "There Are Plenty More Baltimores," *CityLab*, May 4, 2015, www.citylab.com/crime/2015/05/there-are-plenty-more-baltimores/392264. Murders and shootings: Baltimore Neighborhood Indicators Alliance, Jacob France Institute, "Number of Gun-Related Homicides per 1,000 Residents," http://bniajfi.org/indicators/Crime%20and%20Safety/gunhom; *2011 Neighborhood Health Profile: Sandtown-Winchester/Harlem Park*, Baltimore City Health Department, December 2011, http://health.baltimorecity .gov/sites/default/files/47%20Sandtown.pdf.

2. Elizabeth Kneebone, "U.S. Concentrated Poverty in the Wake of the Great Recession," Brookings Institution, March 31, 2016, www.brookings .edu/research/reports2/2016/03/31-concentrated-poverty-recession-kneebone -holmes.

3. Bill Bishop, *The Big Sort: Why the Clustering of Like-Minded America Is Tearing Us Apart* (New York: Houghton Mifflin Harcourt, 2008).

4. On the rise in income segregation in the thirty largest metros between 1980 and 2010, see Paul Taylor and Richard Fry, *The Rise of Residential Segregation by Income* (Washington, DC: Pew Research Center, 2012), www.pewsocialtrends.org/files/2012/08/Rise-of-Residential-Income -Segregation-2012.2.pdf. The Pew study found that 28 percent of lower-income households were located in majority lower-income tracts in 2010, up from 23 percent in 1980, and that 18 percent of upper-income households were located in majority upper-income tracts, up from 9 percent in 1980.

"These increases," the report concluded, "are related to the long-term rise in income inequality, which has led to a shrinkage in the share of neighborhoods across the United States that are predominantly middle class or mixed income—to 76% in 2010, down from 85% in 1980—and a rise in the shares that are majority lower income (18% in 2010, up from 12% in 1980) and majority upper income (6% in 2010, up from 3% in 1980)." For the percentage of urban residents living in economically segregated areas today compared to 1970, see Tara Watson, "Inequality and the Measurement of Residential Segregation by Income in American Neighborhoods," *Review of Income and Wealth* 55, no. 3 (2009): 820–844. On the changing share of American families living in rich and poor as well as middle-class neighborhoods, see Kendra Bischoff and Sean Reardon, "The Continuing Increase in Income Segregation, 2007–2012," Stanford University, Center for Education and Policy Analysis, March 2016, https://cepa.stanford.edu /sites/default/files/the%20continuing%20increase%20in%20income%20 segregation%20march2016.pdf. The study defines middle-class neighborhoods as those where families make between 67 and 150 percent of the median metro income. Affluent neighborhoods are those where families make more than 150 percent of the metro median, and poor neighborhoods are those where families make less than 67 percent of the metro median. Within the middle class, high-income neighborhoods are those where families make between 125 and 150 percent of the metro median, high-middle-income ones make between 100 and 125 percent, low-middle-income areas make between 80 and 100 percent, and low-income ones make between 67 and 80 percent.

5. *America's Shrinking Middle Class: A Close Look at Changes Within Metropolitan Areas*, Pew Research Center, May 11, 2016, www.pew socialtrends.org/2016/05/11/americas-shrinking-middle-class-a-close-look -at-changes-within-metropolitan-areas. The results of our correlation analysis of the Pew data are as follows. Across metros, the middle-class share of the population is positively associated with the working class (0.37), the white share of the population (0.34), and conservatism (with a correlation of 0.27 to the metro share of Trump voters in 2016)—all features of economically declining places. Conversely, the middle-class share of the population is negatively associated with density (−0.22), the creative class (−0.20), diversity (with correlations of −0.46 to immigrants, −0.47 to Latinos, and −0.37 to the gay and lesbian community), and liberalism (with a correlation of −0.33 to the metro share of Clinton voters in 2016)—all basic features of economically vibrant places. The middle-class share of the population

is negatively associated with income inequality (–0.64), wage inequality (–0.38), economic segregation (–0.43), and having a large lower-class share of population (–0.62). There is a negative and statistically significant correlation (–0.48) between the middle-class share in 2000 and the change in the middle-class share between 2000 and 2014.

6. The indexes for specific types of economic segregation are absolute measures, where higher values indicate higher levels of segregation: a value of 1 indicates complete segregation, while a value of 0 indicates no segregation at all. The measures for the combined or composite indexes are relative measures, which compare the extent of those types of segregation in a metro to all other metros. The Appendix provides a detailed description of our variables, data, and methodology. Also see Richard Florida and Charlotta Mellander, *Segregated City: The Geography of Economic Segregation in America's Metro Areas* (Toronto: Martin Prosperity Institute, Rotman School of Management, University of Toronto, 2015), http://martinprosperity.org/media/Segregated%20City.pdf.

7. The poverty line as defined by the US Census Bureau, "Poverty," www.census.gov/hhes/www/poverty/about/overview/measure.html; US Census Bureau, "Poverty Thresholds," www.census.gov/data/tables/time-series/demo/income-poverty/historical-poverty-thresholds.html.

8. Income segregation is positively correlated with population (0.53), density (0.44), the creative class (0.35), and high-tech industry (0.48).

9. Carmen DeNavas-Walt and Bernadette D. Proctor, *Income and Poverty in the United States: 2013*, US Census Bureau, 2014, www.census.gov/content/dam/Census/library/publications/2014/demo/p60-249.pdf; Kendra Bischoff and Sean Reardon, *Residential Segregation by Income, 1970–2009* (New York: Russell Sage Foundation, 2013).

10. The segregation of the poor is positively correlated with population (0.43), density (0.54), the creative class (0.48), and high-tech industry (0.47).

11. William Julius Wilson, *The Truly Disadvantaged* (Chicago: University of Chicago Press, 1987).

12. The segregation of the wealthy is positively correlated with population (0.38) and high-tech industry (0.26).

13. This is based on our calculation of mean segregation scores. Higher values indicate higher levels of economic segregation. The mean segregation score for the wealthy (0.456) is significantly higher than the mean segregation score for the poor (0.324). In fact, the mean segregation score for the wealthy is the highest of any of the groups in our analysis.

14. Michael J. Sandel, *What Money Can't Buy: The Moral Limits of Markets* (London: Macmillan, 2012); Michael J. Sandel, "What Money Can't Buy: The Skyboxification of American Life," *Huffington Post*, April 20, 2012, www.huffingtonpost.com/michael-sandel/what-money-cant-buy _b_1442128.html.

15. At the national level, see Robert J. Barro, "Economic Growth in a Cross Section of Countries," *Quarterly Journal of Economics* 106, no. 2 (1991): 407–443; Robert J. Barro, *Determinants of Economic Growth: A Cross-Country Empirical Study* (Cambridge, MA: MIT Press, 1997). At the city and regional level, see Jane Jacobs, *The Economy of Cities* (New York: Random House, 1969); Robert Lucas, "On the Mechanics of Economic Development," *Journal of Monetary Economics* 22, no. 1 (1988): 3–42; Richard Florida, *The Rise of the Creative Class* (New York: Basic Books, 2002); Edward Glaeser and David Maré, "Cities and Skills," *Journal of Labor Economics* 19, no. 2 (2001); Edward Glaeser and Albert Saiz, "The Rise of the Skilled City," *Brookings -Wharton Papers on Urban Affairs* 1 (2004): 47–105; James Rauch, "Productivity Gains from Geographic Concentration of Human Capital: Evidence from Cities," *Journal of Urban Economics* 34, no. 3 (1993): 380–400.

16. The segregation of the highly educated is positively correlated with population size (0.54), density (0.39), the creative class (0.43), and high-tech industry (0.50).

17. The segregation measures are closely related to one another. The Overall Segregation Index is closely correlated with income segregation (0.83), educational segregation (0.94), and occupational segregation (0.95).

18. Appendix Table 4 provides the rankings for all 350-plus US metros on the Overall Economic Segregation Index.

19. The correlation between the Overall Economic Segregation Index and population size is 0.64.

20. The Overall Segregation Index is positively associated with density (0.56) and the share of commuters who use transit (0.49) and negatively associated with the share of commuters who drive to work alone (–0.22).

21. The Overall Economic Segregation Index is positively associated with wages (0.46) and economic output per capita (0.41).

22. The Overall Economic Segregation Index is positively associated with high-tech industry (0.62) and the creative class (0.53) and negatively associated with the share of workers in blue-collar, working-class occupations (–0.37).

23. The Overall Economic Segregation Index is positively associated with the share of voters who cast their ballots for Clinton in 2016 (0.47) and negatively associated with the share that voted for Trump (−0.44).

24. Appendix Table 4 provides full rankings for all US metros on this combined Segregation-Inequality Index.

25. The correlations for the Segregation-Inequality Index are as follows: 0.50 with density, 0.60 with population size, 0.31 with per capita income, 0.42 with economic output per capita, 0.46 with average wages, 0.61 with high-tech industry, 0.57 with the creative class, and 0.53 with share of adults who are college grads. Conversely, the Segregation-Inequality Index is negatively correlated with the share of the workforce that is blue-collar working-class (−0.44). The Segregation-Inequality Index is positively correlated with the share of metro voters who voted for Clinton in 2016 (0.47) and negatively correlated with the share who voted for Trump (−0.42).

26. The Overall Economic Segregation Index is closely correlated with income inequality (0.52) and wage inequality (0.62). The correlations between inequality and each of the other individual measures of economic segregation are also positive, and many of the correlations are highly significant, with the majority in the range of the high 0.40s to 0.50.

27. Watson, "Inequality and the Measurement of Residential Segregation."

28. Tiit Tammaru, Szymon Marcińczak, Maarten van Ham, and Sako Musterd, eds., *Socio-Economic Segregation in European Capital Cities: East Meets West* (London: Routledge, 2015). Also see Richard Florida, "Economic Segregation and Inequality in Europe's Cities," *CityLab*, November 16, 2016, www.citylab.com/work/2015/11/economic-segregation-and-inequality-in-europes-cities/415920.

29. Rebecca Diamond, "The Determinants and Welfare Implications of US Workers' Diverging Location Choices by Skill: 1980–2000," *American Economic Review*, 106, no. 3 (March 2016): 479–524; Rebecca Diamond, "U.S. Workers' Diverging Locations: Policy and Inequality Implications," Stanford University, SIEPR Policy Brief, July 2014, https://siepr.stanford.edu/?q=/system/files/shared/pubs/papers/briefs/PolicyBrief-7-14-Diamond_0.pdf.

30. Robert J. Sampson, "Individual and Community Economic Mobility in the Great Recession Era: The Spatial Foundations of Persistent Inequality," in *Economic Mobility: Research and Ideas on Strengthening Families, Communities, and the Economy* (St. Louis: Federal Reserve Bank, 2016).

31. The definition of the creative class by race is based on US Census data on shares of black and white (non-Hispanic) workers in management,

business, science, and arts occupations. The correlations for the black creative class are as follows: density (0.32), creative class overall (0.39), college grads (0.31), high-tech firms (0.27), share of adults who are foreign-born (0.34), and share who are gay and lesbian (0.36). In nearly every case, these numbers are significantly lower than the ones for the white creative class. See Richard Florida, "The Racial Divide in the Creative Economy," *CityLab*, May 9, 2016, www.citylab.com/work/2016/05/creative-class-race-black-white-divide/481749.

32. Edward Glaeser and Jacob Vigdor, *The End of the Segregated Century: Racial Separation in America's Neighborhoods, 1890–2010*, Manhattan Institute, 2012, www.manhattan-institute.org/pdf/cr_66.pdf.

33. The Overall Economic Segregation Index is positively associated with the share of population that is black (0.29), Latino (0.24), or Asian (0.30), and negatively associated with the share of population that is white (−0.43). The same pattern holds for the Segregation-Inequality Index, which is positively associated with the share of population that is black (0.30), Latino (0.29), or Asian (0.25), and negatively correlated with the white share of population (−0.42).

34. There is no statistical association between the black creative class and income inequality based on the Gini coefficient, compared to a correlation of 0.40 for the white creative class. The black creative class is modestly associated with my measure of overall economic segregation (0.20), but this correlation is much more modest than that for the white creative class (0.66).

35. The Overall Segregation Index is positively associated with the concentration of gay and lesbian households (0.42) and the share of adults who are foreign-born (0.38).

36. Nate Silver, "The Most Diverse Cities Are Often the Most Segregated," *FiveThirtyEight*, May 1, 2015, http://fivethirtyeight.com/features/the-most-diverse-cities-are-often-the-most-segregated.

37. Paul A. Jargowsky, "Architecture of Segregation: Civil Unrest, the Concentration of Poverty, and Public Policy," Century Foundation, August 9, 2015, http://apps.tcf.org/architecture-of-segregation.

38. Racially concentrated areas of poverty are defined as census tracts where more than half of the population is non-white and more than 40 percent live below the poverty line. Racially concentrated areas of affluence are those that are more than 90 percent white with median incomes that are at least four times the poverty level adjusted for cost of living. Edward G. Goetz, Tony Damiano, and Jason Hicks, "Racially Concentrated

Areas of Affluence: A Preliminary Investigation," University of Minnesota, Humphrey School of Public Affairs, May 2015, www.cura.umn.edu /publications/catalog/niweb1; Alana Semuels, "Where the White People Live," *The Atlantic*, April 10, 2015, www.theatlantic.com/business/archive /2015/04/where-the-white-people-live/390153.

39. E-mail conversation with Patrick Sharkey, July 2013. Also see his book *Stuck in Place: Urban Neighborhoods and the End of Progress Toward Racial Inequality* (Chicago: University of Chicago Press, 2013); Richard Florida, "The Persistent Geography of Disadvantage," *CityLab*, July 25, 2013, www .citylab.com/housing/2013/07/persistent-geography-disadvantage/6231.

40. Sean Reardon, Lindsay Fox, and Joseph Townsend, "Neighborhood Income Composition by Household Race and Income, 1990–2009," *Annals of the American Academy of Political and Social Science* 660, no. 1 (July 2015): 78–97.

41. Jonathan Rothwell and Douglas Massey, "Geographic Effects on Intergenerational Income Mobility," *Economic Geography* 91, no. 1 (2014): 3–106; Richard Florida, "How Your Neighborhood Affects Your Paycheck," *CityLab*, January 16, 2015, www.citylab.com/work/2015/01/how -your-neighborhood-affects-your-paycheck/384536.

42. Raj Chetty, Nathaniel Hendren, Patrick Kline, and Emmanuel Saez, "Where Is the Land of Opportunity? The Geography of Intergenerational Mobility in the United States," *Quarterly Journal of Economics* 4 (2014): 1553–1623; Raj Chetty, Nathaniel Hendren, Patrick Kline, Emmanuel Saez, and Nick Turner, "Is the United States Still a Land of Opportunity? Recent Trends in Intergenerational Mobility," *American Economic Review Papers and Proceedings* 104, no. 5 (2014): 141–147; Chetty and Hendren, "The Impacts of Neighborhoods on Intergenerational Mobility"; Raj Chetty, Nathaniel Hendren, and Lawrence Katz, "The Effects of Exposure to Better Neighborhoods on Children: New Evidence from the Moving to Opportunity Experiment," NBER Working Paper, National Bureau of Economic Research, May 2015.

43. Raj Chetty, Michael Stepner, Sarah Abraham, Shelby Lin, Benjamin Scuderi, Nicholas Turner, Augustin Bergeron, and David Cutler, "The Association Between Income and Life Expectancy in the United States, 2001–2014," *Journal of the American Medical Association* 315, no. 16 (April 26, 2016): 1760–1766.

44. Chetty et al., "The Effects of Exposure"; also see Pat Rubio Goldsmith, Marcus L. Britton, Bruce Reese, and William Velez, "Will Moving to a Better Neighborhood Help? Teenage Residential Mobility, Change of

Context, and Young-Adult Educational Attainment," *Urban Affairs Review* (March 4, 2016) online edition; Molly W. Metzger, Patrick J. Fowler, Courtney Lauren Anderson, and Constance A. Lindsay, "Residential Mobility During Adolescence: Do Even 'Upward' Moves Predict Dropout Risk?" *Social Science Research* 53 (2015): 218–230.

CHAPTER 7: PATCHWORK METROPOLIS

1. Charles Murray, *Coming Apart: The State of White America, 1960–2010* (New York: Crown Forum, 2012); Robert Putnam, *Our Kids: The American Dream in Crisis* (New York: Simon and Schuster, 2015).

2. Alan Ehrenhalt, *The Great Inversion and the Future of the American City* (New York: Knopf, 2012).

3. We mapped the residential locations of the three classes by using census tracts and plotting the neighborhoods where each class has a plurality of residents. Very small tracts—those with fewer than five hundred people—were excluded from our analysis. Data for US metros is from US Census Bureau, American Community Survey, 2010, www.census.gov/programs-surveys /acs/#. The data for London cover its Lower Level Super Output Areas (LSOAs), which are roughly comparable to US census tracts. The data were supplied to us by the United Kingdom's Office for National Statistics for the year 2011. The data from Canada are from Statistics Canada, "2006 Census Data Products," http://www12.statcan.gc.ca/census-recensement/2006 /dp-pd/index-eng.cfm. We also mapped the locations of the urban core (defined as the area within two miles of the city hall); major transit lines; universities and knowledge-based institutions; and natural amenities such as parks, open space, riverfronts, and coastlines, which I do not include here for reasons of space and legibility. See Richard Florida and Patrick Adler, "The Patchwork Metropolis: The Morphology of the Divided Post-Industrial City," Martin Prosperity Institute, Rotman School of Management, University of Toronto, September 2015, http://martinprosperity .org/media/2015-MPIWP-006_Patchwork-Metropolis_Florida-Adler .pdf; see also Richard Florida, Zara Matheson, Patrick Adler, and Taylor Brydges, *The Divided City and the Shape of the New Metropolis* (Toronto: Martin Prosperity Institute, Rotman School of Management, University of Toronto, 2014), http://martinprosperity.org/content/the-divided -city-and-the-shape-of-the-new-metropolis.

4. Terry Clark, Richard Lloyd, Kenneth Wong, and Pushpam Jain, "Amenities Drive Urban Growth," *Journal of Urban Affairs* 24, no. 5 (2002):

493–515; Richard Florida, "The Economic Geography of Talent," *Annals of the Association of American Geographers* 92 (2002): 743–755; Edward Glaeser, Jed Kolko, and Albert Saiz, "Consumer City," *Journal of Economic Geography* 1, no 1 (2001): 27.

5. See Robert Owens, "Mapping the City: Innovation and Continuity in the Chicago School of Sociology, 1920–1934," *American Sociologist* 43, no. 3 (September 2012): 264–293; Martin Bulmer, *The Chicago School of Sociology: Institutionalization, Diversity, and the Rise of Sociological Research* (Chicago: University of Chicago Press, 1986).

6. Robert Ezra Park, Ernest W. Burgess, and Roderick D. McKenzie, *The City* (Chicago: University of Chicago Press, 1925). Burgess also published a seminal study of residential segregation; see Ernest W. Burgess, "Residential Segregation in American Cities," *Annals of the American Academy of Political and Social Science* 140, no. 1 (November 1928): 105–115.

7. Homer Hoyt, "The Structure and Growth of Residential Neighborhoods in American Cities," Federal Housing Administration, 1939; Chauncy Harris and Edward Ullman, "The Nature of Cities," *Annals of the American Academy of Political and Social Science* 242 (1945): 7–17.

8. On the flight from destiny, see Edgar Hoover and Raymond Vernon, *Anatomy of a Metropolis: The Changing Distribution of People and Jobs Within the New York Metropolitan Region* (Cambridge, MA: Harvard University Press, 1959). Vernon later developed his classic product cycle model of industrial location to explain how the rise of standardized manufacturing technologies and automation were allowing factories to move to suburban green-field and foreign offshore locations, where land and labor were cheaper. Raymond Vernon, "International Investment and International Trade in the Product Cycle," *Quarterly Journal of Economics* 80, no. 2 (May 1966): 190–207. On the edge city, see Joel Garreau, *Edge City: Life on the New Frontier* (New York: Anchor Books, 1991). Reflecting upon these changes in the postindustrial metropolis, urban theorists who came to be called the "LA School" argued that metropolitan areas such as LA and other Sunbelt regions no longer grew in a ring-like fashion from the urban center but in a less coherent and more spread-out pattern with a multiplicity of industrial, commercial, and residential zones. See Michael Dear, "The Los Angeles School of Urbanism: An Intellectual History," *Urban Geography* 24, no. 6 (2003): 493–509.

9. J. David Hulchanski, "The Three Cities Within Toronto: Income Polarization Among Toronto's Neighborhoods, 1970–2005," Cities Centre,

University of Toronto, 2010, www.urbancentre.utoronto.ca/pdfs/curp/tnrn/Three-Cities-Within-Toronto-2010-Final.pdf.

10. Sam Bass Warner, *Streetcar Suburbs: The Process of Growth in Boston, 1870–1900*, 2nd ed. (Cambridge, MA: Harvard University Press, 1978).

11. AnnaLee Saxenian, *Regional Advantage: Culture and Competition in Silicon Valley and Route 128* (Cambridge, MA: Harvard University Press, 1994).

12. Richard Florida, "Detroit Shows Way to Beat Inner City Blues," *Financial Times*, April 9, 2013; Richard Florida, "Don't Let Bankruptcy Fool You: Detroit's Not Dead," *CityLab*, July 22, 2013, www.theatlanticcities.com/jobs-and-economy/2013/07/dont-let-bankruptcy-fool-you-detroits-not-dead/6261; Tim Alberta, "Is Dan Gilbert Detroit's New Superhero?" *National Journal*, February 27, 2014, www.nationaljournal.com/next-economy/america-360/is-dan-gilbert-detroits-new-superhero.

13. Thomas Sugrue, *The Origins of the Urban Crisis: Race and Inequality in Postwar Detroit* (Princeton, NJ: Princeton University Press, 2005).

14. Richard Florida, "Visions of Pittsburgh's Future," *Pittsburgh Quarterly* (Fall 2013), http://pittsburghquarterly.com/pq-commerce/pq-region/item/82-visions-of-pittsburgh-s-future.html.

15. Plurality creative-class tracts are negatively correlated with both plurality service-class tracts (−0.62) and plurality working-class tracts (−0.77). Plurality creative-class tracts are highly correlated with average income (0.75) and the share of adults who are college graduates (0.90). Plurality service-class tracts are negatively correlated with average income (−0.49) and the share of adults who are college graduates (−0.45). Plurality working-class tracts are also negatively correlated with average income (−0.56) and the share of adults who are college graduates (−0.78).

CHAPTER 8: SUBURBAN CRISIS

1. Dis, "The Nixon-Khrushchev 'Kitchen Debate,'" Everything2, April 26, 2000, http://everything2.com/title/The+Nixon-Khrushchev+%2522Kitchen+Debate%2522.

2. On dead malls, see Nelson D. Schwartz, "The Economics (and Nostalgia) of Dead Malls," *New York Times*, January 3, 2015, www.nytimes.com/2015/01/04/business/the-economics-and-nostalgia-of-dead-malls.html. The term slumburbia is from Timothy Egan, "Slumburbia," *New York Times*, February 10, 2010, http://opinionator.blogs.nytimes.com/2010/02/10/slumburbia.

3. Jed Kolko, "How Suburban Are Big American Cities?," *FiveThirty-Eight*, May 21, 2015, http://fivethirtyeight.com/features/how-suburban-are-big-american-cities.

4. Jed Kolko, "Urban Revival? Not for Most Americans," JedKolko.com, March 30, 2016, http://jedkolko.com/2016/03/30/urban-revival-not-for-most-americans; Jed Kolko, "City Limits: How Real Is the Urban Jobs Comeback?" JedKolko.com, January 29, 2016, http://jedkolko.com/2016/01/19/city-limits-how-real-is-the-urban-jobs-comeback. See also Karyn Lacy, "The New Sociology of Suburbs: A Research Agenda for Analysis of Emerging Trends," *Annual Review of Sociology* 42 (July 2016): 369–384, www.annualreviews.org/doi/full/10.1146/annurev-soc-071312-145657.

5. Alan Berube, William H. Frey, Alec Friedhoff, Emily Garr, Emilia Istrate, Elizabeth Kneebone, Robert Puentes, Adie Tomer, and Howard Wial, "State of Metropolitan America," Brookings Institution, 2010, www.brookings.edu/research/reports/2010/05/09-metro-america; William H. Frey, "The End of Suburban White Flight," Brookings Institution, July 23, 2015, www.brookings.edu/blogs/the-avenue/posts/2015/07/23-suburban-white-flight-frey.

6. Elizabeth Kneebone and Alan Berube, *Confronting Suburban Poverty in America* (Washington, DC: Brookings Institution Press, 2013).

7. Mary O'Hara, "Alan Berube: We Are Moving Poverty to the Suburbs," *The Guardian*, May 6, 2015, www.theguardian.com/society/2015/may/06/alan-berube-moving-poverty-to-suburbs.

8. Elizabeth Kneebone, "The Growth and Spread of Concentrated Poverty, 2000 to 2008–2012," Brookings Institution, July 31, 2014, www.brookings.edu/research/interactives/2014/concentrated-poverty; Richard Florida, "The Living-in-the-Basement Generation," *Washington Monthly* (November/December 2013), www.washingtonmonthly.com/magazine/november_december_2013/features/the_livinginthebasement_genera047358.php; Kristen Lewis and Sarah Burd-Sharps, "Halve the Gap by 2030: Youth Disconnection in America's Cities," Social Science Research Council, 2013, http://ssrc-static.s3.amazonaws.com/moa/MOA-Halve-the-Gap-ALL-10.25.13.pdf.

9. William H. Frey, "Demographic Reversal: Cities Thrive, Suburbs Sputter," Brookings Institution, June 29, 2012, www.brookings.edu/research/opinions/2012/06/29-cities-suburbs-frey; William H. Frey, "Will This Be the Decade of Big City Growth?," Brookings Institution, May 23, 2014, www.brookings.edu/research/opinions/2014/05/23-decade-of-big-city-growth-frey.

10. Cody Fuller, "Rockin' the Suburbs: Home Values in Urban, Suburban, and Rural Areas," Zillow Research, January 16, 2016, www.zillow.com /research/urban-suburban-rural-values-rents-11714.

11. Elizabeth Kneebone and Steven Raphael, "City and Suburban Crime Trends in Metropolitan America," Brookings Institution, 2011; Cameron McWhirter and Gary Fields, "Crime Migrates to Suburbs," *Wall Street Journal*, December 30, 2012, www.wsj.com/articles/SB1000142412788732 330040457820687317942749 6.

12. Data on Ferguson are from Elizabeth Kneebone, "Ferguson, MO, Emblematic of Growing Suburban Poverty," Brookings Institution, August 15, 2014, www.brookings.edu/blogs/the-avenue/posts/2014 /08/15-ferguson-suburban-poverty; James Russell, "Ferguson and Failing Suburbs," Jamessrussell.net, August 17, 2015, http://jamessrussell.net /ferguson-and-failing-suburbs; Stephen Bronars, "Half of Ferguson's Young African-American Men Are Missing," *Forbes*, March 18, 2015, www.forbes.com/sites/modeledbehavior/2015/03/18/half-of-fergusons -young-african-american-men-are-missing.

13. On the connection between commuting time and economic mobility, see Reid Ewing, Shima Hamidi, James B. Grace, and Yehua Dennis Wei, "Does Urban Sprawl Hold Down Upward Mobility?" *Landscape and Urban Planning* 148 (April 2016): 80–88.

14. On the delivery of local services to the suburbs, see Arthur Nelson as cited in Leigh Gallagher, *The End of the Suburbs: Where the American Dream Is Moving* (New York: Portfolio Penguin, 2013). For the UCLA study, by the California Center for Sustainable Communities, see Laura Bliss, "L.A.'s New 'Energy Atlas' Maps: Who Sucks the Most Off the Grid," *CityLab*, October 6, 2015, www.citylab.com/housing/2015/10/las-new -energy-atlas-maps-who-sucks-the-most-off-the-grid/409135. Of course, nearly 20 percent of Bell's population lives below the poverty line, which means that its residents use less air conditioning, fewer computers, and so on. On the overall cost of sprawl to the US economy, see Todd Litman, "Analysis of Public Policies That Unintentionally Encourage and Subsidize Urban Sprawl," London School of Economics and Political Science, for the Global Commission on the Economy and Climate for the New Climate Economy, 2015, http://static.newclimateeconomy.report/wp-content /uploads/2015/03/public-policies-encourage-sprawl-nce-report.pdf.

15. Christopher Ingraham, "The Astonishing Human Potential Wasted on Commutes," *Washington Post*, February 25, 2016, www.washingtonpost

.com/news/wonk/wp/2016/02/25/how-much-of-your-life-youre-wasting-on
-your-commute.

16. On the health costs of sprawl, see Reid Ewing, Gail Meakins, Shima
Hamidi, and Arthur C. Nelson, "Relationship Between Urban Sprawl and
Physical Activity, Obesity, and Morbidity: Update and Refinement," *Health
and Place* 26 (March 2014): 118–126; Reid Ewing and Shima Hamidi,
"Measuring Sprawl, 2014," Smart Growth America, April 2014, www
.smartgrowthamerica.org/documents/measuring-sprawl-2014.pdf; Jane E.
Brody, "Commuting's Hidden Cost," *New York Times*, October 28, 2013,
http://well.blogs.nytimes.com/2013/10/28/commutings-hidden-cost. On
commuting as life's most undesirable activity, see Daniel Kahneman and
Alan B. Krueger, "Developments in the Measurement of Subjective Well-
Being," *Journal of Economic Perspectives* 20, no. 1 (Winter 2006): 3–24.

17. On Brooklyn, see Justin Fox, "Want a Job? Go to Brooklyn,"
Bloomberg View, January 21, 2016, www.bloombergview.com/articles
/2016-01-21/want-a-job-go-to-brooklyn. On the growth in jobs in areas
close to the urban center between 2007 and 2011, see Joseph Cortright,
Surging City Center Job Growth (Portland, OR: City Observatory, 2015),
http://cityobservatory.org/wp-content/uploads/2015/02/Surging-City-Center
-Jobs.pdf. The urban centers grew jobs at a 0.5 percent annual rate between
2007 and 2011, compared to just 0.1 percent for peripheral suburban areas.
On higher pay in urban centers, see Jed Kolko, "The Urban Jobs Comeback,
Continued: Follow the Money," JedKolko.com, January 20, 2016, http://
jedkolko.com/2016/01/20/the-urban-jobs-comeback-continued-follow-the
-money. The suburbs are home to 54 percent of all jobs in large metros (the
ones with more than a million people, which account for the lion's share of
all jobs across the country)—with 38 percent in higher-density suburbs close
to the urban core and 16 percent in farther-out lower-density suburbs and
exurbs. See Kolko, "City Limits."

18. The cutoff is based on geographer Stephen Higley's rankings of America's 1,000 richest neighborhoods. The list is based on US Census data on
contiguous block groups with mean household incomes of $200,000 or
more. Stephen Higley, "The Higley 1000," Higley1000.com, February 17,
2014, http://higley1000.com/archives/638.

19. These data are from Zillow's research data site, www.zillow.com
/research/data. As I mentioned in Chapter 2, these data exclude the nondisclosure states of Alaska, Idaho, Indiana, Kansas, Louisiana, Maine, Mississippi,
Missouri, Montana, New Mexico, North Dakota, Texas, Utah, and Wyoming.

20. Jed Kolko, "No, Suburbs Aren't All the Same; The Suburbiest Ones Are Growing Fastest," *CityLab*, February 5, 2015, www.citylab.com/housing /2015/02/no-suburbs-arent-all-the-same-the-suburbiest-ones-are-growing -fastest/385183.

21. Richard Florida, "Welcome to Blueburbia and Other Landmarks on America's New Map," *Politico* (November 2013), www.politico.com /magazine/story/2013/11/welcome-to-blueburbia-and-other-landmarks -on-americas-new-map-98957.html; Richard Florida, "The Suburbs Are the New Swing States," *CityLab*, November 29, 2013, www.citylab.com /politics/2013/11/suburbs-are-new-swing-states/7706.

22. Richard Florida, "The Geography of the Republican Primaries," *CityLab*, April 12, 2016, www.citylab.com/politics/2016/04/the-geography -of-the-republican-primaries/477693; Neil Irwin and Josh Katz, "The Geography of Trumpism," *New York Times*, March 12, 2016, www.nytimes .com/2016/03/13/upshot/the-geography-of-trumpism.html.

23. On the class lines of Trump's support, see Andrew Flowers, "Where Trump Got His Edge," *FiveThirtyEight*, November 11, 2016, http://five thirtyeight.com/features/where-trump-got-his-edge; Jon Huang, Samuel Jacoby, K. K. Rebecca Lai, and Michael Strickland, "Election 2016: Exit Polls," *New York Times*, November 2016, www.nytimes.com/interactive /2016/11/08/us/politics/election-exit-polls.html. On the geographic divide, see Jed Kolko, "The Geography of the 2016 Vote," jedkolko.com, November 11, 2016, http://jedkolko.com/2016/11/11/the-geography-of-the-2016 -vote; and Jed Kolko, "Trump Support Was Stronger Where the Economy Is Weaker," *FiveThirtyEight*, November 10, 2016, http://fivethirtyeight.com /features/trump-was-stronger-where-the-economy-is-weaker.

24. Andrew Gelman, *Red State, Blue State, Rich State, Poor State: Why Americans Vote the Way They Do* (Princeton, NJ: Princeton University Press, 2009).

25. Dave Troy, "The Real Republican Adversary? Population Density," Davetroy.com, November 19, 2012, http://davetroy.com/posts/the-real -republican-adversary-population-density. See also Richard Florida and Sara Johnson, "What Republicans Are Really Up Against: Population Density," *CityLab*, November 26, 2012, www.citylab.com/politics/2012/11 /what-republicans-are-really-against-population-density/3953.

26. My own analysis of state-level voting showed Clinton's vote shares to be positively correlated with density (0.71) and the urban share of state land area (0.63), as well as wages (0.82), share of college grads (0.77), and the

creative class (0.72), while Trump's vote shares were negatively correlated with density (–0.61) and the urban share of state land area (–0.54) as well as wages (–0.81) and college grads (–0.81). See Richard Florida, "It's Still About Geography and Class," *CityLab*, November 17, 2016, www.citylab.com/politics /2016/11/americas-great-divide-of-class-and-geography/507908/. At the metro level, the correlations between density and the Democratic share of the presidential vote across counties increased from 0.61 in 2000 to 0.75 in 2016. See Kolko, "Geography of the 2016 Election."

27. Jefferey Sellers, "Place, Institutions and Political Ecology of U.S. Metropolitan Areas," in Jefferey Sellers, Daniel Kübler, Alan Walks, and Melanie Walter-Rogg, *The Political Ecology of the Metropolis: Metropolitan Sources of Electoral Behaviour in Eleven Countries* (Colchester, UK: ECPR Press, 2013), 37–85. Sellers has compiled a large time-series dataset on what he dubs the "metropolitanization" of American politics, which includes data on local voting patterns in Atlanta, Birmingham, Cincinnati, Detroit, Fresno, Kalamazoo, Los Angeles, New York, Philadelphia, Seattle, Syracuse, and Wichita. On Trump in 2016, see Emily Badger, Quoctrung Bui, and Adam Pearce, "This Election Highlighted a Growing Urban-Rural Split," *New York Times*, November 11, 2016, www.nytimes.com/2016/11/12 /upshot/this-election-highlighted-a-growing-rural-urban-split.html; Lazaro Gamio and Dan Keating, "How Trump Redrew the Electoral Map, from Sea to Shining Sea," *Washington Post*, November 9, 2016, www.washington post.com/graphics/politics/2016-election/election-results-from-coast-to-coast.

28. Eva Jacobs and Stephanie Shipp, "How Family Spending Has Changed in the U.S.," *Monthly Labor Review* (March 1990): 20–27.

CHAPTER 9: THE CRISIS OF GLOBAL URBANIZATION

1. Medellín Declaration, "Equity as a Foundation of Sustainable Urban Development," UN-Habitat, Seventh World Urban Forum, April 2014, http://wuf7.unhabitat.org/Media/Default/PDF/Medell%C3%ADn%20 Declaration.pdf.

2. Joseph Parilla, Jesus Leal Trujillo, Alan Berube, and Tao Ran, *Global Metro Monitor*, Brookings Institution, 2015, www.brookings.edu/research /reports2/2015/01/22-global-metro-monitor.

3. According to UN-Habitat, slums are places where people lack one or more of the following: access to clean water, access to a toilet, adequate and safe housing, sufficient living space with not more than two people sharing the same room, and reasonable protections from being thrown out or evicted.

See UN-Habitat, *Streets as Tools for Urban Transformation in Slums: A Street-Led Approach to Citywide Slum Upgrading*, UN-Habitat, 2012, http://unhabitat.org/books/streets-as-tools-for-urban-transformation-in-slums, 5.

4. McKinsey Global Institute, *Urban World: Mapping the Economic Power of Cities*, March 2011, www.mckinsey.com/insights/urbanization/urban_world.

5. Brandon Fuller and Paul Romer, "Urbanization as Opportunity," World Bank, 2013, http://documents.worldbank.org/curated/en/2013/11/18868564/urbanization-opportunity, 1–13.

6. For the data projections out to 2030, see *Organisation for Economic Co-Operation and Development, The Metropolitan Century: Understanding Urbanisation and Its Consequences* (Paris: OECD, 2015), www.oecd.org/greengrowth/the-metropolitan-century-9789264228733-en.htm. For the projections out to 2150, see Robert H. Samet, "Complexity, the Science of Cities, and Long-Range Futures," *Futures* 47 (2013): 49–58.

7. The comparison is for a 16GB iPhone 6 in 2015. See Catey Hill, "This Is How Long It Takes to Pay for an iPhone in These Cities," Marketwatch, September 24, 2015, www.marketwatch.com/story/this-is-how-long-it-takes-to-pay-for-an-iphone-in-these-cities-2015-09-24.

8. Parilla et al., *Global Metro Monitor*.

9. UN-Habitat, *State of the World's Cities 2012/2013: Prosperity of Cities* (New York: Routledge, 2013), http://mirror.unhabitat.org/pmss/listItemDetails.aspx?publicationID=3387. The good news is that the share of the urban population living in slums in the developing world fell from 39 percent in the year 2000 to 32 percent in 2010—meaning that some 227 million slum-dwellers gained access to improved water and sanitation and better housing over this period. The bad news is that the world's slum population nevertheless actually grew, swelling alongside the rapid growth in population across the developing world. See UN-Habitat, *State of the World's Cities 2010/2011: Bridging the Urban Divide* (New York: Routledge, 2010), https://sustainabledevelopment.un.org/content/documents/11143016_alt.pdf, 7. Also see UN-Habitat, *Urbanization and Development: Emerging Futures*, World Cities Report 2016, http://wcr.unhabitat.org/wp-content/uploads/sites/16/2016/05/WCR-%20Full-Report-2016.pdf; Eugenie L. Birch, Shahana Chattaraj, and Susan M. Wachter, eds., *Slums: How Informal Real Estate Markets Work* (Philadelphia: University of Pennsylvania Press, 2016).

10. "UPA's Target: A Slum-Free India in 5 Years," *The Times of India*, June 5, 2009, http://timesofindia.indiatimes.com/india/UPAs-target-A-slum-free-India-in-5-years/articleshow/4618346.cms?referral=PM.

11. Benjamin Marx, Thomas Stoker, and Tavneet Suri, "The Economics of Slums in the Developing World," *Journal of Economic Perspectives* 27, no. 4 (2013): 187–210.

12. On this point, see Edward Glaeser, "A World of Cities: The Causes and Consequences of Urbanization in Poorer Countries," Paper no. 19745, National Bureau of Economic Research, 2013, www.nber.org/papers/w19745; Richard Florida, "Why So Many Mega-Cities Remain So Poor," *CityLab*, January 16, 2014, www.citylab.com/work/2014/01/why-so-many-mega-cities-remain-so-poor/8083.

13. Remi Jedwab and Dietrich Vollrath, "Urbanization Without Growth in Historical Perspective," *Explorations in Economic History* 57 (July 2015): 1–94.

14. Ibid.; Richard Florida, "The Problem of Urbanization Without Economic Growth" *CityLab*, June 12, 2015, www.citylab.com/work/2015/06/the-problem-of-urbanization-without-economic-growth/395648.

15. Richard Florida, "Why Big Cities Matter in the Developing World," *CityLab*, January 14, 2014, www.citylab.com/work/2014/01/why-big-cities-matter-developing-world/6025.

16. The data are from Richard Florida, Charlotta Mellander, and Tim Gulden, "Global Metropolis: Assessing Economic Activity in Urban Centers Based on Nighttime Satellite Images," *Professional Geographer* 64, no. 2 (2010): 178–187. On the broader issue of using satellite data to estimate economic output, see J. Vernon Henderson, Adam Storeygard, and David N. Weil, "Measuring Economic Growth from Outer Space," *American Economic Review* 102, no. 2 (2012): 994–1028. As they note, "Night lights data are available at a far greater degree of geographic fineness than is attainable in any standard income and product accounts."

17. Jane Jacobs, *The Economy of Cities* (New York: Random House, 1969).

18. John F.C. Turner, "Housing as a Verb," in John F.C. Turner and Robert Fichter, eds., *Freedom to Build: Dweller Control of the Housing Process* (New York: Macmillan, 1972).

19. Doug Saunders, *Arrival City: How the Largest Migration in History Is Reshaping Our World* (New York: Pantheon, 2010); Doug Saunders, "Liu Gong Li: Inside a Chinese Arrival City," Arrival City video, n.d., http://arrivalcity.net/video.

20. Janice Perlman, *Favela: Four Decades of Living on the Edge in Rio de Janeiro* (Oxford: Oxford University Press, 2010); Janice Perlman, "Global Urbanization and the Resources of Informality: Moving from Despair to

Hope," Presented at the Humanity, Sustainable Nature: Our Responsibility Workshop, Vatican, May 2–6, 2014.

21. "SFI Takes First Steps Toward a Science of Slums," Santa Fe Institute, February 6, 2013, www.santafe.edu/news/item/gates-slums-announce; Rebecca Ruiz, "Scientists Looking to Solve the Problem of Slums Devise a New Way to Look at Big Data," Txchnologist.com, January 22, 2013, http://txchnologist.com/post/41201839670/scientists-looking-to-solve-the-problem-of-slums; Luis Bettencourt, "Mass Urbanization Could Lead to Unprecedented Human Creativity, but Only If We Do It Right," *Huffington Post*, August 29, 2014, www.huffingtonpost.com/luis-bettencourt/mass-urbanization-creativity_b_5670222.html?1409329471.

22. The study proposes providing small grants or developing business incubators to help the urban poor develop and scale their rudimentary enterprises. Laura Doering, "Necessity Is the Mother of Isomorphism: Poverty and Market Creativity in Panama," *Sociology of Development* 2, no. 3 (Fall 2016): 235–264; Phyllis Korkki, "Attacking Poverty to Foster Creativity in Entrepreneurs," *New York Times*, March 12, 2016, www.nytimes.com/2016/03/13/business/attacking-poverty-to-foster-creativity-in-entrepreneurs.html.

23. These data on population growth, urban expansion and density, and those in the paragraph below on streets are from Shlomo Angel, *Atlas of Urban Expansion*, Lincoln Institute of Land Policy, 2016.

24. UN-Habitat, *Streets as Tools for Urban Transformation in Slums.*

25. Mark Swilling, "The Curse of Urban Sprawl: How Cities Grow and Why This Has to Change," *The Guardian*, July 12, 2016, www.theguardian.com/cities/2016/jul/12/urban-sprawl-how-cities-grow-change-sustainability-urban-age.

26. Letty Reimerink, "Medellín Made Urban Escalators Famous, but Have They Had Any Impact?," *Citiscope*, July 24, 2014, http://citiscope.org/story/2014/medellin-made-urban-escalators-famous-have-they-had-any-impact; "City of the Year," *Wall Street Journal Magazine*, 2012, http://online.wsj.com/ad/cityoftheyear.

27. "Sustainable Cities and Communities" is Goal 11 of the UN Sustainable Development Goals as outlined in its 2030 Agenda for Sustainable Development, www.un.org/sustainabledevelopment/sustainable-development-goals.

CHAPTER 10: URBANISM FOR ALL

1. Russell Berman, "Hillary Clinton's Modest Infrastructure Proposal," *The Atlantic*, December 1, 2015, www.theatlantic.com/politics/archive

/2015/12/hillary-clintons-modest-infrastructure-proposal/418068; Paul Krugman, "Ideology and Investment," *New York Times*, October 26, 2014, www.nytimes.com/2014/10/27/opinion/paul-krugman-ideology -and-investment.html; Ezra Klein, "Larry Summers on Why the Economy Is Broken—and How to Fix It," *Washington Post*, January 14, 2014, www.washingtonpost.com/blogs/wonkblog/wp/2014/01/14/larry-summers -on-why-the-economy-is-broken-and-how-to-fix-it.

2. The New Urban Crisis Index is positively associated with the population size (0.61) and population density (0.55) of metros. It is also positively associated with the share of commuters who take transit to work (0.42), a proxy measure of density, and it is negatively associated with the share of commuters who drive to work alone (−0.38), a proxy measure for sprawl. It is positively associated with wages (0.50), income (0.34), and economic output per capita (0.34). In addition, the New Urban Crisis Index is positively associated with the concentration of high-tech industry (0.61), the creative-class share of the workforce (0.55), and the share of adults who hold college degrees (0.55). Conversely, it is negatively associated with the share of the workforce in blue-collar working-class jobs (−0.55). As with inequality and segregation, the New Urban Crisis Index is positively associated with two key markers of diversity—the adults who are foreign-born (0.52) and the share who are gay or lesbian (0.61). In addition, the New Urban Crisis Index tracks the political affiliations and voting patterns of metros: it is positively associated with more liberal metros (0.59), measured as the share of voters who voted for Clinton in 2016, and negatively associated with more conservative metros (−0.55), measured as the share of voters who voted for Trump in 2016. See Appendix Table 4 for the full rankings of all 350-plus metros on the New Urban Crisis Index.

3. On the concept of secular stagnation, see Timothy Taylor, "Secular Stagnation: Back to Alvin Hansen," *Conversable Economist*, December 12, 2013, http://conversableeconomist.blogspot.ca/2013/12/secular-stagnation-back -to-alvin-hanson.html; Larry Summers, "U.S. Economic Prospects: Secular Stagnation, Hysteresis, and the Zero Lower Bound," *Business Economics* 49, no. 2 (2014): 65–73, http://larrysummers.com/wp-content/uploads/2014/06/ NABE-speech-Lawrence-H.-Summers1.pdf. On the decline in American innovation and productivity more broadly, see Robert J. Gordon, *The Rise and Fall of American Growth* (Princeton, NJ: Princeton University Press, 2016).

4. Krugman, "Ideology and Investment."

5. Frederick Jackson Turner, "The Significance of the Frontier in American History," Paper presented at American Historical Association

meeting, Chicago, July 12, 1893, World Columbian Exposition, http://national
humanitiescenter.org/pds/gilded/empire/text1/turner.pdf; Frederick Jackson
Turner, *The Frontier in American History* (New York: Henry Holt, 1921);
Kenneth Jackson, *Crabgrass Frontier: The Suburbanization of the United
States* (New York: Oxford University Press, 1987).

6. Gerald Gamm and Thad Kousser, "No Strength in Numbers: The Failure of Big-City Bills in American State Legislatures, 1880–2000," *American Political Science Review* 107, no. 4 (2013): 663–678. The study, which
tracked 1,700 pieces of legislation from 1881 to 2000 that dealt with cities
or counties in thirteen state legislatures, found that bills dealing with cities
of 100,000 or more were far less likely to pass than those aimed at smaller
places; bills that were introduced by legislators from smaller places were
twice as likely to pass as ones that originated in big cities.

7. Richard Florida, "Is Life Better in America's Red States?," *New York
Times*, January 3, 2015, www.nytimes.com/2015/01/04/opinion/sunday/is
-life-better-in-americas-red-states.html.

8. Tyler Cowen, "Market Urbanism and Tax Incidence," Marginal Revolution, April 19, 2016, http://marginalrevolution.com/marginalrevolution
/2016/04/market-urbanism-and-tax-incidence.html.

9. As quoted in Stephen Wickens, "Jane Jacobs: Honoured in the
Breach," *Globe and Mail*, May 6, 2011, www.theglobeandmail.com/arts
/jane-jacobs-honoured-in-the-breach/article597904.

10. Henry George, *Progress and Poverty* (New York: Robert Schalkenbach
Foundation, 1997 [1879]). For more on George, see Edward T. O'Donnell,
Henry George and the Crisis of Inequality (New York: Columbia University
Press, 2015); "Why Henry George Had a Point," *The Economist*, April 1,
2015, www.economist.com/blogs/freeexchange/2015/04/land-value-tax.

11. David Schleicher, "City Unplanning," *Yale Law Journal* 122, no. 7
(May 2013): 1670–1737.

12. Enrico Moretti and Chang-Tai Hsieh, "Why Do Cities Matter? Local
Growth and Aggregate Growth," April 2015, http://faculty.chicagobooth
.edu/chang-tai.hsieh/research/growth.pdf.

13. Richard Florida, "The Mega-Regions of North America," Martin
Prosperity Institute, Rotman School of Management, University of Toronto,
March 11, 2014, http://martinprosperity.org/content/the-mega-regions-of
-north-america.

14. These time estimates are from Richard Florida, "Mega-Regions
and High-Speed Rail," May 4, 2009, *The Atlantic*, www.theatlantic.com
/national/archive/2009/05/mega-regions-and-high-speed-rail/17006.

15. Todd Sinai and Joseph Gyourko, "The (Un)Changing Geographic Distribution of Housing Tax Benefits, 1980 to 2000," NBER Working Paper no. 10322, National Bureau of Economic Research, February 2004, www .nber.org/papers/w10322.pdf; Robert Collinson, Ingrid Gould Ellen, and Jens Ludwig, "Low-Income Housing Policy," NBER Working Paper no. 21071, National Bureau of Economic Research, 2015, www.nber.org /papers/w21071; Richard Florida, "The U.S. Spends Far More on Home-owner Subsidies Than It Does on Affordable Housing," *CityLab*, April 17, 2015, www.citylab.com/housing/2015/04/the-us-spends-far-more-on-home owner-subsidies-than-it-does-on-affordable-housing/390666.

16. Richard Florida, "How the Crash Will Reshape America," *The Atlantic*, March 2009, www.theatlantic.com/magazine/archive/2009/03/how-the -crash-will-reshape-america/307293; Richard Florida, *The Great Reset: How the Post-Crash Economy Will Change the Way We Live and Work* (New York: Harper Business, 2010); Nick Timiraos, "U.S. Homeownership Rate Falls to 20-Year Low," *Wall Street Journal*, January 29, 2015, http://blogs.wsj .com/economics/2015/01/29/u-s-homeownership-rate-falls-to-20-year-low.

17. Data on the increase in renting and on rent burdens below are from Harvard's Joint Center for Housing Studies. See *America's Rental Housing: Expanding Options for Diverse and Growing Demand*, Joint Center for Housing Studies of Harvard University, December 2015, www.jchs.harvard .edu/research/publications/americas-rental-housing-expanding-options -diverse-and-growing-demand.

18. Richard Florida, "The Steady Rise of Renting," *CityLab*, February 16, 2016, www.citylab.com/housing/2016/02/the-rise-of-renting-in-the-us /462948.

19. Miriam Zuk and Karen Chappel, "Housing Production, Filtering, and Displacement: Untangling the Relationships," University of California–Berkeley, Institute of Governmental Studies, Research Brief, May 2016, www.urbandisplacement.org/sites/default/files/images/udp_research_brief _052316.pdf.

20. Arindrajit Dube, "The Minimum We Can Do," *New York Times*, November 30, 2013, http://opinionator.blogs.nytimes.com/2013/11/30/the -minimum-we-can-do; Arindrajit Dube, T. William Lester, and Michael Reich, "Minimum Wage Effects Across State Borders: Estimates Using Contiguous Counties," *Review of Economics and Statistics* 92, no. 4 (2010): 945–964.

21. Richard Florida, "The Case for a Local Minimum Wage," *CityLab*, December 11, 2013, www.citylab.com/work/2013/12/why-every-city-needs -its-own-minimum-wage/7801; Arindrajit Dube, "Proposal 13: Designing

Thoughtful Minimum Wage Policy at the State and Local Levels," Brookings Institution, 2014, www.brookings.edu/research/papers/2014/06/19 -minimum-wage-policy-state-local-levels-dube.

22. James Womack, Daniel T. Jones, and Daniel Roos, *The Machine That Changed the World* (New York: Free Press, 1990).

23. Zeynep Ton, *The Good Jobs Strategy: How the Smartest Companies Invest in Employees to Lower Costs and Boost Profits* (Boston: Houghton Mifflin Harcourt, 2014); Richard Florida, "The Business Case for Paying Service Workers More," *CityLab*, March 3, 2014, www.theatlanticcities .com/jobs-and-economy/2014/03/case-paying-service-workers-more/8506.

24. Michael Erard, "Creative Capital? In the City of Ideas, the People with Ideas Are the Ones with Day Jobs," *Austin Chronicle*, February 28, 2003 www.austinchronicle.com/news/2003-02-28/147078.

25. Robert J. Sampson, "Individual and Community Economic Mobility in the Great Recession Era: The Spatial Foundations of Persistent Inequality," in *Economic Mobility: Research and Ideas on Strengthening Families, Communities, and the Economy* (St. Louis: Federal Reserve Bank, 2016).

26. On early childhood education, see James J. Heckman, "Skill Formation and the Economics of Investing in Disadvantaged Children," *Science* 312 (June 2006): 1900–1902; William Dickens, Isabell Sawhill, and Jeffrey Tebbs, "The Effects of Investing in Early Education on Economic Growth," Brookings Institution, June 2006; Timothy Bartik, "Investing in Kids: Early Childhood Programs and Local Economic Development," Upjohn Institute, 2014, http://research.upjohn.org/up_press/207. On the role of public education in US economic growth, see Claudia Goldin and Lawrence Katz, *The Race Between Education and Technology* (Cambridge, MA: Harvard University Press, 2008).

27. See Robert A. Moffit, 'The Negative Income Tax and the Evolution of U.S. Welfare Policy," *Journal of Economic Perspectives* 17, no. 1 (August 2003): 119–140.

28. One commentator calls it venture capital for the people. Steven Randy Waldman, "VC for the People," Interfluidity, April 16, 2014, www .interfluidity.com/v2/5066.html.

29. Richard Florida, "How Stronger Cities Could Help Fix Fragile Nations," *CityLab*, November 19, 2015, www.citylab.com/politics/2015/11 /how-stronger-cities-could-help-fix-fragile-nations/416661.

30. Brandon Fuller, "Rethinking Refugee Camps: A Practical Approach to Solving an Intractable Problem," *City Journal*, December 11, 2015, www .city-journal.org/2015/eon1211bf.html.

31. Royal Society for the Encouragement of Arts, Manufactures and Commerce, "Unleashing Metro Growth: Final Recommendations of the City Growth Commission," London, October 2015, www.thersa.org /discover/publications-and-articles/reports/unleashing-metro-growth-final -recommendations.

32. See Benjamin Barber, *If Mayors Ruled the World: Dysfunctional Cites, Rising Nations*, Yale University Press, 2013; Barber, "Can Cities Counter the Power of President-Elect Donald Trump?" *The Nation*, November 14, 2013, www.thenation.com/article/can-cities-counter-the-power-of -president-elect-donald-trump/.

EPILOGUE

1. This chapter draws on a wide range of my thinking and writing since this book was published. See Richard Florida, "A Declaration of Urban Independence," *Politico*, July-August 2017, www.politico.com/magazine/ story/2017/06/23/richard-florida-cities-independent-donald-trump-215288; Richard Florida and Steven Pedigo, "The Case for Inclusive Prosperity," NYU Shack Institute of Real Estate, Urban Lab, September 2017, http:// scps.nyu.edu/content/dam/scps/pdf/200/200-4/200-4-15/Urban-Lab/ NYUSPS-Shack-Urban-Lab-The-Case-for-Inclusive-Prosperity.pdf; Richard Florida, "What the New Urban Anchors Owe Their Cities," *CityLab*, September 21, 2017, www.citylab.com/equity/2017/09/what-the-new-urban -anchors-owe-their-cities/540588; Richard Florida, "The Unaffordable Urban Paradise," *Technology Review*, June 20, 2017, www.technologyreview .com/s/607957/the-unaffordable-urban-paradise; Richard Florida, "Silicon Valley Needs to Be a Better Neighbor," *Financial Times*, August 2, 2017, www.ft.com/content/5be7c806-6e23-11e7-b9c7-15af748b60d0; Richard Florida, "A Tale of Two Cities, and Two Companies," *CityLab*, October 17, 2017, www.citylab.com/equity/2017/10/a-tale-of-two-cities-and-two -companies/543405; Richard Florida and Jodie McLean, "What Inclusive Urban Development Can Look Like," *Harvard Business Review*, July 11, 2017, https://hbr.org/2017/07/what-inclusive-urban-development-can-look-like.

2. This section draws from Florida, "A Tale of Two Cities, and Two Companies." The open letter, "Support a Non-Aggression Pact for Amazon HQ2," is at change.org, https://www.change.org/p/elected -officials-and-community-leaders-of-amazon-hq2-finalist-cities-support -a-non-aggression-pact-for-amazon-s-hq2. Also see, Richard Florida,

"Mayors Say No to Amazon," *Wall Street Journal*, January 28, 2018, https://www.wsj.com/articles/mayors-say-no-to-amazon-1517175734.

3. This section draws from Florida and Pedigo, "The Case for Inclusive Prosperity."

4. Meagan M. Ehlenz, "Neighborhood Revitalization and the Anchor Institution: Assessing the Impact of the University of Pennsylvania's West Philadelphia Initiatives on University City," *Urban Affairs Review*, no. 52 (September 2015): 714–750, http://journals.sagepub.com/doi/abs/10.1177/1078087415601220.

5. See Richard Florida and James Goodnight, "Managing for Creativity," *Harvard Business Review*, July-August 2005, https://hbr.org/2005/07/managing-for-creativity.

6. See Julian Gross, Greg LeRoy, and Madeline Janis-Aparicio, "Community Benefits Agreements: Making Development Projects Accountable," Good Jobs First, 2002, http://community-wealth.org/sites/clone.community-wealth.org/files/downloads/report-gross.pdf; Patricia Salkin and Amy Lavine, "Negotiating for Social Justice and the Promise of Community Benefits Agreements: Case Studies of Current and Developing Agreements," *Journal of Affordable Housing* 17 (Fall 2007 / Spring 2008), https://papers.ssrn.com/sol3/papers.cfm?abstract_id=1117681; Laura Wolf-Powers, "Community Benefits Agreements and Local Government: A Review of Recent Evidence," *Journal of the American Planning Association* 76, no. 2 (2010), www.tandfonline.com/doi/full/10.1080/01944360903490923.

7. Benjamin Barber, "Jihad vs. McWorld," *The Atlantic*, March 1992, www.theatlantic.com/magazine/archive/1992/03/jihad-vs-mcworld/303882; Benjamin Barber, *If Mayors Ruled the World* (New Haven, CT: Yale University Press, 2013); Benjamin Barber, *Cool Cities* (New Haven, CT: Yale University Press, 2017).

8. The Global Parliament of Mayors, https://globalparliamentofmayors.org.

9. Yuval Levin, *The Fractured Republic* (New York: Basic Books, 2016).

10. Alice M. Rivlin, *Reviving the American Dream* (Washington, DC: Brookings Institution Press, 1993).

11. Organisation for Economic Co-operation and Development (OECD), *OECD Regional Outlook 2016: Productive Regions for Inclusive Societies* (Paris: OECD, 2016); OECD, *Governing the City: Policy Highlights* (Paris: OECD, 2015). Also see Philip McCann and Raquel Ortega-Argilés, "Transforming European Regional Policy: A Results-Driven Agenda and Smart

Specialization," *Oxford Review of Economic Policy* 29, no. 2 (2013): 405–431; Philip McCann and Raquel Ortega-Argilés, "Smart Specialization, Regional Growth and Applications to European Union Cohesion Policy," *Regional Studies* 49, no. 8 (2015): 1291–1302.

12. Charles Tiebout, "A Pure Theory of Local Expenditures," *Journal of Political Economy* 64, no. 5 (October 1956): 416–424.

13. Jenna Bednar, "The Resilience of the American Federal System," in Mark Tushnet, Sanford Levinson, and Mark Graber, eds., *Handbook of Constitutional Law* (London: Oxford University Press, 2014), www-personal .umich.edu/~jbednar/WIP/handbook.pdf; Jenna Bednar, "The Political Science of Federalism," *Annual Review of Law and Social Science* 7 (2011): 269–288.

14. Gallup, "Americans Still More Trusting in Local over State Government," *Gallup News*, September 19, 2016, http://news.gallup.com/ poll/195656/americans-trusting-local-state-government.aspx; Pew Research Center, "Beyond Distrust: How Americans View Their Government," Pew Research Center, November 2015, www.people-press.org/2015/11/23/4 -ratings-of-federal-agencies-congress-and-the-supreme-court.

15. Michael Greve, "Federalism and the Constitution: Competition Versus Cartels," George Mason University, Mercatus Center, 2015.

16. See Heather Gerken, "A New Progressive Federalism," *Democracy Journal* 24 (Spring 2012), http://democracyjournal.org/magazine/ 24/a-new-progressive-federalism.

17. See Karl Marx, *Das Kapital* (New York: Penguin Classics, 1992 [1867]; Karl Marx and Friedrich Engels, *The Communist Manifesto* (New York: International Publishers, 2014 [1848]); Joseph Schumpeter, *Capitalism, Socialism and Democracy* (New York: Harper and Brothers, 1942); Jane Jacobs, *The Economy of Cities* (New York: Random House, 1969). See also Richard Florida, "The Creative Class and Economic Development," *Economic Development Quarterly* 8, no. 3 (August 2014): 196–205; Richard Florida, Charlotta Mellander, and Patrick Adler, "The City as Innovation Machine," *Regional Studies* 51, no. 1 (2017): 86–96.

18. See Erik Olin Wright, *Class, Crisis and the State* (London: New Left Books, 1978); Erik Olin Wright, *Classes* (New York: Verso, 1987); Erik Olin Wright, *Class Counts: Comparative Studies in Class Analysis* (Cambridge: Cambridge University Press, 1996); Daniel Bell, *The Coming of Post-Industrial Society* (New York: Basic Books, 1973); Daniel Bell, *The Cultural Contradictions of Capitalism* (New York: Basic Books, 1976); Peter Drucker, *The Age of Discontinuity* (New York: Harper and Row, 1960).

See also, Fritz Malchup, *The Production and Distribution of Knowledge in the United States* (Princeton, NJ: Princeton University Press, 1962). My thinking about occupations and class was also influenced by the work of the urban economist Wilbur R Thompson. See Wilbur R. Thompson, *Preface to Urban Economics* (Baltimore: Johns Hopkins Press for Resources for the Future, 1965); Wilbur R. Thompson and Phillip R. Thompson, "From Industries to Occupations: Rethinking Local Economic Development," *Economic Development Commentary* 9, no. 3 (Fall 1985): 12–18; Wilbur R. Thompson and Phillip R. Thompson, "National Industries and Local Occupational Strengths: The Cross-Hairs of Targeting," *Urban Studies* 24, no. 6 (December 1987): 547–560.

19. Karl Marx, *The Grundrisse: Foundations of the Critique of Political Economy*, originally published in 1857, is available at www.marxists.org/archive/marx/works/1857/grundrisse/ch14.htm.

20. Richard Florida, "The New American Dream," *Washington Monthly*, March 2003; Richard Florida, *The Flight of the Creative Class: The Global Competition for Talent* (New York: HarperBusiness, 2005).

21. See Richard Florida and Martin Kenney, *The Breakthrough Illusion: Corporate America's Failure to Move from Innovation to Mass Production* (New York: Basic Books, 1990); Martin Kenney and Richard Florida, *Beyond Mass Production: The Japanese System and Its Transfer to the United States* (New York: Oxford University Press, 1993).

22. Richard Florida, "Toward the Learning Region," *Futures: The Journal of Forecasting and Planning* 27, no. 5 (June 1995): 527–536.

23. See Richard Florida and Marshall Feldman, "Housing in U.S. Fordism," *International Journal of Urban and Regional Research* 12, no. 2 (June 1988): 187–210; Richard Florida and Andrew Jonas, "U.S. Urban Policy, the Postwar State, and Capitalist Regulation," *Antipode* 23, no. 4 (1991): 349–384. On the concept of the spatial fix see, David Harvey, "The Spatial Fix: Hegel, Von Thunen and Marx," *Antipode*, 13, no. 3 (December 1981): 1–12.

APPENDIX

1. Paul D. Allison, "Measures of Inequality," *American Sociological Review* 43, no. 6 (December 1978): 865–880.

2. On the Dissimilarity Index, see Douglas Massey and Nancy Denton, "The Dimensions of Residential Segregation," *Social Forces* 67, no. 2 (1988): 281–315.

3. On the Milken Tech-Pole Index, see Ross DeVol, Perry Wong, John Catapano, and Greg Robitshek, *America's High-Tech Economy: Growth, Development, and Risks for Metropolitan Areas* (Santa Monica, CA: Milken Institute, 1999).

4. Barry Hirsch and David MacPherson, "Union Membership and Coverage Database from the CPS," Union Stats, 2014, http://unionstats.com.

5. On population-weighted density, see Steven G. Wilson, David A. Plane, Paul J. Mackun, Thomas R. Fischetti, and Justyna Goworowska et al., *Patterns of Metropolitan and Micropolitan Population Change: 2000 to 2010*, 2010 Census Special Reports, September 2012 (Washington, DC: US Census Bureau), www.census.gov/prod/cen2010/reports/c2010sr-01.pdf.

6. State-level election data are from standard media sources like CNN. Metro-level data are compiled from county-level sources based on Dave Leip's "Atlas of U.S. Presidential Elections" for 2012 and 2016, http://us electionatlas.org.

INDEX

Chicago School models of,
125–127, 127 (fig.)
economic inequality in, xvi–xix,
2–7, 12, 18–20, 31–33, 39,
78–95, 88, 89 (fig.), 109, 112,
192–194, 209–210, 218
edge, 128, 152
empowered, 11, 211–215
geography of class divide and, 12,
121–122, 149
global super-rich in, 38–42, 40
(fig.), 41 (fig.)
hollowed-out center of, 5, 7
importance of, 214–216
metabolism of, 17
parasitic, 26
policymakers neglecting, 185–186
refugee, 210–211
3Ts of economic development in,
xv
See also knowledge hubs;
Rustbelt cities; startup cities;
Sunbelt cities; superstar cities;
specific cities
Cities of Tomorrow, 13
The City (Park, Burgess, and
McKenzie), 126
class. See creative class; middle
class; service class; working
class
class divide, xix, 5
economic segregation and,
121–123
gentrification and, 78
geography of, 12, 121–122, 149
in Patchwork Metropolis, 12,
122–124
in suburbs, 121–122, 154,
162–163

in superstar cities, 123–124
Clinton, Hillary, xx, 164, 185, 188
clustering
back-to-the-city movement and,
124
in capitalism, 33
contradictions of, 8–9, 33
economic growth from, 166, 191
factors in, 123–124
of firms and industries, 21, 33
New Urban Luddism limiting, 28
of talent, xiv, xvii–xviii, xx, 8,
15, 21, 33, 42, 149
in winner-take-all urbanism,
13–14
working for all, 11, 191–195
CMU. See Carnegie Mellon
University
college graduates
educational segregation of,
103–104, 105 (table), 111, 219
middle class and, 203
variable of, 220
colleges, 66
Coming Apart (Murray), 121–122
commuting, 158–160
Composite Inequality Index, 88, 89
(fig.), 192, 218
congestion charges, 198
connectivity, 181–183
conservatism, 112, 190, 204, 222
Cook, Philip J., 14
corporations, real estate owned by,
39
cost of living
minimum wage and, 205
in superstar cities, 18–19
Council of Cities, 211
Cowen, Tyler, 192

© Lorne Bridgman

Richard Florida is University Professor and Director of Cities at the Martin Prosperity Institute at the University of Toronto's Rotman School of Management and a Distinguished Fellow at New York University's Schack Institute of Real Estate. He is Senior Editor at *The Atlantic*, cofounder and editor at large for *The Atlantic*'s *CityLab*, and founder of the Creative Class Group. He can be found on Twitter at @Richard_Florida and online at www.richardflorida.com.